Scotland – th

Scotland – the Brand

The Making of
Scottish Heritage

David McCrone, Angela Morris
and Richard Kiely

EDINBURGH UNIVERSITY PRESS

© David McCrone, Angela Morris and
Richard Kiely, 1995

Edinburgh University Press Ltd
22 George Square, Edinburgh

Typeset in ITC Garamond
by Pioneer Associates, Perthshire, and
printed and bound in Great Britain by
The Cromwell Press, Melksham

A CIP record for this book is available
from the British Library

ISBN 0 7486 0615 7

Contents

List of Illustrations

Acknowledgements

There are many people who have contributed to this study, wittingly or unwittingly. Above all, we are grateful to the Leverhulme Trust who funded the study on which this book is based. Truly, without their support it would not have happened. We are grateful too for their flexible way of working, given the vagaries of research in which the real world is a much messier place than the one which appears on research proposals.

We are also indebted to the National Trust for Scotland, especially to Lester Borley, and Walter Simpson and his staff, for their vital support in contacting life members. The ways of the research academy are rarely those of other organisations, and they coped with our requests for batches of names and addresses with good humour and patience.

The life members we interviewed were helpful and interesting, and we are grateful for the time, effort and cups of tea they made for us. We hope that we have managed to capture some of their abiding interest in heritage.

We are grateful too to the Scottish Tourist Board, Historic Scotland, Scottish Civic Trust, Scottish Natural Heritage and the Scottish Museums Council for the helpful way they explained what they did, and for giving so freely of their time and materials. Many individuals helped us. Special mention should be made of Jenni Calder, Tim Edensor, Jennifer Trimarchi, Fred Coalter, Murray McGregor and Nick Lilwall of the Scottish Agricultural College, as well as our many students, colleagues and friends who have had our enthusiasm for heritage inflicted on them.

Our publisher, Edinburgh University Press, and especially

Vivian Bone, Jackie Jones and Penny Clarke, are owed a debt of thanks for their enthusiasm and efficiency with which they saw the book through to publication.

An earlier version of Chapter 5 was published in *Scottish Elites,* edited by Tom Devine, and published by John Donald Ltd. We are grateful for permission to include some of that paper in this volume.

Finally, we wish to thank our own families, partners and spouses who are probably to blame for our individual interests in heritage in the first place, and who possibly regretted this as we dragged them round yet another heritage site in less than perfect Scottish weather. We promise to find something else to bore them with from now on.

October 1994

Chapter 1

The Rise and Rise of Heritage

Heritage is a thoroughly modern concept. Much as sexual intercourse was, according to the poet Philip Larkin, invented in 1963, so heritage belongs to the final quarter of the twentieth century. It is true, of course, that in one sense heritage, like sex, is as old as the world itself. All property which is not forcibly taken by conquest but has been passed on by means of some contract or other is heritage. Strictly speaking, heritage refers to that which has been or may be inherited, anything given or received to be a proper possession, an inherited lot or portion. But heritage has outgrown its legal definition. It has come to refer to a panoply of material and symbolic inheritances, some hardly older than the possessor. We have constructed heritage because we have a cultural need to do so in our modern age. Heritage is a condition of the late twentieth century.

The aim of *Scotland – the Brand* is to address this condition. It will try to describe and explain the extraordinary phenomenon through which the past is opened not only to reconstruction but to invention. We will discover that heritage has only a tenuous connection to actual events, to history. It has a much stronger one with the past, that is to say our interpretation formed in the context of the present. If there has been a boom in interest in history and archaeology, it has been because of what we want to use them for in the context of our own lives, and their potential for mapping out the future. How are we to account for this growing cult of the past?

THE GROWTH OF HERITAGE

Let us first establish that heritage is now part of our modern consciousness. The past twenty years or so have seen the rapid growth of 'heritage' centres and heritage-based attractions. When the British parliament passed the Ancient Monuments Act in 1882, it listed sixty-eight monuments deemed to be significant. A century later, these numbered over 12,000. There were, in addition, 330,000 listed buildings, and in excess of 5000 conservation sites (Hewison, 1987). This growth in heritage, however, is largely a feature of the 1970s and 1980s. Half of Scotland's 400 museums have been opened since the late 1970s, and these attract around 12 million visitors annually (STB Visitor Attractions n.d.: 2). The public demand for heritage is striking. Most of us include heritage-visiting as an important part of our leisure patterns and around 35 per cent of the population visit a museum, gallery or historic building at least once every three months with an average frequency of two to two-an-a-half visits per quarter (Henley Centre for Leisure Forecasting, 1986) .

Museums too have moved out of their musty past and have been a major growth area in post-industrial Britain, with an attendant academic spin-off, 'the new museology' (the title of a collection of essays by Vergo in 1989). The Scottish Museums Council, for example, which is the main channel of central government finance for the sector, supports more than 300 local museums in Scotland, and has seen its annual allocation of grant aid rise from just £6000 in 1975/6 to almost £400,000 in the early 1990s. By the late 1980s, museums in Britain were not only being opened at a rate of one every fortnight, even more frequently in America and Japan (Lumley, 1988), but they also began to become multi-functional – places for studying, attending lectures, having discussions, meeting, eating and drinking (Walsh, 1992). 'Museum,' Lumley suggests, is a word acquiring new significance at the end of the twentieth century. It no longer refers to an institution or building, but functions as a time-machine, 'as a potent social metaphor and as a means whereby societies represent their relationship to their own history and to that of other cultures' (1988:2).

By the mid-1980s, tourism had become the UK's second biggest earner of foreign currency. By the late 1980s, 330 million site visits were being made, compared with 200 million in 1984. These included 3.25 million to Westminster Abbey, and 2.7 million to the Tower of London and Tower Bridge (Fowler, 1992). Around 40 per cent of foreign tourists in 1989 gave visiting historic sites, cities and towns as an important reason for visiting the UK. Peter Fowler, who is Professor of Archaeology at Newcastle University, commented: 'The whole island is for practical purposes a single archaeological site rather than a tract of land containing hundreds of thousands of sites' (1992:7).

Scotland has its own version of this heritage explosion. The key sites are Edinburgh Castle and Glasgow's Art Gallery and Museum with 1 million visitors each, the Burrell Collection (with 750,000) and around 500,000 to the People's Palace in Glasgow and Edinburgh's Royal Museum of Scotland. Holyrood Palace attracted 330,000, to say nothing of the 350,000 which the Loch Ness Monster Exhibition claims to have had through its doors. It seems to matter little which of these exhibits are 'real' or not, because as we shall see, the key measure is 'authenticity', a commodity which can easily be manufactured with the aid of special effects. Thus, the Amish in Lancaster County, Pennsylvania, employ life-size fibre-glass replicas of themselves and their wagons so that tourists can photograph the 'authentic' lifestyle, allowing the Amish to get on with their daily chores unencumbered (MacCannell, 1992).

The consumption of heritage has its informed cadres as well as its infrequent foot-soldiers. Bodies such as The National Trust (covering England, Wales and Northern Ireland), the National Trust for Scotland, English Heritage and Historic Scotland have large and important memberships. The National Trust enrolled its 2 millionth member in 1990 (its member-ship doubled in the 1980s) and is the largest conservation organisation in the world, needing £80 million per annum just to keep going at its present level, and a staff of over 2,000, sup-plemented by 20,000 volunteers. By 1993, the National Trust for Scotland (NTS) had over 230,000 members and an annual income of over £13 million, of which over £3 million came from membership subscriptions. We should, of course, be careful about how we interpret these figures. Membership of these heritage bodies, as Fowler (1992) observes, may be closer in form to supporters' clubs than active and involved participants. In other words, members of heritage associations (like football clubs) appear in the roles of cheer-leaders rather than decision-makers, a feature we encountered during our interviews with NTS members.

Scotland, then, mirrors the explosion in heritage which is taking place across the western world. But there is another deeper and more important reason than this for studying heritage here. To put it simply, the whole idea of heritage has its origins in nineteenth-century Scotland and the revolution in the writing of history brought about by Sir Walter Scott.

Scott's lifetime spanned a period of great historical change. In the words of Marinell Ash, he lived through 'the tensions and contradictions of a traditional Scotland merging into a great world empire' (1980:13). Scott spent part of his child-hood on his grandfather's farm at Sandyknowe, near Smail-holm in Roxburghshire. At an early age he was exposed to the oral history tradition of the Borders. These early childhood experiences were to provide the inspiration for his novels. In these, Scott created a highly romantic and fictitious picture of the Scottish past. He then encouraged nineteenth-century Scottish historians to recover and study historical documents and records, and recreate for themselves similar pictures of the past. It was this activity which led the Hungarian philo-sopher Georg Lukacs to describe Scott's work as the first literary expression of world-historical consciousness (Ash, 1980: ch. 1).

Scott's historical revolution gave birth to a new way of thinking about the past which turned out to be extremely important in the context of nineteenth- and early twentieth-century European social development (Nairn, 1975). It intro-duced the idea of past and present as two very different entities. In the words of David Lowenthal: 'This new past gradually came to be cherished as a heritage that validated and exalted the present. And the new role heightened concern to save relics and restore monuments as emblems of communal identity, continuity and aspiration' (1985:xvi). We will argue that there are special benefits to be had by looking at heritage from a Scottish perspective. Scotland is clearly a nation which is not a conventional state. For much of its history over the last 300 years its population has been very aware of the difference between its cultural and political identities.

We might even argue that Scotland suffers from too much heritage rather than too little. Its iconography includes tartan, Glencoe, Bonnie Prince Charlie and Culloden, Bannockburn, Burns, Mary Queen of Scots, whisky, Edinburgh Castle and much more. It has become an *idée fixe* of many Scottish intellectuals that Scotland suffers from a deformation of its culture; that it has sold out its political birthright for a mess of cultural pottage (Nairn, 1975; Beveridge and Turnbull, 1989). It is argued that instead of a rounded thought-world in which culture and politics work together in gear, the prevalent images of Scotland are adrift from their political moorings. All manner of imaginings have been allowed to gather around the country's representation, of which perhaps the best-known is the Hollywood concoction, Brigadoon. Genuine Scottish culture has truly been 'eclipsed' (Beveridge and Turnbull, ibid.).

Even the Scottish Tourist Board is reported as having tired of the tartanry and tourism image (*The Herald*, 17 August 1994). In a campaign to attract English visitors north of the border, its search for 'Scotland the Brand' involved an advertising campaign which played down the images of kilted bagpipe players in favour of Scotland's poetry, music and landscape. It is now a commonplace to assert that much of tartanry is Victorian fabrication (Trevor-Roper, 1984; Cheape, 1991), that it owes more to the heritage industry than to history. Some, like Beveridge and Turnbull (op. cit.), argue that much of conventional Scottish culture is so utterly tainted that it is best left alone. However, it is also clear that most Scots are ambivalent about Scottish heritage icons like tartan. For example, it is frequently worn at sporting events, notably at Hampden and Murrayfield, in assertions of Scottish sporting nationalism, and even those central icons of the British imperial past, the Highland regiments, have their vociferous defenders in the Scottish National Party. All is not what it seems. The heritage icons are malleable. They take on radical as well as conservative meanings.

At the centre of Scottish heritage stands the country itself, Scotland as theme-park. Its landscape is a social and cultural product in the words of Denis Cosgrove: '. . . a way of seeing projected on to the land, and having its own techniques and compositional forms; a restrictive way of seeing that diminishes alternative modes of experiencing our relations with nature' (1984:269). The capture, both materially and culturally, of Highland estates for sporting purposes in the nineteenth century has bequeathed an iconography of Scottish landscape which is largely bereft of people. Landseer's painting, *The Monarch of the Glen*, sets the framework for our expectations of Scotland. Raymond Williams has pointed out that a working country is hardly ever a 'landscape' (1973). Neither is it likely to be 'heritage'. The material power of the nineteenth century aristocracy and its monarchy was translated into the cultural representation of Scottish landscape. The 'stag at bay' image of the Highlands is probably so deeply embedded that it makes radical land reform to restore the land to a 'working' environment all the more difficult. Cleared estates have come to represent landscape in Scotland just as soldiers in kilts inform our image of what it is to be a Scot.

The power of heritage seems unduly onerous in Scotland. Indeed, it seems at times as if Scotland only exists as heritage: what singles it out for distinction is the trappings of its past while its modernity seems to make it little different from elsewhere. At a lecture in Aberdeen, we were once asked why we thought it had been so difficult to establish a heritage centre in the city devoted to North Sea oil. Our answer was that this would not happen unless and until North Sea oil was 'over' as an economic phenomenon. If Scotland is heritage-rich, then it could be because it has a past but not a present or future. That is perhaps why many Scottish writers attack the cultural representations of Scotland as overly obsessed with what has passed, and why the nationalist party presents itself as a modernist, economistic one. Heritage in Scotland seems to many to be too tainted, too heavy.

It is, however, a crucial cultural repository for answers to the identity question. Like many 'stateless nations' such as Catalonia and Quebec, Scotland cannot rely on a pragmatic definition in terms of its political statehood. Indeed, given that it currently has no meaningful level of democratic control over its administration, it has even more of an identity crisis than the other two nations. There is no shortage of cultural accoutrements, however, in this search for collective identity. In spite of the high degree of institutional autonomy afforded to Scotland (Paterson, 1994), there is a continuous questing for identity. The old joke has it that Canadians are defined as a people who constantly pull up their roots to find out who they are. How much more does this apply to Scotland which does not have formal political sovereignty?

In the quest for national (as opposed to state) identity, heritage is a vital source of legitimacy. The iconography of nationalism is replete with sacred objects such as flags, emblems and sites which are often contested and fought over (as Jerusalem is by Israelis and Palestinians, and Kosovo by Serbs and Albanians). In asking who we are, the totems and icons of heritage are powerful signifiers of our identity. We may find tartanry, Bonnie Prince Charlie, Mary Queen of Scots, Bannockburn and Burns false descriptors of who we are, but they provide a source of ready-made distinguishing characteristics from England, our bigger, southern neighbour.

Heritage of this sort also communicates a powerful sense of glamour. We have grown accustomed to thinking of glamour as a fairly superficial show-biz quality of the late twentieth century. It also has its deeper meaning of magic or delusion which it has retained in Scotland. The glamour of an object originally referred in the eighteenth century to its magical powers, to enchantment and witchcraft, even the power to bamboozle or deceive. The etymology of the word derives from the same root as 'grammar' - 'grimoire' - a sorcerer's book (Oxford English Dictionary). The painter Allan Ramsay is quoted in OED as defining glamour as follows: 'when devils, wizards or jugglers deceive the sight, they are said to cast glamour o'er the eyes of the spectator' (OED, 1983:855), and Sir Walter Scott, who did so much to create Scottish heritage, is attributed with using it to refer to delusive or alluring charm.

All of this may seem highly suspicious to late twentieth-century rationalist eyes. If heritage has to do with 'glamour', with deceit and fabrication, then 'history' is much to be preferred. To make such a distinction, however, would be to ignore the salience of glamour afforded by modern tourism. The Australian writer Donald Horne has referred to modern tourist guidebooks as 'devotional texts', to the sightseer as pilgrim, the object as relic, and the photograph as the equivalent of holy icon (1984). The modern tourist, he argues, relies on 'authenticity', the 'magical glow' which 'can illuminate meanings that justify power or claim prestige' (ibid.:34). Above all, authenticity is conferred by interpretation, not the object per se. Central icons - what Horne calls monuments - acquire a special glamour to convey their special status; it is all about presentation and interpretation. Most of us have had the deflating experience of queuing to see a sacred icon only to wonder what all the fuss was about. No one can understand the significance of the black madonna of Monserrat without knowing what that icon means for Catalan identity, both religious and national. The key to heritage is to sacrilise its objects. The anthropologist, Annette Weiner, put it this way:

> An individual's role in social life is fragmentary unless attached to something of permanence. The history of the past, equally fragmentary, is concentrated in an object that, in its material substance, defies destruction. Thus, keeping an object defined as inalienable adds to the value of one's past, making the past a powerful resource for the present and the future. (1985)

HERITAGE AND AUTHENTICITY

History like heritage has become less and less synonymous with professional historians and the realm of books. This is reflected in the shift away from narrow scholarly appreciation towards history as a form of entertainment, as 'info-tainment'. It also has employment pay-offs. As Robert Hewison has observed, the heritage movement has been a godsend to the Manpower Services Commission, creating 'jobs that otherwise would not have existed, such as weaving, grinding corn, and living in a reproduction Iron Age round house at Manchester Museum' (1987:102). Heritage presents new challenges as well as problems for academics such as historians and archaeologists. It is no longer enough to let the artefacts speak for themselves; indeed, it is often vital that the artefacts 'speak' by means of holograms on to which images are projected. The demand is for authenticity rather than 'fact', for the believable over the actual. Peter Fowler points out that this frequently runs the risk of creating a past that never existed, and he quotes Joseph Heller's observation about a statue that 'it was an authentic Hellenistic imitation of a Hellenic reproduction . . . for which there had never been an authentic original subject' (1992:13). But then again, Fowler comments, 'there is more to the past than authenticity' (ibid.:17).

The search for the authentic through heritage is aided by technological advances which allow more active participation for the spectator. People are now much more willing to 'dress up and do', by taking part in enactments of battles by joining military reconstruction associations like the Sealed Knot Society, or role-playing in country house reconstructions. At its extreme, there is double reflexivity; tourists and natives perform their allocated roles for each other in the context of 'watching me watching you'. The Zuni Pueblo Indians in North America, according to MacCannell, have developed a typology of tourists – a New York type, a Texas type, a Hippy type, a 'save the whale' type. These figures have begun to be represented in Indian dances. Texas types wear cowboy boots and drive Cadillacs. Hippies wear tie-dyed T-shirts, and join uninvited in the dancing, while the 'East Coast' tourist is played by a male Indian wearing high heels, wig, dress, mink coat, dime-store jewelry, clutch purse and pill-box hat. 'Ex-primitives', MacCannell comments, 'knowingly overdose tourists with unwanted pseudo-authenticity' (1992:31). We may find this far-fetched and overly cynical until we remember the instance closer to home of the authenticity of tartan and the 'Scottish experience'. It seems that the desire to believe too easily overcomes the counter-evidence that much of this 'tradition' is of recent origin. It is even possible to acknowledge pastiche while believing in it. Somehow, simulacra pretences, presented as the real, for example the Scottish ceilidh experience, have the power to overcome our cynicism.

Such talk of pastiche and simulacrum has helped to develop a fresh interest in the culture of tourism in the late twentieth century. The commercialisation of culture may be obvious enough, but perhaps more insidiously, as MacCannell points out 'it is also an ideological framing of history, nature and tradition' (1992:1). In other words, when people are defined as tourist attractions, do they not tend to relate to each other by way of commercially enforced stereotypes of themselves? How much of a meaningful identity do people have beyond that which is required by the touristic framework?

MacCannell ties the threat to identity into the power of 'spectacle' over 'sights'. Mass tourism in its early twentieth-century phase required tourists to observe in a fairly passive manner – to see the sights, as it were. Late twentieth-century tourism is much more focused on spectacle, on a degree of active involvement, whether it is joining in a make-believe version of a 'native' dance, or having a go at pot making (Note the extension of this into 'activity holidays', and the denial of the passive tourist role in favour of the persona of 'the traveller'.) In these events re-enactment is a form of remaking the past for the purposes of the present.

As a result of the demand for active involvement, the traditional custodians of heritage are placed in a dilemma. They are forced to choose between defending their traditional activities and sites by letting stones speak for themselves, as it were, or becoming more interpretative of what they guard. So a controversy develops as to whether it is acceptable to build a replica of a Roman fort at Vindolanda on Hadrian's Wall – to give visitors a sense of 'what it must have been like to be a Roman soldier' – or to take refuge in the strictly scholarly and dry account, or to represent the past in some other way. Traditionalists may point out that this notion of heritage simply and quickly deteriorates into pastiche and 'Disneyfication'. They might argue that what is created is simply an archaeological zoo along with a theme park mentality which threatens the careful and scholarly attempts to build up knowledge from fragmentary evidence. 'Conceptualisation' takes liberties with time and telescopes history, as in the action-packed and breathless experience on offer at Timespan (sic), a Highland heritage centre at Helmsdale in Sutherland (a centre financially assisted by Highland and Islands Enterprises). Its brochure carries this appeal:

> Experience our Highland heritage, fashioned over centuries. From Picts and Vikings, murders at Helmsdale castle, last burning of a witch, the harrowing Highland Clearances, the 19th century Sporting Scene, the Kildonan goldrush, and through our crofting and fishing past to the present day and our neighbouring oilfields.

Admittedly this hands-on heritage has its appeal and it is reinforced by two other developments. Firstly, technology today permits reconstruction not simply in real space, but in 'virtual' space by means of computer-aided design. So it is now possible to view the major icons of western civilisation, for example, its fortresses, palaces and monasteries, not as heaps of rubble requiring imagination and maybe a degree in architectural history as well, but as virtual reality. With the required equipment, it is possible to 'be' at medieval Cluny Abbey in France, or at the second battle of Manassas in the American Civil War, without leaving your armchair. The second development which takes heritage from the hands of professional scholars is the rediscovery of 'people's history'. The new configurations of English economic history at Beamish or Ironbridge may simply be collections of industrial pastiche owing little to the actual site itself (Beamish did not exist before the present reconstruction, although Ironbridge was 'real' enough as a site although it has been restored and doctored), but, as Peter Fowler comments 'they symbolise the common man's past of labour, neighbour and netty, as distinct from the national past of Blenheim and the Tower of London' (1992:132).

Whether we are talking about actual or invented heritage sites, they have key features in common: they are, of course, places out of time for they operate in the here and now while involving visits to 'time past'. Crucially, they allow and encourage us to play for a while in another age and so they seem to deny the possibility of decay and death for there is no passage of time allowed to occur between 'then' and 'now', and by implication 'we' and 'they' are not separated, either across the years or, by definition, in place (Sorensen, 1989). In his view, 'in these changing and disturbing times historic theme parks and heritage centres probably tell us as much about ourselves as about the past – indeed probably more' (ibid.:65).

Is there anything new, however, about this cult of the past? Is it not the case that the late twentieth-century heritage industry is simply a modern version of the late eighteenth- and early nineteenth-century Romantic nostalgia for the past, but with technological updates? Certainly, the concern with heritage is not new. Two hundred years ago the idea of Progress was central to the modernist project of Improvement – culturally, economically and socially. The past was a fixed point from which to measure that Progress. In the late twentieth-century, however, this faith has waned, and the intellectual paradigm of modernism has receded (Giddens, 1990).

In the late twentieth century evocation of the 'past' even when it is an essentially mythical past, we catch a glimpse of the appeal of 'post-modernism' as an intellectual framework for making sense of disparate meanings and activities, as well as the everyday and the mundane. As we shall see later in this chapter, the rise and rise of heritage is driven by a set of commercial, political and intellectual motors which help to give it an unusual salience in the late twentieth century.

HERITAGE: THE INTERNATIONAL CONTEXT

Although we are primarily concerned with heritage in Scotland, and in Britain generally, Scottish heritage is one aspect of an international phenomenon. While there are the inevitable national variations in manifestations and emphases of heritage, there is also much transmission of ideas, presentation and marketing techniques across national boundaries.

As a form of commodification, heritage has its roots in the restructuring of the world economy, a process which began in the 1970s and paved the way for the development of international mass tourism (Urry, 1990). Heritage and tourism have always been first cousins, as the following extract from a paper by the European Travel Commission/Europa Nostra written in the '70s makes clear:

> While sun, sea, sand, and decent accommodation are essential ingredients of many tourist industries (especially in attracting visitors from outside Europe) scenery, historic sites, ancient towns, and land and buildings in the local vernacular are also important. They are in fact the essence of the travel brochure, the poster, the guide, the package deal . . . the interests of tourism demand the protection of the scenic and historic heritage. (1974:2)

International thinking about heritage has been heavily influenced by the introduction of a 'new cult of the past' (Hoyau, 1988) which came out of the celebrations surrounding France's 'Heritage Year' in 1979. The effect of this new cult of the past was 'to promote new values on the basis of a thoroughly transformed conception of tradition and the national heritage' (ibid.:27-8).

Central to this new cult of the past was the twentieth century notion of heritage. As the then Minister of Culture, J. P. Lecat, observed:

> The notion of heritage has been expanded. The national heritage is no longer merely a matter of cold stones or of

exhibits under glass in museum cabinets. It now includes the village wash-house, the little country church, local songs and forms of speech, crafts and skills (ibid.:28)

It is an equally broad definition of heritage which informed the thinking of those responsible for administering the British National Heritage Memorial Fund when it was set up at the beginning of the 1980s:

> The national heritage of this country is remarkably broad and rich. It is simultaneously a representation of the development of aesthetic expression and a testimony to the role played by the nation in world history. The national heritage also includes the natural riches of Britain - the great scenic areas, the fauna and flora - which could so easily be lost by thoughtless development. (Annual Report 1980-1)

While the growth of heritage is an international phenomenon there are marked differences in the way heritage is organised in different countries. In republican France, for example, the impetus for looking after heritage comes mainly from the state, and the role of voluntary institutions is small. What is conveyed is a strong sense of national inheritance, or '*patrimoine*', closely allied with the rural imagery and peasant culture which is of continuing political importance in the French Republic. In monarchist Britain, on the other hand, the role of the state is relatively small compared to that of voluntary organisations such as the National Trust and National Trust for Scotland, which, as we shall see in Chapter 4, convey an organic, even aristocratic, ethos.

The situation is different yet again in the United States of America where heritage has a long history of exploitation as a business resource. Despite this single impetus, there are nevertheless competing definitions of heritage and how it should be handled. In 1993, for example, the Disney Corporation announced a new heritage venture in the form of a $650 million American history amusement park outside Washington DC. Disney's Vice-President vowed: 'This is not a Pollyana view of America. We want to make you a Civil War soldier. We want to make you feel what it was to be like to be a slave or what it was like to escape through the underground railroad' (*The Guardian*, 27 December 1993). This view sat somewhat uneasily with that of the park's general manager: 'The idea is to walk out of Disney's America with a smile on your face. We don't want people to come out with a dour face. It is going to be fun with a capital F' (ibid.). The president of the US National Trust for Historic Preservation observed:

> What will Disney's America mean for the authentic historic sites that depend on visitation for their survival? It's bound to be bad news for Mount Vernon and Monticello or quasi-public institutions such as the Smithsonian or national parks such as the Manassas Civil War battlefield – this is one project that should not be driven by economics alone. (ibid.)

By September 1994, the project had been scrapped as a result of public opposition.

This episode shows how central heritage is to a nation's self-identity, and yet what complex and contradictory pressures play upon it. Nowhere is that clearer than in Britain. In 1973 the then Secretary of State for Education, Margaret Thatcher, forced the introduction of compulsory charges for admission to national museums, a move which was reversed by an incoming Labour government three months later. Nevertheless, this move marked a major shift by museums and monuments into the market place. It opened the flood gates for a new wave of 'independent museums' which perceived themselves as part of the leisure and tourism industry. Entertainment rather than education or their hybrid 'Infotainment' was all important because these museums needed to draw the crowds in order to justify their existence. The result is that in Britain today these new-style, independently funded 'heritage attractions' exist alongside traditional heritage 'sites' which are in the care of state or semi-state bodies.

Heritage is now a political phenomenon despite the reluctance of British politicians to acknowledge this. Patrick Cormack, the Conservative MP for South-West Staffordshire and author of 'Heritage in Danger', has been quoted as saying: 'it is vital for the preservation of our heritage that it should never become a political football' (Wright, 1985:43). Labour politicians have also been keen to place heritage above politics. Andrew Faulds, for, example, publicly praised Lady Birk and Lord Donaldson because they 'took up cudgels' for heritage (ibid.). In Britain, the politicisation of heritage began in 1946 when Labour Chancellor Hugh Dalton established the National Land Fund in memory of those who died in the Second World War: 'the beauty of England, the famous historical houses, the wonderful stretches of still unspoilt open country, surely it would be a fitting memorial that these might become part of the heritage of all of us' (ibid.:45).

The National Land Fund existed from 1946 to 1980 when it was replaced by the National Heritage Memorial Fund under the 1980 National Heritage Act. Wright points out there was considerable controversy surrounding this memorial to the war dead because not once was it used as an emergency or contingency fund to protect the heritage it claimed to represent. When it was set up in 1946 the National Land Fund stood at £50 million, a sum which came into the exchequer from the sale of surplus war materials. In 1957 Enoch Powell, then a junior minister in the Tory government, reduced it to £10 million, claiming that in 1946 the Exchequer had merely lent itself £50 million.

Powell's actions in 1957, coupled with the recognition that the National Land Fund had never once been used in the way that Dalton had intended was the impetus behind the National Heritage Act 1980. The legislative reform regarding the National Heritage Bill was planned under the Callaghan administration, was modified by the Tories when they took over in 1979, and finally went forward with all-party support to become the National Heritage Act 1980. This Act with its appeal across the political spectrum serves as the classic reminder that however easily heritage appears to fit with a Conservative world-view it cannot simply be dismissed as right-wing rhetoric.

One particularly important aspect of the 1980 Act is that it established the National Heritage Memorial Fund grafted on to the remains of the National Land Fund so paying lip service at least to Dalton's hortatory vision of the National Land Fund as a way to honour those who fell in the Second World War. At the same time it acted as a vehicle for the political project of Mrs Thatcher. Patrick Wright comments:

> There is nothing hortatory about the National Heritage Memorial Fund; all it indicates is a generalised and everyday sense of the way things used to be, and in this respect it stands as an early engagement with that anxious

and vernacular sense of historical existence which
Thatcher has deliberately gone on to make the ground of
so many spuriously 'historical' gestures and pleas.
(1985:46)

The 1980 National Heritage Act did not itself attempt to
define heritage. Instead it gives heritage an indefinable quality
as the following passage taken from the first annual report of
the National Heritage Memorial fund for 1980–1 illustrates:

> We could no more define the national heritage than we
> could define, say, beauty or art. Clearly, certain works of
> art created by people born in this country were part of
> the national heritage – paintings by Turner and Constable,
> for instance, or sculptures by Henry Moore or Barbara
> Hepworth – as were buildings such as Chatsworth or
> Edinburgh Castle. But, beyond that, there was much less
> assurance. So we decided to let the national heritage
> define itself.

In 1983, Parliament established English Heritage and
CADW (Welsh Historic Monuments), and the Historic
Buildings and Monuments Directorate in Scotland in 1984. All
three institutions gained executive agency status in 1991,
which meant that while they were government-owned, they
had the freedom to manage along with the responsibility to
return a profit to the government. The Historic Buildings and
Monuments Directorate in Scotland changed its name to
Historic Scotland in that year.

This brief review of heritage in Britain reveals one of the
key themes of this book. While the state needs to mobilise
heritage as a key icon of its political legitimacy, this is quite
problematic in these islands, for there is no single 'national'
heritage on offer. Since there is no simple correspondence
between the nation and the state heritage will have the potential of acting to bolster the state while also helping to provide
an alternative, competing version of nationhood. In Scotland,
it is inevitable that such a conflict exists in a civil society
which retains so many of its distinctive institutional identities.
The existence of a separate suite of de facto national heritage
bodies is indicative of this. The way key bodies – National
Trust for Scotland, Historic Scotland, the Scottish Tourist
Board – operate north of the border will be analysed in
Chapter 4.

UNDERSTANDING HERITAGE

Our aim is to provide a sociological account for the rise and rise of heritage, focusing on Scotland as a particular but not unique instance of the general phenomenon. We are intrigued by the fact that while the explosion of heritage centres and heritage-based tourist attractions throughout the world during the past twenty years or so has been the subject of much academic attention (Wright, 1985; Hewison, 1987; Lumley, 1988; Hoyau, 1988; Sorensen, 1988; Urry, 1990) Scotland itself has received short shrift, despite the fairly intense debate about its culture and development during the same period. We will also have something to say about the meaning of heritage, but as we are sociologists not cultural critics, it should be stressed that deciphering or decoding heritage is not our aim.

Four main themes will run through the book – the commodification of heritage; the consumption of heritage; the politics of heritage; and the ideology of heritage. Let us unfold each of these in turn.

Heritage as Commodity

First of all, we are interested in the commodification of heritage, how it has been mobilised by private and public capital, in the context of a rapidly changing economy. It is clear that something fundamental has happened to economic structures and relations in the last few decades of the twentieth century. We may choose to call it a 'post-industrial' or a 'service' economy, but it manifestly is one in which manufacturing industry is far less significant as an employer. The process whereby service sector jobs have replaced those in manufacturing has been variously described as 'de-industrialisation' and 'post-Fordist' in recognition of the fact that large-scale omnibus production is no longer the norm (Lash, 1990). A key part of this argument is that culture itself becomes a commodity in this new economy which is now internationalised – or 'globalised'. The question as to how this operates, and in whose interests, will be developed in the next chapter when we look at the insights into heritage afforded by aspects of sociology.

Another aspect of this commodification of heritage and culture relates to the process of economic regeneration, especially at the local level. Local authorities in particular have not been slow to recognise the economic and political potential of heritage. In many British cities, the talk is of the 'heritage option' as a means of economic regeneration, and the 'culture economy' as a way of achieving post-industrial city status. These culture industries include traditional ones like museums and cathedrals, but also art galleries, concert halls, orchestras, community arts, TV franchises and the performing arts. This is not, in the main, politically contentious, for the Labour Party has given this strategy its blessing, arguing that developing urban arts and a local heritage industry helps to redistribute resources away from London (Fisher and Owen, 1991). Cities in turn have invented new titles or adopted existing ones by way of badges of regeneration, a point we will develop in the next chapter: Glasgow as European City of Culture in 1990, Dundee as City of Discovery, Lancaster as Heritage City, to say nothing of the heritage attractions of Wigan Pier, a joke within a joke.

Undoubtedly, the doyen of this strategy is Glasgow which has sought to diversify its economy away from traditional heavy engineering and shipbuilding (the irony is that Glasgow was always much more of a commercial than an industrial city, compared with Dundee which was the industrial city par excellence in Scotland in terms of the proportion employed in manufacturing industries). The pay-off of Glasgow's regeneration through culture came in 1993 when the city council ran a campaign to persuade the trustees of the National Galleries of Scotland to site the proposed Gallery of Scottish Art not in the capital, Edinburgh, but in Glasgow. The campaign itself was successful, although the Secretary of State for Scotland vetoed the project in 1994 largely on grounds of cost. In general terms, Glasgow's mobilisation of culture for economic regeneration is reflected in the dramatic increase by 90 per cent in the numbers of overseas visitors to the city over the last eight years. The figures given in the 1992 international passenger survey carried out by the Department of National Heritage (a UK body) revealed that Glasgow now lay third in the league table (with 420,000), behind London (with 8.8 million visitors), and Edinburgh (with 820,000). The view has now taken hold that, in the words of the city's director of performing arts: 'Over the last two or three years Glasgow has been used as a model for many European cities that are trying to copy the regeneration process that is taking place' (*The Scotsman*, 27 December 1993).

Closely connected with urban images are industrial ones. These are not simply images to escape from, but ironically in a post-industrial age, to recover, albeit in a sanitised form. A direct result of the French Minister of Culture expanding the definition of heritage in 1979 and cutting it free from its attachment to beauty was the development of industrial heritage. Hoyau sees this as 'the infrastructure taking its revenge'. The result is that:

> By being assimilated into the nation's heritage, material production once again finds its place in the cultural landscape: efforts are then made to prevent the destruction of factories, industrial archaeology sight-seeing tours are organised, and children are initiated into the mysteries of hydraulic pumps. (1988:29)

In Britain examples of industrial heritage abound. Ironbridge Gorge Museum, Beamish Open Air Museum, The Black Country Museum, and The Scottish Mining Museum are among the most well known. Industrial heritage has attracted considerable criticism both from academics and from people working within the museum business. The historian Robert Hewison sees industrial heritage in general as a poor attempt to cope with industrial decline. Others are critical of the way the Ironbridge Gorge Museum (the first of its kind) has become part of the historical tourism 'business'. Tony Bennett regards the Beamish Museum in north east England as exemplifying a British ability 'to transform industrialism from a set of ruptural events into a mere moment in the unfolding of a set of harmonious relations between rulers and people' (1990:72–3).

The urban and industrial opportunities have been matched by rural and agricultural ones. Cookson Country, Hardy Country, even Land O' Burns, have been virtually created by local councils and entrepreneurs as places which do not actually exist, sometimes, as the playwright Alan Bennett pointed out, with alarming consequences:

> The village in Yorkshire where I spend all too little of my time now sports one of those DoE brown heritage signposts declaring it a 'Dales Village' and it's only a matter of time before the inhabitants start playing it up as 'Dales Folk'. We're fortunate not to be in 'Herriot Country' or

the temptation to act the part may be even greater. But it's toytown now on every hand, dignified and stately barns converted into bijoux residences with bottle glass windows and carriage lamps that bring with them a view of the countryside that is equally folksy. The Village shop becomes The Village Shop, the confectioners The Village Bakery; it won't be long now before some well-meaning parish council will be employing some of those turfed out of psychiatric hospitals as Village Idiots. (Bennett, 1989)

There is, of course, more scope to elaborate heritage themes in rural areas, because as Raymond Williams observed (1973), 'the country' is more easily treated as the essence of The Country or nation. It is but a short step from there to the use of heritage as a means of 'cultural capital', a symbolic resource with a capacity for power. Life styles may come with implicit social values built into them. Peter Fowler coins the term 'Ashleyism' to refer to the ethos one 'buys' with the Laura Ashley product: 'It harks back from an urban viewpoint not just to a rural underpinning of a former life-style but to assumptions about, a reading of, social hierarchies and the mores which went with it.' To underscore his point, he cites the producer herself: 'I did not set out to be Victorian but it was a time when people lived straightforward, balanced lives, when everything was clear-cut and respectable' (1992:40).

Yorkshire is also the home of possibly one of the most bizarre heritage sites in Britain, a reconstructed prisoner-of-war camp near Malton, North Yorkshire. Making use of huts left over from the war, it advertises itself as 'the only modern history theme museum of its type in the world', in which the visitor will be transported back to wartime Britain: 'You will experience the sights, the sounds, even the smells of those dangerous years', it promises, and the twenty-nine huts become mini-theme parks, each devoted to a war battle, or specific feature such as 'the Eden Camp Music Hall', and '1946 prefab'. Given war nostalgia, this reconstruction of war heritage looks set to be a sure-fire success.

Heritage as Consumption

Our second theme is closely related to the commodification of heritage. It is the consumption of heritage. The concept of

'the heritage industry' implies a product, a set of entrepreneurs, a manufacturing process, a set of social relations structured around this process, a market, and, of course, consumers.
The transition from a manufacturing to a service-based economy helps bring to the fore the consumption of culture and
heritage. John Urry (1990) identifies a 'new middle class' as
especially susceptible to heritage. By implication, those who
work in the cultural and education industries, the so-called
'service class', would seem to be likely consumers of heritage
given its potential for linking economic and social interests,
that is, class and status or life style. We have here a hypothesis which is worth testing, rather than a firm finding, for
Urry's account of the social base of heritage consumption is
sketchy and ill-defined (1990). An important part of our study
has been a careful examination of the meaning of heritage for
those who are members of the National Trust for Scotland,
and this is reported in Chapters 6 and 7.

Heritage as Politics

The third theme which runs through the book is that of the
politics of heritage. It is this aspect of the whole business of
heritage which probably attracted most attention in the
1980s. In 1985, Patrick Wright published his book *On Living
in an Old Country*, the somewhat horrified observations of
an Englishman returning to Thatcher's Britain after living in
North America. In the book he made the point that while heritage was not unknown in the United States (after all, this was
the culture which gave us Disneyworld), heritage in modern
Britain had taken on deeply conservative and Conservative
resonances rather than simply being a commodity in the marketplace. In the context of economic restructuring, Wright
argued, heritage not only represented a cultural capital to be
exploited for commercial gain, but was used by the regime to
paper over some fundamental ideological and political cracks
in the fabric of the state. Wright's book was followed two
years later by *The Heritage Industry: Britain in a Climate of
Decline*, by the journalist Robert Hewison. This book remains
the most explicit commentary to date on the public's apparently growing obsession with the past, and its desire to consume cultural events and artefacts which reflect the past in
ways relevant to the present. For Hewison, like Wright, the
cultural and political perspective dominates. He stresses how,

during her term of office, Mrs Thatcher and the ideologues of the New Right were able to mobilise and manipulate a set of thoroughly conservative ideas: 'Nostalgia is profoundly conservative. Its emphasis on order and tradition relies heavily on appeals to the authority of the past' (1987:47).

National Heritage: the Rediscovery of the Nation

Everyday life, Patrick Wright argues, is informed by a vernacular and informal sense of history which is often expressed through the powerful symbolism of the public world, but which is not swamped or rendered impotent by it. It is to this informal and vernacular sense of history that ideas about national heritage appeal. The following passage from Patrick Cormack's *Heritage in Danger* illustrates this point:

> When I am asked to define our heritage I do not think in dictionary terms, but instead reflect on certain sights and sounds. I think of a morning mist on the Tweed at Dryburgh where the magic of Turner and the romance of Scott both come fleetingly to life; of a celebration of the Eucharist in a quiet Norfolk Church with the mediaeval glass filtering the colours, and the early noise of harvesting coming through the open door; or of standing at any time before the Wilton Diptych. Each scene recalls aspects of an indivisible heritage, and is part of the fabric and expression of our civilisation. (1976:14)

This passage is interesting because Cormack links heritage firmly into what Patrick Wright has described as 'a well established and broadly Conservative tradition' of writing (1985:82). Other examples of this tradition, he argues, can be found in the writings of Stanley Baldwin, G. K. Chesterton, H. A. L. Fisher, and even Ramsay MacDonald.

Wright argues that common to all such writings is the theme of the celebration of an 'indivisible heritage' as 'a kind of sacrament encountered only in fleeting if well remembered experiences which go without saying to exactly the extent they are taken for granted by initiates, by true members of the ancestral nation' (1985:83). Such writings, Wright argues, are ethnocentric bordering on racist and intensified by the experience of war. They are also, we would like to add, most definitely anglocentric. The ancestral nation Wright is talking about includes Scotland only as part of a greater England.

We can make two criticisms of the approach to heritage by Wright and Hewison. First, there is an assumption that consumers are passive recipients of this kind of ideological hegemony. Secondly, both authors over-emphasise the rightward and inevitably anglocentric thrust of heritage. Historians like Raphael Samuel have argued that a variety of heritages are on offer, both local and national, including those suspectible to leftist and radical interpretations. After all, as we pointed out earlier in this chapter, the origins of the National Trust lay in a popular movement to protect access to land and rights of way in England, and it was only later that the Trust took on a more conservative disposition following its 'capture' in the post 1945 period (Wright, 1986). In any case, within the UK, there are in addition to local/regional and radical heritages, a rich variety of alternative and competing national heritages – English, Scottish, Welsh, and Irish/Northern Irish – each with considerable political potential to mobilise different constitutional outcomes. The images and icons of heritage north of the border are not English ones; the mythopoeic narrative of Scotland is not that of England. In the words of the English geographer Nigel Thrift: 'It is . . . important to recognise that the 'national' traditions of countryside and heritage so beloved of the "service class" are not truly national (despite the casual equation of "Britain" with "England")' (1989:39).

Our concern here is with the Scottish dimension of heritage, and we will examine the extent to which it connects with the cultural and political meanings of Scotland. Wright's later work (*The Guardian*, 18 August 1993) has shown how notions of English heritage have leant themselves to conservative even racist political accounts, and it is one of the interesting features of 'Englishness' that it has often been employed as part of a reactionary political discourse. Even Mrs Thatcher's successor, John Major, has chosen to highlight heritage themes in his 'back to basics' campaign which conjures up a highly stylised world of England in the 1950s:

> Fifty years from now, Britain will still be the country of long shadows on county grounds, warm beer, invincible green suburbs, dog lovers, and – as George Orwell said – old maids bicycling to holy communion through

the morning mist. And, if we get our way, Shakespeare will still be read – even in school. Britain will survive unamendable in all essentials. (speech to the Conservative Group for Europe, 22 April 1993)

It is only recently that a debate has begun on concepts of Englishness, and its associated landscapes of the mind. The work of the political geographer Peter Taylor at Newcastle University is particularly important here. (It is also significant that both Taylor and the archaeologist Peter Fowler are based at Newcastle insofar as it gives them a sense of geographical and cultural distance from the southern centre of power.) Taylor argues that an apparently homogeneous English national identity covers up considerable internal variation, and especially systems of power. He points out, for example, that the geographical core of England is called the 'Home Counties' whereas peripherality is built into the descriptions of other territories, for example, The North, the West Country and so on, all lumped together as 'the provinces'. Insofar as the Conservative heartland lies in the south of England, it surprises Taylor little that the core cultural metaphor is a southern one.

The travel writer, Ian Ousby, reinforces this point about the cultural construction of 'England' in his book *The Englishman's England*, in which he seeks to show how movements in taste have led to patterns of travel, and how in turn, these patterns of travel have been expanded and systematised into a tourist industry. He comments:

> Our communal sense of England has been codified into the familiar images of the travel poster and the accompanying rhetoric of the guidebook far more than we care to admit, making the countryside into cottage gardens with larkspurs, London into bowler hats, pigeons, buses and policemen, leaving the industrial cities of the north conveniently hidden from view by the curve of the earth's surface and reducing our history and culture to a list of representative sights or specially selected attractions. (1990:4)

As regards the Scottish dimension of heritage, it is obvious that it is doubly peripheral to the dominant but often implicit English one. It is plainly not English, but it also escapes hierarchical ordering in a way the North of England ('The North') does not. It has the capacity to generate an alternative political and cultural consciousness, and it will be an important part of our argument that this capacity has grown rather than diminished in the late twentieth century. This is not simply because the cultural and political power of the British state has waned, although it undoubtedly has, but because most modern state formations are under scrutiny. Globalisation of the economy, supra-national political agreements (such as the European Union), and the impact of multinational media on 'national' cultures have all eroded the power of national states to control their own economic, political and cultural affairs. In the context of this broad debate, we can place the revival of regionalism and nationalism. The latter, and even the former, have a capacity to mobilise aspects of heritage for political purposes, and it is this process perhaps more than any other which has helped to bring heritage to prominence. In the late twentieth century when issues of identity become especially problematic, there is a search for roots, for discovering where we have come from. The focus on heritage is bound to be one expression of this search.

Heritage as Ideology

The final central theme of this book focuses on the ideology of heritage. We have already seen that heritage lends itself to pastiche, to reconstruction if not to construction *de novo*. The concept has also become caught up in a wider debate about modernism and post-modernism. Heritage seems to express neatly Jean Baudrillard's statement (1983) that the real is no longer real, as well as Umberto Eco's observation that 'absolute unreality is offered as real presence' (1987). Both writers are referring to the dissociation between what is actual and what is believable. It is a central tenet of post-modern thought that the latter has become more important than the former in influencing social action. The key association between heritage and the post-modern lies in MacCannell's notion of 'staged authenticity' (1974), where the sign and the real are treated as equivalent; indeed, the sign has priority over the real if it carries more magic or authenticity. MacCannell picks up the idea of front/back stage from Erving Goffman (1973), and implies in his work that the 'unstaged' authentic lies in the back region where things are not arranged for tourists, and are therefore 'real'. As we shall see in the next chapter, there are considerable criticisms to be made of MacCannell's work, but it has undoubtedly been influential. In this book, we will not be arguing for a post-modern conception of heritage, but we will argue that the revival of academic interest in heritage reflects its ideological potential in the late twentieth century.

THE ARGUMENT

There are, then, four basic themes in this book on heritage: its commodification, its consumption, the politics in which it has become embedded, and the ideological, that is to say the part it plays in the debate about post-modernism. It is as if heritage finds itself at the confluence of a much broader debate about about who we are and where we are going. The four themes act as supports for our study rather than as chapters in themselves. They will run through each of the chapters. Chapter 2 reviews the literature on the sociology of heritage, its treatment as a concept, and the way it has become embedded in sociological debate.

The third chapter will focus on Scottish heritage, and the debates about its authenticity. The relationship between culture and politics has always been a key one in Scotland – to what extent, for example, does the success of the SNP in the last three decades relate to a forefronting of the Scottish cultural dimension? Where do the images and icons of Scotland come from, and why do they function as they do, and for whom? Is Scottish heritage deeply flawed and alienating, helping to keep Scots politically within the British state?

Chapter 4 examines the manufacture of Scottish heritage by the key agencies responsible for it. We will focus on three competing discourses on Scottish heritage. First, on how it is treated as a product to be sold in the marketplace. This manipulation of heritage evokes the vocabulary of commerce, and is largely the preserve of the Scottish Tourist Board. We will examine the assumptions about and presentations of Scottish heritage by STB. The second discourse concerning heritage is that of inheritance, or '*patrimoine*'. This evokes a vocabulary of social and cultural order, and is most closely associated with the National Trust for Scotland, with its strongly patrician ethos and culture. In the broadest sense, this is a 'political' discourse on heritage. The third discourse is more strongly associated with the 'academy', with the vocabulary of technique and knowledge, and we will examine the role of Historic Scotland and its concern with artefacts and ruins as a fitting representative of this discourse. No account of heritage is possible in these islands without an examination of the 'stately homes' industry. Here is a very profitable and burgeoning sector which has allowed the landed gentry and aristocracy to find a means of economic and ideological defence for its social position. In Chapter 5 we will examine how Scottish lairds in particular have insinuated themselves into public consciousness as the keepers of the national heritage.

The following two chapters, 6 and 7, will focus on the consumption of heritage among those who have made a financial commitment to Scottish heritage, namely life members of the National Trust for Scotland. In these chapters we will be able to test out ideas about the social appeal of heritage to the 'service class', and the degree to which it fits into this class's wider conception of its social image and that of Scotland.

In the final chapter, we will discuss the broader meaning of heritage in the context of cultural and political changes in Scotland. Does heritage allow us to break the linear time-chain between past, present and future? How does heritage fit with the revival of interest in identity and nationalism? In what ways does heritage contribute to ways of imagining ourselves both culturally and politically at the end of the twentieth century?

In this book we will treat the debate about heritage in Scotland as a specific version of a broader one which occurs in all modern societies. 'Heritage' is a word which is powerful, persuasive, and ideologically loaded. It is also ethnocentric. Our interest in heritage in Scotland grew out of curiosity about the explosion in its local and national manifestations, coupled with a dissatisfaction with the conventional, largely anglocentric, explanations to hand. These are good grounds, albeit not the only ones, on which to make a case for focussing our study on the growth of heritage in Scotland. We trust though that our analysis of heritage will carry with it messages for elsewhere, for that is both the intention of this book and our justification for writing it. Let us begin our task by reviewing the analytical tools which a sociological perspective gives us.

Chapter 2

The Sociology of Heritage

This chapter will review the intellectual tools at our disposal for analysing heritage. Ours is a sociological approach which focuses on the social, economic and political interests which drive the 'heritage' industry. There are four ways of looking at heritage which we want to examine: first, how the rise of heritage fits into the changing political environment of the last fifteen years; second, how and why heritage has been commercialised; third, the extent to which heritage fits into a 'post-modern' perspective; and finally, how heritage has become a key marker for social identity. It is important to stress that the heritage literature does not conveniently fall into such neat categories, but it seems to us that for analytical purposes this is a helpful way to proceed.

THE POLITICS OF HERITAGE

There is little doubt that, from the late 1970s, heritage fits into an analysis of the rise of the New Right in general and Thatcherism in particular. This is reflected in the two most significant critiques of heritage to appear in the mid to late 1980s, namely, those by Patrick Wright, *On Living in an Old Country* (1985), and Robert Hewison's *The Heritage Industry* (1987). Both set heritage in the general context of British politics in that period. Put simply, they both argue in different ways that the British state in the 1980s sought to mobilise national identity in its project to change British society. In other words, heritage, in the form of a 'remembered past' of events and processes symbolised through monuments and artefacts, was mobilised by the state to effect social and economic change. The icons and symbols of a perceived 'common heritage' were important levers of political and social legitimation.

Wright's book is the starting point chronologically and conceptually for most academic accounts of the sociology of heritage. He argues that since 1979 a political conscription of the past has taken place in Britain, and that a preoccupation with 'the nation' rather than the state is indicative of a deep crisis in which traditions and customs were being destroyed by economic development. At the same time, an ever-deepening source of cultural meaning is sought with which this changing society can legitimate itself. In this situation, Wright argues: 'tradition appears as an artifice, articulated not in particular or essential connection to people's experience, but at the generalised and diffused level of an overriding 'national identity' (1985:141-2).

Wright had spent most of the 1970s in North America, and on returning to Britain, found the country 'full of precious and imperilled traces – a closely held iconography of what it is to be English' (1985:2). That distinction between Britain and England is at one level unconsciously anglocentric, but it also indicates an awareness that the nation which was being mobilised by Thatcherism was undoubtedly the latter. Neo-Conservative authoritarianism was a strategy of presenting a 'national identity', a spirit of England, to which all had to return. Wright drew on a national obsession with 'stately homes' and the preservation of landscapes and buildings in which the National Trust had become 'an ethereal kind of holding company for the dead spirit of the nation' (1985:56). He found evidence in the experience of the Falklands War with its accompanying resonances of British imperial power ('remembered war', in his phrase), as well as the raising of the Tudor warship the Mary Rose. Both the Falklands War and the raising of the Mary Rose occurred in the same year – 1982 – at a point of low political fortunes for the Thatcher government. Having resort to heritage, however, was not simply a convenient political expediency. Rather, it reconnected current events with a 'deep history', one which was geared to restoring a grander and older identity of some imaginary Britain. 'History becomes, more urgently, the object of ceremonies of resonance and continuity when it seems actively to be threatened and opposed by an inferior present epoch'

(1985:166). The seizure and manipulation of heritage for political purposes was also reflected in the battle over the English schools curriculum (learning 'facts', the key events of Anglo-British history) rather than interpretations.

The view that heritage had become a political touchstone for the Thatcher government in the 1980s was shared by Hewison. He wrote: 'In the face of apparent decline and disintegration, it is not surprising that the past seems a better place. Yet it is irrecoverable, for we are condemned to live perpetually in the present' (1987:43). His book, *The Heritage Industry,* remains the most explicit commentary to date on the public's apparently growing obsession with the past reflected in its desire to consume cultural events and artefacts which reflect the past in different ways. For Hewison as well as Wright, the cultural and political perspectives dominate. He stresses how Mrs Thatcher and the New Right were able to mobilise and manipulate a set of thoroughly Conservative ideas about 'deep England', an England which has to be defended against the enemy within and without.

There is perhaps a temptation in this analysis simply to see heritage as offering a political expediency to a government in trouble. There is also the apparent contradiction that a New Right government wedded to extending the marketplace against the state should have recourse to such a thoroughly statist device as nationalism. This would be to oversimplify the Thatcherite project. Thatcherism had two main strands, fundamentally contradictory, a neo-liberal one of reducing as many social relations as possible to the cash nexus, and a neo-Conservative one which sought not less but more power for the central state. Such a political strategy was not all that easy to maintain, given its basic philosophical contradictions. In this regard, heritage has two useful functions. On the one hand, it represents considerable cultural capital which can itself be bought and sold, as well as a means whereby commodities can be traded as 'authentic'. Both involve commodifying the past. Heritage and enterprise, Corner and Harvey point out, form a 'mythic couplet for preserving hegemonic equilibrium and momentum during a period of major national reorientation' (1991:46). We need only look at how useful 'oldness' is as a marketing strategy to make that connection. On the other hand, heritage is a cultural device for managing as well as for 'stage managing' economic change. Conservative regimes in Britain since 1979 have had recourse to claiming the past as a goal for the future. Mrs Thatcher had her 'Victorian Values', and John Major his 'Back to Basics', while the broad goal of Conservatism since 1979 has been to effect major economic and social change.

Other commentators like Tom Nairn have analysed heritage icons like the monarchy (1994). He points out that the institution has sought to modernise itself in the twentieth century by transforming the impersonal Crown into the intimate Royal Family. Monarchism and royal ritualism become the receptacle of heritage. Royalty's further function is to stand as one of the few British (as opposed to English) institutions thereby helping to incorporate national differences within the Kingdom. Just as everyone can identify with a family, so the vocabulary of home and domesticity has the potential to encourage identification with the stately 'homes' of the aristocracy. The mobilisation of these aspects of heritage help to explain the survival of both monarchy and aristocracy in the United Kingdom (even the country's name is redolent of heritage).

Patrick Wright uses the connections between heritage, nostalgia and the intimate to draw out the deeper significance of living in an 'old country'. He makes the point that the actual depth of historical experience is irrelevant to the mobilisation of heritage. What matters are current concerns:

> The national past is above all a modern past, and as the events of recent years have indicated very clearly, it is defined not just in relation to the general disappointment of earlier historical expectation, but also and more pointedly around the leading tensions of the contemporary political situation. (1985:2)

Heritage has the power to make the connection with 'everyday life'. Using the work of the Hungarian philosopher, Agnes Heller, Wright argues that heritage becomes an intimate part of individual identity because 'everyday life' is experienced as intimate and personal, but is highly structured and institutionalised. Everyday life above all is, in Heller's word, 'situated'. It also has its own forms of (everyday) historical consciousness in which stories play a crucial part. These narratives rely for truth-status on authenticity rather than objectivity, on their plausibility rather than their veracity. Western modernity, says

Wright, has its own versions of nostalgia which testify to the destabilisation of social life in a rapidly changing society. There emerge golden ages or rural idylls in which old, 'remembered' forms of security, such as the family, become alluring. So too in a different way does the fascination of 'remembered war' which connects up the personal and the national. Such remembering touches those on the left as well as the right; the symbolism of the Second World War crosses the whole political spectrum in Britain. (At this stage we might recall the 'war heritage' project in North Yorkshire we discussed in the previous chapter.) Wright observes:

> The nation is the modern integration par excellence, and it is in the service of the nation that public images and interpretations of the past circulate . . . The rags and tatters of everyday life take on the lustre of the idealised nation when they are touched by its symbolism. (1985:24)

Here we have the connection between national and personal heritage, for 'the nation works to re-enchant a disenchanted everyday life' (ibid.).

There can be little doubt that the New Right has managed to mobilise heritage as a vital part of its political project since 1979, despite the fundamental contradictions between neo-liberalism and neo-conservatism. Liberalising social and cultural relations leaves little time for paying reverence to sacred icons. The impatience of free-market liberals with the monarchy is just one indication of this. Nevertheless, it is necessary to be careful before associating heritage irredeemably with the New Right. As Wright points out, nostalgia for the 1939–45 war and the ensuing welfare state are central icons of Labour heritage in the UK. Similarly, Raphael Samuel in a review of Hewison's book observed that the first great wave of conservation, that is to say the mania for railway preservation in the 1950s and steam traction rallies in the 1960s were plebeian rather than patrician in character (*The Guardian*, 9 October 1987). Samuel regards conservation not simply as a reflex of economic decline, but as an 'antiphon', a counter-chant, to the modernisations of the 1950s and 1960s. He comments:

> On a larger timespan . . . the heritage industry could be seen as a picking up of ancient threads. Historically, it is

modernism - a self-conscious aesthetic of the new - rather than revivalism which appears as an oddity. Economically, modernisation and traditionalism are not necessarily alternatives: as Mrs Thatcher is [sic] teaching us in the contemporary restructuring of capital and class, they are two sides of the same coin. (ibid.)

Undoubtedly, setting heritage in the context of the political and economic upheavals of the 1980s has much to commend it. History as pageant becomes heritage, and with political purpose. In the words of the Scottish historian, Christopher Harvie:

History in the government's sense is ideology, rather like the 'history of the regiment' that soldiers are subjected to, directed at preserving a centralised state which is otherwise under threat - and possibly turning choice parts of an otherwise decaying social and material fabric into marketable 'heritage'. (1991:78)

Nevertheless, there is nothing inevitable about the rightward thrust of heritage. In addition to those of a radical or leftist disposition, there are alternative national heritages on offer, while for those of a post-modern disposition, blurring the boundaries between Right and Left is part of the postmodern condition. In any case, it is our view that seeing heritage in terms of the political dimensions of Right and Left is to miss the complexities involved. To grasp those we must· broaden our perspective.

THE COMMERCE OF HERITAGE

Another sociological approach to heritage is to focus on its commercial exploitation rather than its political manipulation. Writers such as Hewison build into their critique the view that culture and commerce have become increasingly intertwined. He comments:

It is ironic that while those of marxisant persuasion have difficulty in convincing people that we must think of art as a form of cultural production, the non-marxisant bureaucracy that manages the arts thinks more and more of the arts as 'product'. Product that is offered to 'consumers', for whose purchasing power the various art forms are increasingly in competition. (1991:163)

In large part this is due to the changes in funding for the arts as the result of political decisions. Museums and galleries have been forced into the marketplace at least since 1979, and increasingly compete for funds in the public and private sectors. As Hewison points out, the philosophy behind the British Museum Act of 1753 to make the great national museums a public responsibility has been superseded.

Broadening the argument, it has been argued that the overall restructuring of British capital in the context of global changes has ushered in a new form of 'late capitalism' (Jameson, 1984). In this form, culture, not simply conventionally manufactured items, is a major commodity, and, as we shall explore in the next section, becomes a defining characteristic of post-modernism. The angle here is less on the cultural content or the political message of heritage and more on the economic opportunities it affords. It is this perspective which has given us the notion of heritage as an 'industry' which implies a product, a set of entrepreneurs, a manufacturing process, a set of social relations structured around this process, a market and consumers.

John Urry's book *The Tourist Gaze* (1990) sets an analysis of heritage within the broader conspectus of tourism. He argues that there has been a major reorientation of cultural products set in the context of a shift from Fordist production and consumption which was based on mass forms of manufacture and mass leisure (such as the late nineteenth century seaside resort) to post-Fordist differentiated consumption, where there is no single mass tourist market. This shift has brought an increase in consumption as a proportion of national income, a rise in consumer indebtedness, the commodification of virtually all aspects of social life, including charity, greater volatility and differentiation of consumer markets and the politicisation of consumption. Whereas the holiday camp and annual holidays at the seaside typified Fordist holiday making, the emphasis on contemporary tourism is on 'freedom' and choice. New tourism, says Urry, is segmented, packaged and customised.

The title of Urry's book indicates why tourism is important. The concept of the 'gaze' is borrowed from Foucault's analysis of the 'medical gaze'. By this he meant that doctors were not simply observers but that what they saw was structured and justified by the institutionalising of medicine. The doctor was trained to 'see' things which ordinary observers could not. Hence, the tourist in the late twentieth century is in some sense trained, or at least predisposed, to look at scenes and sights in the expectation that they are out of the ordinary. This environment 'speaks to us in ways we appreciate, or at least we anticipate that it will do so. In other words, we gaze at what we encounter' (1990:1). The tourist gaze, then, is socially organised and systematised, especially in contrast with other social practices based on home and paid work.

Urry sets out to examine the processes whereby the gaze is constructed and reinforced; who or what authorises it; what its consequences are for the 'places' which are its object; and how it relates to a variety of other social practices. Tourism, he observes, is essentially a twentieth-century phenomenon, succeeding the more ideologically and socially limited pilgrimages of the Middle Ages, and the aristocratic Victorian Grand Tour. Modern tourists are to be treated as semioticians, reading the landscape for certain pre-established notions or signs. The tourist gaze gathers in those sights which are deemed to be out of the ordinary, and objectified through, say, a postcard or photograph. Urry comments: 'The gaze is constructed through signs, and tourism involves the collection of signs' (1990:3).

The seaside resort typified the first wave of twentieth-century mass Fordist consumerism. The working class of northern England found in Blackpool and Morecambe the antitheses of factory work in northern mills. Their successors took their solace in the holiday camps of Butlins and Pontins, and in the second half of the century on the beaches of Spain. By the late twentieth century, a new breed has been formed, the 'post-tourist'. Post-tourists, as Urry understands them, know that there is no authentic tourist experience, merely a series of games and texts than can be played. To use Urry's own example, a miniature of the Eiffel Tower can be simultaneously a piece of kitsch, an exercise in geometric formalism, and a socially revealing artefact. The post-tourist is self-conscious, cool and role-distanced. Heritage has particular appeal for the post-tourist because it allows different layers of appreciation. Wigan Pier, for example, is a piece of joke-heritage both because it is and yet is not a 'real' place and because we catch the allusion to George Orwell. Urry is critical of Hewison's assumption that a straightforward nostalgia is transferred from object to the gazer and he points out that different visitors can 'read' quite different meanings into the same set of objects. His comment about Wigan Pier is well taken:

> The Wigan Pier centre is, after all, scholarly and educational; it presents a history of intense popular struggle; it identifies the bosses as partly to blame for mining disasters; it celebrates a non-elite popular culture; and it is organised by a council with the objective of glorifying 'heroic labour'. (1990:111)

The explosion in heritage holidays and activities fits into a post-tourist mentality. We ought, however, to treat the concept of the post-tourist with caution. Few tourists are likely to be as sophisticated as this, and more fundamentally, how one would identify (and self-identify) a post-tourist is not at all clear (Bruner, 1991).

Although it is true that visitors to museums are three times more likely to be members of the service class than the manual working class, there has been rising interest in 'industrial' heritage and in the lives of self-styled 'ordinary people', witness the popularity of sites like Beamish in the North of England, the People's Palace in Glasgow, and Albert Dock in Liverpool. The attractions of mining museums, steel works and industrial sites generally testify that the de-industrialisation process has generated a sense of loss both for the kind of work itself and for the social and community processes in which it was embedded. The demise of traditional mills, docks and factories has also released new kinds of properties onto the development market; warehouses, tenements and workshops have been converted to new non-industrial uses. Virtually all towns and cities in Britain have their sites of gentrification around former industrial spaces and far from their previous legacy being obliterated, it is built into the meaning of the place in a deliberate if sanitised way.

A large part of the reason for this is that much of the burden for economic regeneration falls upon the local authorities. Regeneration through culture has been an obvious device because it builds (often literally) on the legacy of the past while promising economic diversification. It also fits in with the culture and politics of conservation which has taken hold in the last two decades, promising to attract upper-income groups into those parts of cities in need of economic regeneration. Such redevelopment brings in funds from private developers and central government as well as heritage bodies and the European Union. Local authorities have found themselves in new forms of competition for art galleries, TV and radio franchises, shopping complexes, conference centres and the apparatus of cultural capital in alliance with private capital.

Scottish cities have been in the vanguard of these developments, its towns and cities have had the advantage over their English counterparts in having central government funds channeled to them via Scottish Enterprise, formerly the Scottish Development Agency. Edinburgh, for example, has invested considerable funds in the regeneration of its former port of Leith with the aid of local and central enterprise money: 'Leith Sur Mer' is its ironic local title. And Dundee, Scotland's premier industrial city, with its far higher proportion of workers in manufacturing than Glasgow, has actively exploited its manufacturing past. Many of its former jute warehouses, close to the city centre, have been turned into small apartments. However, much more enterprising than that, it has acquired an old sailing ship, *The Discovery*, bought very cheaply from the Greater London Council as it was being closed down. The exact claim of Dundee to the ship does not bear too close scrutiny, but it is strong enough to allow the city to moor the ship in a disused wharf and thus proclaim itself 'City of Discovery', a title nicely suited to a project of local economic regeneration.

It is Glasgow, however, which is the leading example of 'place boosterism'. Glasgow built its reputation in imperial Britain as the second city of the Empire, and was strongly associated in the public mind with heavy engineering, notably shipbuilding and locomotive manufacture. A city with a strong sense of itself – it has been called Scotland's city-state – Glasgow had a vibrant local culture as well as ethnic and social divisions. By the 1970s, though, it was defined by itself and central government as in urgent need of economic regeneration. Securing considerable public funds from central government (the Scottish Development Agency), Strathclyde Regional Council, as well as the local Glasgow District Council, the city embarked in the early 1980s on a campaign to change its reputation for industrial and political militancy, religious sectarianism, squalor and urban violence.

The Mr Men symbol from New York was adopted with the nicely ambiguous slogan 'Glasgow's Miles Better'. Better than what? Better than it used to be? Better than its old rival in the East, Edinburgh? In 1988 the slogan was verified as the city won the competition to hold the National Garden Festival, a legacy of Michael Heseltine's semi-corporatist sojourn at the Department of the Environment. This success was capped in 1990 when a new regenerated Glasgow was made European City of Culture (slogan: 'There's a lot of Glasgowing going in 1990', with the aid of graphics in the style of Rennie Mackintosh, Glasgow's early twentieth-century artist. So pervasive was the house-style that it became known to its critics as 'Mockintosh'). Neither of these titles, National Garden Festival nor City of Culture, caused such a stir before or after Glasgow's stint (who can remember who preceded and succeeded the city in these competitions?), but the city used them to the full as devices in its assault on a mean reputation which it saw as the key reason for its economic decline. The leader of the Labour Council, Pat Lally, made no apologies 'for milking 1990 in the interests of the people, for all the development and investment we can'. He became so identified with the strategy that the concert hall built for 1990 is locally known as Lally's Palais.

His programme was not without its critics inside and outside the council. By 1992, when the party was over and the bills had to be paid, Lally was ousted as council leader by a rival who had a less boosterist image, only to win the leadership back again in 1994 (*The Scotsman*, 8 July 1994). Outwith the council, critics on the left, notably in the group Workers City, pointed out that Glasgow's considerable legacy for political struggle as well as its deep and abiding forms of social deprivation were being airbrushed out of the picture by the image-merchants. The official exhibition 'Glasgow's Glasgow' was a financial failure, and had relegated the city's history of political and religious strife to a footnote in a lengthy text. At the same time, the struggle over Glasgow's heritage had surfaced in a conflict over the keeper of the People's Palace Museum, Elspeth King, who had been turned down for a promoted post in the city's museums service. The high-profile political and social museum which King ran seemed to be at odds with the new sanitised image which the city authorities wanted to present to developers. Ultimately, King resigned to run a local museum in the east of Scotland.

Glasgow was quick to seize on reports which placed it high in league tables for 'quality of life', and employed economic consultants to show the direct and indirect effects on employment of becoming 'culture city' (Myerscough, 1991). The 1993 report showing the rapid rise of Glasgow up the tourist league table is simply the latest in its sustained campaign to regenerate its economy through tourism and heritage. The fact that this heritage does not correspond too closely to its actual history helps to make the point that in the culture politics of the 1990s this is not required. The city had embarked on a strategy of economic change by means of image-building, and cultural tourism was perceived as the way to the promised land.

The self-proclaimed 'internationalising' of the city by the 1990 festival director, Bob Palmer, now the director of performing arts in Glasgow, reveals the strategy for economic regeneration. So does his comment that the city 'has been used as a model for many European cities that are trying to copy the regeneration process that is taking place' (*The Scotsman*, 27 December 1993). Glasgow has acted as an entrepreneur for translating to a European setting the North American strategy of 'culture bootstrapping' as a means of economic regeneration, and by employing what Urry calls the 'festival marketplace'. In this context, heritage and history serve as the raw materials rather than as the benchmarks against which all claims have to be judged. Hewison's critique of heritage is that it drives history out, a process which can only be redressed by bringing the two into alignment. So 'the open story of history has become the closed book of heritage' (Corner and Harvey, 1991:175). By contrast Urry (1990) recognises that both concepts operate in quite different form-fields. Just as historians have little control over what people think happened, what we might call their conception of the 'past', so heritage might rely on a bit of history but it cannot be mistaken for it. As Hoyau (1988) points out, the past is an imaginary object formed around the family, conviviality (community life), and a spirit of place, which can, without too much difficulty, be connected into heritage as well as everyday life.

The growth in museums, then, is explicable in terms of the fascination with heritage. Urry points out that museums are central to the tourist experience: 'The fame of the object becomes its meaning. There is thus a ceremonial agenda, in which it is established what we should see and sometimes even the order in which they should be seen' (1990:129).

He argues that museums have traditionally been founded on the aura of the authentic historical artefact (speaking for itself, as it were). However, the museum gaze has changed in a number of ways: there is now a much broader range of objects, and a proliferation of alternative 'histories' to be encountered; partly as a result, the nature of museums have changed – they no longer resemble churches and encourage passivity; and finally there is a changed relationship between the museum and other social institutions. Shops, for example, resemble museums (with titles like 'The Way We Were' and 'Past Lives' and so on), museums have become shops, and 'factory tourism' has developed as an integral part of business. In Scotland, for example, virtually all tartan and woollen mills carry their own exhibitions giving the 'history' of the cloth, delivered to you with its aura intact. Urry doubts whether the term 'museum' can even survive insofar as it 'stems from a period of high art and auratic culture well before 'heritage' had been invented' (1990:134).

Urry's *The Tourist Gaze* is more explicitly concerned than either Wright or Hewison with the commerce of heritage and its consumption. Using the ideas of Bourdieu, he identifies the 'new middle class' as especially susceptible to heritage consumption because as a class it is stronger on 'cultural' than on 'economic' capital, and because its boundaries with other classes are more malleable. The powers of all social classes, according to Bourdieu, are founded as much on symbolic as on economic and political power. These symbolic goods have their own 'economy' *vis-à-vis* other classes and social struggle takes place between these goods as much as it does on the material level. Classes seek to impose their own *habitus*, their system of classification regarding taste and life style, on others. Culture and education are vital aspects of these struggles. Hence, the use of culture is both the result of class position and a means of fighting for dominance. It is both an outcome and a mechanism. A number of social changes have altered this class struggle in the course of the century. First, the size of the service class has grown as the tertiary sector of the economy has grown and as manual labour has diminished. Second, the culture of this class is much more accessible and less elitist than that of the traditional bourgeoisie. Third, the *habitus* of this service class is more fluid and permeable than others. Fourth, it occupies a strategically important position between the 'vulgarity' of the working class, and the 'elitism' of the upper class.

This service class does not own substantial amounts of capital; it operates within social institutions which service capital, it enjoys superior market, work and status situations within the context of its members careers and it has been able so far to regulate entry into occupations by means of credentials. The middle-class groupings who cluster in the service class have, according to Urry, a number of important features: the centrality of symbolic work; the dominating role of the media in determining fashion and taste; freedom and incentive to innovate cultural patterns; status ranking which accrues from fashionability rather than respectability; and the declining importance of economic over cultural capital (1990:91).

As we have already pointed out, Urry's account of the sociological base of heritage is somewhat sketchy and ill-defined, but he does, nevertheless, provide a firmer base than either Wright or Hewison. Above all, his account forefronts the need to focus on the consumption rather than simply the production of heritage. It is one of the main failings of the literature on culture generally and heritage in particular that it implies a fairly undifferentiated and passive reception of what is manufactured. This neglect often expresses itself in the assumption, in Hewison, for example, that the presentation of heritage can only be read in a single, uniform way. In fact, there is little work on the consumption of heritage, and our study later in the book of a sample of life members of the National Trust for Scotland is an attempt to redress this balance.

The neglect of cultural consumption is, however, part of a much broader tendency within sociology to attribute causality to aspects of production. Daniel Miller, in his important

book *Material Culture and Mass Consumption* (1987), criticised academics for neglecting consumption in preference to
production as the key generative arena within which dominant social relations emerge in modern societies. In our society, there is far more interest in the level of wages and salaries,
the relation between public and private services in generating
income, than in what people do with their money or services
received. These are deemed to be derivative of their place in
the productive system, an odd and ironic sharing of views
between the two dominant theoretical modes in twentieth-
century Western sociology, Marxism and functionalism.

POST-MODERNISM AND HERITAGE

Throughout this chapter, much of the discussion has brought
us close to the theme of post-modernism, whether we are discussing the political symbolism of heritage, its consumption
and social base, or its commercial exploitation. In this section
we will outline the arguments and criticisms associated with
this concept and its applicability to the study of heritage in a
sociological context.

The argument behind post-modernism is that a new kind
of society has emerged which is very different from the past.
According to Anthony Giddens, the argument usually involves
one or more of the following presumptions: all pre-existing
foundations of epistemology have been shown to be unreli-
able; history has no final goal, and nothing can be known
with certainty; new social movements emerge which presage
a new social and political order. The precise parameters of
this new society are unclear.

How does heritage fit into this post-modernist account?
Two aspects of cultural change are important here. On the
one hand, the boundaries between high and low culture
dissolve; secondly, as Urry comments, 'commerce and culture
are indissolubly linked in the post-modern' (1990:85). Under
post-modernism, everyone is a permanent *emigré* from the
present, a 'sign system in which images and stereotypes from
the past and the future, from the locale and the globe, are
implacably intermingled, admitting no principle of determi-
nancy' (Rojek, 1993:168). Similarly, modernist distinctions
between work and leisure, past and present, public and
private, have lost their force in a process of 'de-differentiation'
(Lash, 1990).

Hewison links the growth of the heritage industry with post-modernism because 'both conspire to create a shallow screen that intervenes between our present lives and our history' (1987:135). The commodity which museums put on the market are called different things by different people: 'hyper-reality' (Eco, 1987), 'simulation' (Baudrillard, 1983), or 'historicism' (Jameson, 1984). In this world, image has replaced reality, and we now live in a world of simulacra, perfect copies of originals which never existed. In this way, these simulacra pass as heritage, which in Hewison's view, is a form of history which never existed. While Urry disputes the idea that history is more knowable and real than heritage, he argues that 'the way in which all sorts of places have become centres of spectacle and display, and the nostalgic attraction of 'heritage' can both be seen as elements of post-modernism' (1990:93–4).

The key assocation between heritage and the post-modern lies in MacCannell's notion of 'staged authenticity' (1974 and 1992) which we introduced in the first chapter. In his earlier work, MacCannell uses Erving Goffman's distinction between front regions and back regions. Front regions are the public areas; back areas are the private ones, and it is only in the back regions that authenticity and the intimacy of social relations can be found. Tourists, MacCannell argues, try to enter via the back regions in their quest for authenticity of experience. Many heritage organisations try to capitalise on this by creating back regions for touristic purposes (such as the kitchens of stately homes). As MacCannell argues, there inevitably remains a 'staged' quality to this encounter:

> the touristic way of getting in with the natives is to enter into a quest for authentic experiences, perceptions and insights. The quest is marked off in stages in the passage from front to back. Movement from stage to stage corresponds to growing touristic understanding. This continuum is sufficiently developed in some areas of the world that it appears as an infinite regression of stage sets. Once in this manifold, the tourist is trapped; his road does not end abruptly in some conversion process . . . as he breaks the bounds of all that is pseudo and penetrates, finally, into a real back region. Tourists make brave sorties out from their hotels hoping, perhaps, for an authentic experience, but their paths can be traced in advance over the

small increments of what is for them increasingly apparent authenticity preferred by tourist settings. Adventuresome tourists progress from stage to stage, always in the public eye, and greeted everywhere by their obliging hosts. (1974:602)

In his later collection of essays *Empty Meeting Grounds* (1992), MacCannell argues that tourism is not simply reducible to commercial activities, but is at the forefront of the production of new cultural forms. He analyses the character of performances (another legacy from the works of Goffman) as crucial to 'authenticity'. In this context, tourism has to manufacture the exotic and the primitive, even though the term 'is increasingly only a response to a mythic necessity to keep the idea of the primitive alive in the modern world and consciousness', and because there are several understandings, commercial and academic, which require its existence (MacCannell, 1992:34). In their quest for the authentic, tourists become contemporary pilgrims in search of the real, the 'sacred', but unlike their religious counterparts, they do not worship at one single shrine, but pay promiscuous homage to a variety of attractions. Above all, these post-modern places 'are designed around a totemic exaltation of the past not as history' (ibid.:95). Festivals or 'traditions' are specifically designed as the bearer of traditional values even although they are the means of their destruction.

MacCannell discusses these processes in the context of the implicit power system surrounding ethnicity. The definition of the ethnic for tourist purposes operates a double-bind for the group subject to the tourist gaze. Typically, the group 'museumises' itself by presenting a stereotype which fits in with tourist expectations. Instead of adapting its values and practices in line with broader social processes, by conforming to required stereotypes group members come to relate to each other predominantly in these ways. MacCannell observes:

> Conforming to the requirements of being a living tourist attraction becomes a total problem affecting every detail of life. . . . Any deviation from the touristic cultural ideal can be read as a political gesture that produces conflict not between groups but within the group. (1992:179)

Ethnicity itself becomes a form of rhetoric read off a dominant white culture which is highly implicit. Hence, there is black but no white consciousness, female but no male, and as we shall see in the next chapter, Scottish but little English culture per se. In other words, ethnicity helps to define the periphery to the centre, rather than the other way round. Here, for example, is a comment written by the then (Conservative) Secretary of State for Scotland, Malcolm Rifkind, in the introduction to *Heritage Scotland*, the magazine of the National Trust for Scotland:

> It is a natural and proper thing for each of us to take a pride in our national identity and the achievements of our native country, but we should do so in a spirit which gives full recognition of the part other countries have played in our cultural and historical development – and the contribution we have made to theirs. (1989:3)

Such sentiments may seem eminently reasonable, but the sub-text to these comments is relevant. It is probable that 'other countries' here means England; and it is unlikely that such sentiments would be reciprocated south of the border. In other words, there is a political agenda contained in seemingly innocuous remarks. We have only to remind ourselves of the implicit hierarchy involved in the vocabulary of naming: there is no National Trust for England, only The National Trust (just as there is 'The Football Association' and 'The Rugby Football Union'). To return to MacCannell's point about ethnicity, an ethnic group defined as such comes to think of itself not as a people but as bearers of an authentic way of life which operates at the behest of others. We shall examine this dilemma in a Scottish context in the next chapter.

In the post-modern conception, the sign and the real are treated as equivalent; indeed, the sign has priority over the real if it carries more magic and authenticity (doubly so, if the participants become what they are playing). In Rojek's words, 'spectacle has replaced meaning and value is dominated by sensation'. In this context, heritage is a matter of signs; authenticity and originality are matters of technique, not 'reality':

> Preserving the past in order to escape into it is therefore seen as impossible. For merely to define something as unchangeable alters our relationship with it. Literary

landscapes, and for that matter heritage sites, do not preserve the past, they represent it. (1993:160)

Authenticity and originality are, above all, matters of technique. Modernist distinctions between the real world and the imaginary world are no longer valid in the post-modern scheme of things. There is no past, no future, no present, instead merely an eclectic historicism.

What is interesting to post-modernists about heritage is that reality depends on how convincing the presentation is, how well the 'staged authenticity' works. (It is interesting how the work of Erving Goffman has been subsumed in this interpretation. Front and back regions, presentations, everyday life, action places, ritual and ceremonial all find their place. His rejection of a paramount reality against which different experiences can be judged clearly strikes a post-modern chord.) The more 'authentic' the representation, the more 'real' it is. Theme parks, literary landscapes and heritage sites reject modernist notions of the distinction between the real and the imaginary, past and present, private and public, action and inaction, and, not least, work and leisure. The television soap opera *Coronation Street*, for example, is more real and thus more authentic than life in Salford, England.

The key problem with the post-modern perspective, however, is a fundamental methodological one, namely, the difficulty of trying to theorise cultural constructs from the inside out, as it were, when the investigator is implicated and ensnared as the bearer of the myths and images which are being investigated. Put another way, because the world of post-modernism is a world of no-history, a world of no absolutes in which everything is part of the discourse and discourses cannot be proved or disproved, then it is impossible to know what constitutes evidence. All relies on plausibility, on authenticity. Critics of post-modernism have attacked this version of authenticity. James Overton observes:

> Authenticity is not 'out there' to be tracked down. It is not a quality which exists in things, but a 'cultural construct', a taste which is part and parcel of a particular aesthetic. Just as 'tradition' and 'the historic' are constructed by particular people in the present, so too with authenticity. It follows that authenticity can never be 'staged' or 'spurious'. (1988:37)

In similar vein, Bruner points out that the tourist pursuit of the exotic has been conceptualised as a quest for authenticity by MacCannell who locates it within a myth of modern decadence. However, says Bruner, there is nothing particularly post-modern about this conception which has its origins at least in the late eighteenth-century Romantic movement. Nor can we simply assume that tourists are alienated from their own societies and have embarked on a search for authenticity elsewhere. Bruner comments:

> After all they are not dupes, and they realize that the native performances on their tour itinerary are constructions for a foreign audience. Tourists are willing to accept a reproduction as long as it is a good one, or as one tourist brochure put it, as long as it is an 'authentic reproduction'. (1991:240–1)

We do not accept that the analysis of heritage and tourism can only be achieved through the framework of post-modernism. We are attracted by Anthony Giddens' critique in which he argues that 'post-modernism' is a term best kept for styles or movements in literature, painting, art and architecture. Giddens argues, on the other hand, that post-modernity means something different from post-modernism. If we are moving into a phase of post-modernity, this means that the trajectory of social development is taking us away from the institutions of modernity towards a new and distinct type of social order. Post-modernism, if it exists in a cogent form, might express an awareness of such a transition, but does not show that it exists. Giddens argues:

> We have not moved beyond modernity but we are living precisely through a phase of radicalisation . . . We do not yet live in a post-modern social universe, but we can still see more than a few glimpses of the emergence of ways of life and forms of social organisation which diverge from those fostered by modern institutions. (1990:51–2).

Above all, Giddens argues, it is the rate of social and cultural change which is important here: 'The modern world is a "runaway world"; not only is the pace of social change much faster than in any prior system, so also is its scope, and the profoundness with which it affects pre-existing social practices and modes of behaviour' (1991:16).

We do not have to 'buy' post-modernism to appreciate this point. Clusters of social, economic and political systems were brought into being from the eighteenth century and are in dissolution in the late twentieth. The classical form of the 'nation-state', for instance, is undergoing radical change even dissolution, and the ideology of nationalism emerges as both a device for bolstering its fading popularity, and as a means for 'imagining', in Benedict Anderson's word, a new form of political community. Either way, the search for 'national heritage' helps to foreground these fundamental changes.

But it is not enough simply to attribute the salience of heritage to this politically abstract level and leave it there. In this chapter we have tried to show how the political, commercial and ideological aspects of heritage are woven inextricably together. The search for the social base of its appeal takes us into an underdeveloped area of sociology, that of consumption. John Urry's endeavours to attribute a susceptibility for heritage to the 'new middle class' represent a step in the right direction. We need to treat seekers after heritage, as with any other form of cultural product, as active interpreters of what they consume. In the next two chapters, we will focus on how heritage in Scotland is manufactured, at the level of historical construction (Chapter 3) and at the contemporary institutional level (Chapter 4). Only then can we explore the social base and cultural meaning of Scottish heritage which we have set out to do.

Chapter 3

Scottish Heritage
Commercialising the Culture

In his account of *Scotland in Film* (1990), Forsyth Hardy tells the story of a visit he had in 1953, while film correspondent of *The Scotsman* newspaper, from the Hollywood producer of *Brigadoon*. The producer was looking for a suitable site for his film, a village in the Highlands which would look unchanged after a hundred years. Hardy, taking a few liberties with the Highland/Lowland distinction, took him to Culross in Fife, Dunkeld and Comrie in Perthshire, and Braemar and Inveraray in the Highlands. The producer returned, disappointed, to Hollywood and commented: 'I went to Scotland but I could find nothing that looked like Scotland' (1990:1).

Hardy's story is significant because it brings into focus probably the two dominant discourses about Scotland, aptly styled Brigadoonery and anti-Brigadoonery. In our discussion of Scottish culture and heritage, we find that these discourses occur and re-occur, and that they have long insinuated themselves into tourism. There is no shortage of Scottish iconography; if anything, it is overwhelming. It appears in films, novels, poems, paintings, photographs, as well as on shortbread tins. It is virtually impossible to escape the imagery, and it has become the stuff of the heritage industry in Scotland. In this chapter, we will discuss the historical and cultural roots of the dominant representations of Scotland, while in Chapter 5 we will focus on how the key heritage organisations order and mobilise them.

Listen to how a professional archaeologist and non-Scot, Peter Fowler, describes, tongue in cheek, part of Scotland as portrayed in tourist leaflets:

The Scottish Highlands and Island tourist leaflet enjoins
you in Argyll and the Isles to 'visit pre-historic standing
stones; go cruising in waters saints and Vikings have
sailed'; in the Heart (where else?) of the Highlands it
offers 'Britain's oldest monster, Nessie' . . . and 'the sites
of ancient battlefields'. In the Northern Highlands and
Islands 'In the course of a day you can come across . . .
stone age remains and magnificent castles . . . And at the
end . . . you can frequently enjoy a ceilidh . . . into the
wee small hours (nae doot). (1992:123)

Much of this, of course, is tourist-speak, but there is no lack
of raw materials. The reader might like to add to this collection: tartan; kilts; heather; haggis; misty landscapes; couthy
(and slightly weird) natives; Jekyll and Hyde; Scottish soldiers;
Take The High Road; MQS (Mary Queen of Scots); BPC
(Bonnie Prince Charlie); Balmorality; Harry Lauder. There are
also counter-images: Glasgow hard men; socialist politics;
legendary meanness. But there is more than a suspicion that
these are simply two sides of the same coin. All of this, as we
shall see in the next chapter, offers rich pickings to heritage
advertisers in Scotland, and all contribute to the image of
Scotland as a single theme park. Probably no other country in
the world has such a rich iconography. What are its origins,
and what are its effects?

The cultural sociologist Raymond Williams referred to 'cultural formations' as: 'effective movements and tendencies, in
intellectual and artistic life, which have significant and sometimes decisive influence on the active development of a culture, and which have a variable and often oblique relation to
formal institutions' (1977:117). In discussions about Scottish
culture, two such formations, tartanry and Kailyardism, are
deemed to be of dominant, yet negative, significance. Such
has been their ideological power, it is argued, that they have
had a baleful effect on Scottish cultural and political life.

TARTANRY AND SCOTTISH HERITAGE

Tartanry has been used as a shorthand for the set of garish
symbols appropriated by Music Hall (and Harry Lauder) in the
1920s and 1930s. It clearly owes its origins to a highland garb
of history, but, the analysis goes, it has over time lost its original significance and has come to stand for a superficial and

sentimental attachment by lowland Scots to an emblem to which historically they have no right. It is also the over-whelming image of Scotland to be had in tourist shops and it is intimately associated with heritage.

It is worth outlining the tartan story before examining its cultural significance. Tartan was 'made' for the modern world in the relatively short time between the late eighteenth and mid-nineteenth century. During this period, a sequence of events occurred which gave tartan its modern meanings. In the first place, the Proscription Act, which had forbidden the wearing of 'highland garb' after the defeat of the Jacobites in 1746 at Culloden, was repealed in 1782 under political pressure from a group of rich and influential 'chieftains' living in London who were becoming conscious of the interest in the Gael, as were Scotland's élite generally. This interest had in large part been generated by the Romantic movement, the search for a suitable 'noble savage', primitive people closer to Nature, without the encumbrance of modern living and manners. The kilt and tartan came to signify the mystery of primitive society and consequently what had been lost since 1746 or had never been known was simply invented.

The élite was encouraged in the wearing of tartan by the visit of George IV to Edinburgh in 1822 at the behest of Sir Walter Scott who had a substantial literary and financial commitment to the tartan venture. Scott, living and dead, became a considerable influence on Scotland's heritage industry since that period. By the 1820s, the commercial production of tartan was in full swing under the auspices of William Wilson of Bannockburn, who developed a list of tartans in a fairly opportunistic way by reclassifying designs to fit clan names. There was little evidence of a systematic association between family names/clans and specific designs such as appear in the sales catalogues of tartan manufacturers of today. Wilson's were also aided by a bit of creative invention in the 1840s from two brothers, John and Charles Allen, who were so caught up in the cause of Jacobitisim that they changed their names to Sobieski Stuart and claimed to be the grandsons of the Young Pretender. Their famous work, *Vestiarium Scoticum*, found a ready market when it was published in 1842. The fact that it was soon proved to be a forgery did little to dampen the determination of polite society to believe in the myth.

The royal associations with tartanry which had begun with

George IV's visit were reinforced by Queen Victoria who helped the tartan enterprise on its way with the purchase of the Balmoral estate in 1848. (Heritage seekers can now follow the Queen Victoria Heritage Trail on Deeside in Aberdeenshire. It is a feature of the heritage business that the myths of one generation become the facts - and then again the myths - of the next.) The Establishment capture of tartan was reinforced by its military associations. After 1746, the only possible public use of tartan was as army colours, and both kilt and tartan were appropriated by the British state to kit out its erstwhile enemies while in its military employ. New muted tones of tartan were invented to make it more seemly (and safer) as a uniform, and its haphazard excesses were reduced through regimentation and standardisation. This proved to be a master-stroke by the British state in literally stealing its enemy's clothes, and helped to incorporate tartanry into an élite rather than a rebel form of dress. By the late nineteenth century, the myth of tartan had been made.

Using the term 'myth' might seem to imply a value judgement, as if the whole thing was a fraud, but myths provide guides to the interpretation of social reality and if we want to know what tartan means today, that is where we have to begin. The attitudes of Scots to tartan and what it stands for are highly ambivalent. On the one hand, it is a common dress for males at ceremonial occasions, like weddings and graduations, for example. It also has its wilder manifestations. Football fans, for example, bedeck themselves in shades of tartan like the colours of the rainbow, wearing what the sports editor of *The Scotsman* newspaper called: 'spectacular lengths of tartan curtain material which stretch from oxter [armpit] to ankle and are worn with plimsolls and ankle socks set off at the neck with a contrasting flag' (6 April 1987).

Manifestations such as Brigadoonery in Hollywood's authorised version (having failed to find a 'real' Scotland, its producer had created his own in the dream factory in Los Angeles), umpteen versions of the fictional hero Rob Roy, White Heather Clubbery, and Harry Lauderism, all seem to verge on the absurd and ludicrous. Sending the whole thing up seems to be the only appropriate gesture: the Tartan Monster can be tamed by laughing at it. However, a number of writers have argued that the Monster has distorted Scottish culture by requiring that all things Scottish have to be tartan,

FIGURE 1 Modelling *Brigadoon.*

Argyll Jacket

Coatee & Vest

Day Outfit

Gauntlet Style
Kilt Jacket

Plain Style
Kilt Jacket

Day Outfit

FIGURE 2 Establishment wear.

and moreover that tartan stands for the trivial, the commercial, the deformation of a nation which has lost its way politically. What Tom Nairn called the 'cultural sub-nationalism of tartanry' has to be exorcised from our culture and from our conception of what it is to be Scottish. Hogmanay Shows,

FIGURE 3 Propping up heritage.

Highland Dancing, endless choruses of 'Roamin' in the Gloamin' have, it is argued, had a pernicious effect on Scottish culture and politics. Such an image of Scotland is condemned utterly. Neal Ascherson's comment probably has considerable support:

> the fringe of glaring tartanry on sale along Princes Street and the High Street, the Gaelic gonks like dwarf descendents of the Town Guard, the joke cards about shooting haggis, lifting kilts and tickling sporrans. Nobody selling this stuff would be seen dead with it at home. But the traders solemnly accept that this is Scotland's authentic, *typisch* fragment of itself for the outside world – much as if French shopkeepers in Paris lined their shelves with plastic frogs in beret and striped vest. (1986:38)

The worst excesses of tartanry verge on the ludicrous, and yet in other manifestations, it is high fashion; it has a 'yuppy' image not only in Britain but throughout Europe and North America. Tartan is chic, and cool, and the uniform of the affluent, albeit not quite in the form kitted out by Vivienne Westwood (as in Figure 1).

CELTICISM AND THE SCOTTISH IDENTITY

The tartan story is, however, one aspect of a broader narrative about Scottish identity. Much of the iconography of Scotland is a Highland phenomenon:

> We know that the Highlands of Scotland are romantic. Bens and glens, the lone shieling in the misty island, purple heather, kilted clansmen, battles long ago, an ancient and beautiful language, claymores and bagpipes and Bonny Prince Charlie – we all know that, and we also know that it's not real. (Womack, 1989:1)

For something which is not real, this image of Scotland is persistent and endemic. And yet it is traceable in history. As Malcolm Chapman (1978) has pointed out, it is only since the late eighteenth century that the Highlands have provided a ready made identity for lowland Scots. At that point, much of the lowlands were becoming urbanised and industrialised (Lanarkshire and Lancashire could easily be mistaken), whereas under the influence of the Romantic movement, the Highlands offered something distinctive and exotic. The symbols, myths and tartans of the Highlands were appropriated by low-land Scots as evidence of their distinctive culture. The irony was until then the Highlands had been reviled as barbaric, backward and savage.

This romanticising of the Highlands (even its creation – the Gaeltachd – is ambiguous in its reference to territory and to language) had an appeal furth of Scotland. James Macpherson's *Ossian* poems of 1760 were a precursor of the Sobieski Stuart's tartan forgeries of the 1840s, and were also, like them, snapped up by a public wishing to believe. The debate about authenticity which followed their publication helped the Scottish Gael to enter the European imagination. Pointing this out Chapman argues, in terms which resonate in the debate about the authenticity of heritage today: 'the inauthenticity of Ossian was part of a more general inauthenticity in the assessment of other cultures which is closely linked to the romantic aesthetic' (1978:24).

More generally, the concept of the 'Celt' which was constructed in this period was largely independent of the way people actually lived. Instead, Chapman observes, it derives from a system of metaphors of great generality which constantly recur in later works concerning the Celts. It became part of an ethnological fiction and system of symbolic appropriation whereby Gaelic culture, life and language became the focus of associations required by the external discourse of wider English and European cultures. In a more recent book entitled *The Celts*, Chapman argues that even the term is a misnomer. For the ancient Greeks, he claims, it simply referred to the 'Other', to foreigners, and there was little evidence that it was a self-appellation. 'The Celts,' he says, 'for ancient Greece were, so to speak, "the wogs of the north"' (1992:33), the equivalent of a modern racist epithet (similar in many ways to the pejorative term *teuchter* – country-bumpkin would be the nearest English term – used by Lowlanders for Highlanders). In a similar vein, in more modern times 'Celtic' became a term for non Anglo-Saxon, an identity constructed around the requirements of modern geo-politics. So, he argues, Scotland 'has, on the whole, settled for a Celtic and Gaelic definition, in pursuit of difference from England. This accounts for the extraordinary efflorescence of Highland and Gaelic imagery in the self-presentation and assumed genealogy of modern Scotland' (1992:92).

A similar process occurred in Ireland, where historically significant interventions by Anglo-Norman and Norman-Welsh incomers as well as the English themselves were all alienated in more recent Irish history by a concentration on a Celtic genealogy, to express the Irish difference from England. Similar geo-political processes appear to have been at work in an exhibition of Celtic art which spent time in London, Dublin and Edinburgh. In all three capital cities, the national relevance was quite different. However, the symbolic capture of the Celtic identity does not simply occur for geo-political purposes. As Chapman points out, there are deeper ideological antinomies being employed in the use of this vocabulary:

> the Anglo-Saxon . . . appears a brutal soulless figure, disfigured by every wart and sore that industry, cities, pollution, capitalism and greed can cast upon the countenance. The Celt, by contrast, is a magical figure, bard, warrior and enchanter, beyond the reach of this world, and an object of love and yearning for those doooomed to wander among material things in the cold light of reason. (1992:253)

We can begin, then, to see the power and meaning of heritage as the carrier of important ideas. It is not enough simply to cast the cold light of history at heritage because it stands for meanings which are not easily extinguished. That is why, for example, Hewison's preference for 'history' over 'heritage' is misplaced. These do not operate on the same plane.

Similarly, Grant Jarvie's analysis of the mythology of Scottish Highland Games have to be understood as the changing cultural form 'of a number of complex traditions and customs which both mediate and are mediated by the unique pattern of social arrangements which have developed within Highland society and in Scottish culture generally' (1991:2). Jarvie usefully analyses four stages of their development: (a) pre-1750, when games had their origins within the patriarchal-feudal set of social relations surrounding the clan; (b) 1740–1850, when Highland gatherings were stripped of their military-social significance as a landlord class emerged in the North; (c) 1840–1920, when the Highlands were celebrated, 'in the glamour of backwardness', as the sporting playground of the élite in the context of Balmorality – loyalty and royalty – and associated with what passed for Highland dress in its more fantastic forms; (d) since 1920, when the games have become more professionalised (the standardisation of rules, payment of competitors) and commodified (commercial sponsorship, e.g. by whisky distillers). Modern Highland games as a cultural form (even Lowland oddities such as the Airdrie Highland Games) have then to be decoded in a careful manner, peeling off layers of cultural accretions. This process of decoding requires careful attention to the social consequences of cultural formations. The imagery of the Highlands, or parts of it, as 'the iast wilderness in Europe' (how are we to judge?) carries with it implicit social expectations. Highland landscapes are presented as 'natural', composed of bare rugged mountains, inhabited only by eagles and stags (at bay, naturally). As the landscape architect, Seumus Filor, points out:

> In fact, scenic qualities which delight the visitor today are largely the result of cultural, social and economic interactions with the natural systems. . . . even a brief historical analysis shows that humankind has played a major role in changing at least the surface mantle of the landscape. (1990:3)

It is above all the 'social gaze' in the Highland landscapes that require attention. The work of the Victorian artist, Landseer, was a major influence, masking 'fundamental changes in the structure of social and economic life over the period 1820 to 1870' (Pringle, 1988:153). The analysis of these peopleless places has recently been developed by Mairi MacArthur in her work on Highland tourism, which shows how people were airbrushed out in favour of 'blasted heaths and hills of mist' (1993). Guidebooks and travel memoirs focused on three themes: the wild grandeur of the landscape, remoteness and peace, coupled with a dash of romantic history. The values celebrated are 'masculine' ones of ruggedness and strength. In the late twentieth century, the Highlands still await 'discovery' in terms of its people and their culture: 'in the past they have been feared as barbarians, pitied for their poverty and scorned for their backwardness' (ibid.:29). Since the late 1980s academic and political attention has been focused on Scotland's crofting communities, rather than simply the landscape, as governments try to evolve new policies to deal with changes in agriculture.

So far in this chapter we have seen that the iconography of tartanry has a powerful if distorted history attached to it. Its significance, however, does not lie simply in that, but in the place it has in the cultural creation of 'Scotland' itself. It cannot be excised by a dose of historical realism, as was attempted by the English Conservative historian Hugh Trevor-Roper in the Hobsbawm and Ranger collection *The Invention of Tradition* (1983). Its significance is anthropological, not historical. Neither is it to the point to assert that there is a better, higher sort of Scottish culture which we should focus on, a 'hagiography of Great Scots Artists' (Wills, 1984). Such is the power and influence of tartanry and Highlandism in the manner and for the reasons we have tried to spell out that it has to be confronted and understood for the powerful discourse that it is.

Scotland has been the subject of an intense 'tourist gaze' at least for the last 150 years. Christopher Smout has shown that whereas in the first half of the nineteenth century the Highlands had at most 100 visitors, by the end of the century and in a good year it could expect a hundred times that number (Durie, 1992). Undoubtedly, the works of Walter Scott did much to bring this about. As the social historian, Alistair Durie, comments: 'Scott did much to expand and popularise tourism in Scotland. He did not create it, any more than he created Romanticism on which his work fed' (1992:48). Durie observes that such had been the increase in tourist visits to Loch Katrine in the Trossachs after 1810 when Scott published *The Lady of the Lake*, that Sir John Sinclair tried to get Scott interested in the adventures of a Caithness mermaid for the same reason. Scott's own home/museum at Abbotsford near Melrose became a mecca for visitors almost immediately after Scott died in 1832. By the late 1850s, over 5,000 visitors annually were coming (often from Europe and America), but only after the house had been extensively refurbished, possibly as the first 'heritage centre'. Today, the house has over 70,000 visitors a year. Abbotsford was an important stopping place on Cook's Tartan Tours (established in 1846) which also took in Loch Lomond, and the Western Isles, and the company estimated that over 40,000 visitors had completed the tour in fifteen years.

Sir Walter Scott was a central figure in romanticising Scotland, and is held responsible by many opposed to the 'deformation' of Scottish culture. He is credited (or blamed) with creating a Scotland divided between the heart, that is to say its romantic Scottish past, and the head, identified with its rational British future. This Caledonian Antisyzygy, the battle between unrestrained fantasy and dour realism, is judged to be at the heart of the Scottish psychiatric-political condition (Nairn, 1977:150). We now turn to the second cultural formation which is deemed to be responsible for cultural repression – the so-called 'kailyard'.

KAILYARDISM AND SCOTTISH HERITAGE

Strictly speaking, kailyardism was a popular literary style from about 1880 until 1914 (E. Anderson, 1979; Carter, 1976; Campbell, 1981) described by the *Penguin Guide to Literature* as consisting of 'minor writers who pursued Scottish country quaintness into whimsical middens'. Tom Nairn has commented:

> Kailyardism was the definition of Scotland as wholly consisting of small towns full of small-town 'characters' given to bucolic intrigue and wise sayings. At first the central figures were ususally Ministers of the Kirk (as were most of the authors) but later on schoolteachers and doctors got into the act. Their housekeepers always have a shrewd insight into human nature. Offspring who leave for the city frequently come to grief, and are glad to get home again (peching and hosting to hide their feelings). (1977:158)

If kailyardism had simply remained a fairly obscure literary movement of dubious value, then we would probably have heard little more about it. However, its significance and impact are judged to be much more than that. In Colin McArthur's phrase, kailyardism along with tartanry has become a 'hegemonic discourse' in Scotland, and with distinctly negative consequences. It is argued that this 'cabbage-patch' tradition affected/infected Scottish literary and cultural life in such as way as to blight Scottish consciousness with narrow minded parochialism. It was also judged, we will see later, to have negative political consequences. It was the critic George Blake who probably coined the term 'kailyard' as a literary genre characterised by domesticity, rusticity, humour, humility, modesty, decency, piety, and poverty (Shepherd, 1988). Not all writers in Scotland in the late nineteenth and early twentieth centuries belonged to the kailyard school, but its key figures included Ian Maclaren (1850–1907), S. R. Crockett (1860–1914), and J. M. Barrie (1860–1937), undoubtedly the best-known as the creator of Peter Pan, the ultimate escape(ist) story.

The kailyard tradition has been analysed as a cultural formation well suited to its age (Carter, 1979). In rural areas especially, peasant agriculture was being destroyed by the further penetration of agrarian capitalism, and with it the social and cultural values which its social structure held. Carter argues that the kailyard was a panegyric for the virtues of independence, hard work, and 'getting on', expressed above all in the social type 'the lad o' pairts', the son of a crofter or peasant farmer who had the ability but not the financial means to benefit from education. It was the role of the local schoolteacher, the dominie, to spot the talent and persuade the affluent of the parish to provide the money to pay the educational fees. The lad o' pairts became a central literary and educational image well into the twentieth century, and an ideological bulwark for the Scottish educational system. The purpose of the social myth was clearly celebratory, but as Allan MacLaren pointed out, its ideology had conservative and radical implications, as well as being heavily gendered:

> the egalitarianism so often portrayed is not that emerging from an economic, social or even political equality; it is equality of *opportunity* which is exemplified. All men are not equal. What is implied is that all men are given the chance to be equal. Whatever the values attached to such a belief, if expressed today, it would be termed elitist not egalitarian. (1976:2)

Kailyardism as a literary genre probably failed to survive the Great War, but its influence on Scottish culture is deemed longlasting and malevolent. Tom Nairn refers to it as 'subcultural Scotchery', produced in part by Scottish emigres with rosy and romantic memories of a simpler, ideal Scotland of their imaginations. Kitsch and kailyard became fused in the process and left a thoroughly negative legacy. As Colin McArthur comments '. . . Scottish artists and intellectuals, where they did not leave Scotland and function solely within the discourses of other cultures, produced works in or about Scotland which were deformed and 'pathological' (1983:2). The dominating discourses were tartanry and kailyard.

In an important critique of these cultural formations entitled *Scotch Reels and After* (1983), a number of authors set about showing how this influence operated through aspects of Scottish culture. The focus of the book is almost all on the visual arts, especially cinema, where the structuring force of tartanry and kailyard in filmic representations of Scotland, emanating especially from England and Hollywood, are strong – witness *Brigadoon*. Cairns Craig points out that we have to make a distinction between the impact of Walter Scott and the kailyard writers themselves. Scott, he argues, 'may have popularised the notion of a romantic Scotland, but he did so without subscribing to that romanticism himself' (1982:9). Above all, says Craig, to Scott 'Scotland is a place in which the highest potentialities of the human spirit can be found and can be striven for', whereas for J. M. Barrie, the apogee of the kailyard school, 'Scotland is a place to escape from, a cultural wasteland whose values are inimical to the imagination' (ibid.). Scott's project of discovering and manufacturing legends, symbols and heroic figures was not out of the ordinary in the European context of his time. What was specific, Craig argues, was that these myths did not come to fruition 'in a cultural nationalism in Scotland such as can be found in Norway or Ireland or many of the areas of the Austro-Hungarian Empire' (ibid.:10).

The essence, then, of the critique of tartanry and kailyard is that it was not linked, as it should have been according to the critics, to the wider political project. Because Scottish identity could not take a political form of expression, it was subverted into a cultural backwater of a deformed nationalism. The key to this critique lies in the relationship between culture and politics. 'Normal' societies are deemed to be those in which national culture and politics are fused. The supposed deformation of Scottish cultural representations are the outcome of this lack of fit. Cairns Craig again:

> Tartanry and kailyard, seemingly so opposite in their ethos, are the joint creations of an imagination which, in recoil from the apparently featureless integration of Scottish life into an industrial culture whose power and whose identity lies outside Scottish control, acknowledges

its own inability to lay hold of contemporary reality by projecting itself upon images of a society equally impotent before the forces of history. (1982:13)

These 'pathological discourses' can then be traced through representations of Scotland, notably the written and the visual arts. Colin McArthur's work on Scotland and the cinema is especially important in this respect. Tartanry had its origins in the Romantic movement of the late eighteenth century, while kailyard belonged to the demi-monde of the late nineteenth. By the twentieth century, modern cultural media were reproducing the stereotypes, or 'discursive positions', as McArthur calls them. In film, it was the decade and a half after the Second World War which laid down the 'definitive modern statements of tartanry and kailyard in the cinema' in Scotland (1983:45). Films such as *Bonnie Prince Charlie* (1948), *Rob Roy, the Highland Rogue* (1953), *Kidnapped* (1960), *Greyfriars Bobby* (1961) and the doyen of them all, *Brigadoon* (1954), were all Hollywood creations and representations of Scotland. McArthur comments on the latter: 'at one level it takes the Romantic representation of Scotland as a given, but at another level . . . this representation is revealed as the dream *par excellence*, as a fiction created to escape from the urban horrors of the twentieth century' (1983:47). The comedies of the late 1940s and 1950s – *Whisky Galore* (1949), *The Maggie* (1953), *Geordie* (1955), and *Rockets Galore* (1958) – were all permeated by the Ealing Studios ethos expressing a detestation of modernity vis à vis the city and the power of capital and the powers of central bureaucracy. McArthur observes: 'the films construct a set of contrary humane values invested in a range of lovable rural eccentrics and non-conformists' (1983:47).

Set against this escapist genre were films in the British documentary tradition, associated with John Grierson. He had been responsible for making a series of documentaries from the 1920s, most notably *Drifters* (1929), *Nightmail* (1936), and a sequence of films in 1938 such as *Wealth of a Nation*, *The Face of Scotland* and *The Children's Story*. By the 1950s, this genre continued in those made for the tourist industry, such as *The Silver City* (1957) for Aberdeen, *Festival in Edinburgh* (1955), and *Enchanted Isles* (1957) for MacBraynes. The documentary and narrative forms were brought together in *The Brave Don't Cry* (1954), an account of the Knockshinnoch pit disaster, very much in the tradition of European naturalism such as Pabst's *Kameradschaft*. In counter-distinction, there is the tradition of what McArthur calls, tongue in cheek, the 'Ur-Tartan Documentary'. It would open, he says:

> accompanied by a clarsach or plaintive Scottish violin tune, on a panorama of lochs and bens, preferably in autumn since the lament is the dominant tone of the form. Against this Landseerian background (the more gross versions actually include a kilted and claymored highlander) the commentary begins to unfold. The choice of narrator is crucial; the voice must call up the cluster of motifs characteristic of the genre: beauty, sadness, dignity, loss . . . The visual, verbal and musical rhetorics are sustained throughout with a frequent closure on a loch at sunset (one notorious film closes with clinking glasses of a Scottish liqueur held, in belaced hands, against the sky. (1983:59)

Taken together, the traditions of 'romantic reactionary' and social realism have been set as two sides of a restricted discourse. McArthur expresses it thus: 'the hegemonic discourses about Scotland within which Scots, including Scots film-makers are interpellated, are set in place as social actors, provide a severely limited set of representations of the country and its people' (1982:58). Bill Douglas's autobiographical film trilogy, which began with *My Ain Folk* (1973), was disliked by the critics of the time for conforming to the British documentary genre. Bill Forsyth's films, starting with *That Sinking Feeling* (1979), and most notably *Local Hero* (1983), have been criticised for an over-reliance on escapist whimsy. The burden shouldered by Scottish fim makers is indeed considerable, and it is doubtful whether any film 'about' Scotland can carry all the required nuances to escape the restricted discourses. Cairns Craig has pointed out that whether it likes it or not, any Scottish film carries the burden of representing Scotland in a way in which American films do not have to 'represent' the United States since these films 'do not need to be consciously about American identity because that identity is constantly being processed and developed and refined and discarded in every American film' (1982:8). On the other hand, he argues, 'Scottish identity is an image powered from without Scottish culture' (ibid.).

The key, we believe, to understanding the discourse on the discourse, as it were, lies in the frequently implicit assumption that because Scotland is a nation, it must have a national culture. This national culture must be derived from the broader political culture, and be home grown, not imposed by outside cultures, but eschewing the 'pathological' discourses of tartanry and kailyard. That may seem unexceptional, but it contains some important assumptions. First of all, it assumes that these are dominant discourses, and that counters are simply the reverse image. In the course of the debate generated by Isabel and Murray Grigor's exhibition on 'Scotch Myths' at the Edinburgh Festival of 1981, the search was on for such a healthier and indigenous discourse, and 'Clydesideism' seemed to be the answer. What it had in its favour was that it was constructed from 'real' images of working class life, from the discourse on class and from naturalism. John Caughie commented in the edited collection, *Scotch Reels* by McArthur (1983), that the tradition is 'based on working class experiences which, since the twenties, have seemed to offer the only real and consistent basis for a Scottish national culture' (1983:121). Critics like Cairns Craig pointed out, however, that Clydesideism was an unlikely candidate because even in its traditional heartland in the West of Scotland it was fast becoming a 'historic discourse' – and even more historic in the 1990s as the city sought to alter its economic base. (This 'heritage' was not one it sought to forefront, as we have argued in previous chapters.)

Since this debate about cultural discourses in Scotland took place in the early 1980s, recent work has called its terms into question. The assumption that the kailyard of the late nineteenth century as it was portrayed in the writings of Barrie, Crockett and MacLaren was typical of vernacular culture of that period has been demolished by T. D. Knowles (1983) and Willie Donaldson (1986). The former argued that the output of kailyard writers was geared to a wider British and North American market with its vogue for religious fiction and sentimental retrospection. The nonconformist press in England encouraged such writing furth of Scotland, and it is significant that many of the Scottish kailyardists were ministers of religion. Knowles argues that the kailyard writers were important outwith Scotland:

> Their work contained British Victorian elements as well as Scottish; they were regionalists, and there is influence from the gothic novel, the fairy tale, 18th century sentimentalism, and the Victorian penchant for dying and death. (1983:64)

Donaldson (1986) makes it clear that the weekly press was much more significant in Scotland than book-publishing (which carried the kailyard novels). There were over 200 weekly titles in Scotland at the end of the nineteenth century, and these were much more willing to use Scots vernacular and to address major political and social issues of the day. Writers like William Alexander (who wrote the novel *Johnnie Gibb of Gushetneuk*, 1871), who tackled the impact of social and economic change in North-East Scotland had, their work serialised in the weekly press. Donaldson concludes:

> On the whole, popular fiction in Victorian Scotland is not overwhelmingly backward-looking; it is not obsessed by rural themes; it does not shrink from urbanisation or its problems; it is not idyllic in its approach; it does not treat the common people as comic or quaint. The second half of the nineteenth century is not a period of creative trauma or linguistic decline; it is one of the richest and most vital episodes in the history of Scottish popular culture. (1986:149)

Given the work by Knowles and Donaldson, it is difficult to sustain the view that Scottish popular culture was fundamentally tainted by parochial and 'pathological' images in the period of its heyday. It is then more difficult to sustain the argument thereafter when kailyard was manifestly in decline.

The 1980s also saw another attack on the view that Scotland was suffering from a deformed Scottish culture. In an important book, *The Eclipse of Scottish Culture* published in 1989, Beveridge and Turnbull argued that such a view belonged to the mind-set of a metropolitan dominated intellectual cadre who had come to believe in the 'inferiorism' of Scottish culture. Their starting point is not that the discourses of tartanry and kailyard have been hegemonic in their impact on Scottish culture, but only on the perspectives of intellectuals who have devalued Scottish culture from the outset. Such intellectuals like Tom Nairn have ended up giving a pessimistic and misleading account of Scottish culture:

> Suspicious of concepts like 'tradition' and 'identity', many tough-minded left-wing nationalists were even prepared to abandon the cultural argument entirely. Scottish nationalism's cultural-intellectual base was therefore altogether too narrow for the nationalist challenge to be sustained over any extended period. (Beveridge and Turnbull, 1989:4)

Beveridge and Turnbull's critique of the critics sought to reinstate the view that particularly in the fields of philosophy and theology, Scotland has in fact produced important and original thinkers. The central task of cultural nationalism is to rescue Scottish ideological practices from the hands of the cultural pessimists with their 'deep aversion to everything native and local' (1989:59). They are also highly critical of accounts like McArthur's analysing popular culture. In terms familiar to those who have followed our argument in this book about heritage, they criticise his view that the discourses are in fact hegemonic, that they are merely passively consumed. They argue:

> There is in reality, no *Sunday Post* reader waiting to soak up the messages conveyed by D. C. Thomson, but only *Sunday Post* readers, people who are also trade unionists, or Kirk-goers, or nationalists, or defenders of animal rights, and their responses to tartanry is not uncritical assimilation, but a complex negotiation dependent on the beliefs and values which are bound up with these concerns. (ibid.:14)

In other words, the problem with the thesis of 'hegemonic discourses' is that it fails to analyse the reception of them, how they are mediated and perceived. Instead, they argue, the discourse which needs contesting is the critical one that Scottish culture is and always has been culturally deformed. In this regard, they are closer to the more orthodox nationalist stance which argues that it was the Union of 1707 which has had a negative impact on how Scots perceive themselves, and that a healthy Scottish national culture can be restored with political independence.

In so arguing, of course, they make the crucial assumption that 'Scottish national culture' can exist, and remains to be rescued from intellectual pessimism. In this discussion about Scottish culture, we might, however, ask a more fundamental question: in the late twentieth century, is a 'national culture' possible? If so, is it desirable? Both the cultural pessimists and optimists answer positively to these questions. They view broader Anglo-American culture as having a negative impact on Scotland, and accept that such a phenomenon as a national culture can exist. The issue at odds is whether it is possible to reinstitute or reconstruct a valid Scottish culture (Beveridge and Turnbull), or whether the task is so riven with negative discourses that it remains only a theoretical rather than a practical possibility. We might consider a more radical view which touches directly on the discussion of heritage more generally. That is, in the conditions of 'late-modernity', to use Giddens' felicitous term, no mono-cultural project is possible. Looking closely, we can identify an older essentially nationalist assumption that all societies worthy of the name should have a distinctive culture. This is in essence an eighteenth-century notion of sovereignty, embodied in the culture of a nation waiting to be brought to political realisation. In key respects, Beveridge and Turnbull criticise the intellectual pessimists for giving up on their 'historic' role of identifying the 'essential character' of a people, and giving it political expression. Such a 'modernist' project has the task of seeking out the essential character of a people and presenting it as distinctive and self-contained.

There are, however, in-built assumptions in such a project. The national identities which are to be produced from this cultural exercise are gendered. It is no coincidence that those diagnosed as typically Scottish – tartanry, kailyard, Clydesidism – are entirely masculinist. The image of tartanry is a male-military one; there is no female equivalent of the 'lad o'pairts'; and the Clydeside icon was a skilled male worker who was man enough to care for his women. As Alex Howson has argued:

> within debates concerning Scottish identity, either those
> which assert that Scotland is framed as inferiorist or
> those which allude to the positive images which may be

provided by a reclamation of working class history, women are marginalised and femininity is selectively deployed as a symbolic category. (1993:48)

The point here is not that the neglect of women is an unfortunate side-effect of the debate, but that it is fundamental to it. All essentialist attempts to create mono-culture will inevitably build in power assumptions, and in this scheme of things gender will be skewed. The same will be true of race, region, class or any other social dimension we examine.

The debate, then, about 'real' Scottish culture is almost inevitably going to be an historical excavation of the 'golden age', or an attempt to construct a pure national character free from alien and inferiorist influences. The search for a truly Scottish culture is inevitably retrospective and romantic, a celebration of the past. There is a growing amount of Scottish historiography which argues that history took a funny turn after the Union of 1707. As Scotland lost its formal statehood, so it appropriated that which had flourished in the currency of the Romantic movement, the Gaelic vision, for example. More recently, Colin Kidd has argued in similar vein (1993) that Scottish Whig historians of the late eighteenth century looked to the Anglo–British state to offer a more progressive and liberating vision of society. This was not another example of the Scottish cringe but a rational assessment of the opportunities for liberty and progress set against those offered by Scotland alone.

That the late twentieth century does not offer Scots the same prospects within the British state does not require the re-writing of history, building in a Scottish 'cringe' factor. Lindsay Paterson's important book, *The Autonomy of Modern Scotland* (1994), argues that Scotland was not 'incorporated' into England by the Union of 1707, but retained and developed a considerable degree of civil autonomy over its social and political institutions, certainly on a par with many similarly small societies which had formal political independence. It was quite logical to have dual identities – Scottish and British. Graeme Morton's recent work shows that far from Scots abasing themselves to Anglo–Britishness in the middle of the nineteenth century, they celebrated it as a means of asserting that the Union had occurred between two equal partners. Scotland, as it were, had had to fight for and win its independence in the fourteenth century in order that it could join the

Union on equal terms (unlike Ireland and Wales). Such a view of the Union was recently expressed in 1993 by the Conservative Secretary of State for Scotland, Ian Lang, and if it seems somewhat odd to our late twentieth-century ears, that is probably because being Scottish and being British no longer seem as complementary as they did 150 years ago (Morton, 1993).

The late twentieth century is not made for homogeneous, mono-cultural 'nation states'. States no longer have the political, economic or cultural power to imagine and then enforce national self-determination. This is not a failure of will (a concept orthodox nationalists find appealing) but a realisation of limited autonomy and multiple identity. Those who argue that intellectuals have let Scotland down are reluctant to endorse the view that people have much more control over how they choose their identities, and the way they play them. Without a systematic set of beliefs, they argue, societies cannot cohere, and abhore the pathology of what they see as alienation.

Colin McArthur, one of those criticised by Beveridge and Turnbull for adopting an 'inferiorist' stance to Scottish culture, has recently made an important defence of his view that Scottish culture is dominated by hegemonic discourses (1993). He argues that the Scottish film media, which has such an effect on the visual arts generally, still operates within an 'elegaic' discourse, expressed in images of Glencoe and Culloden, which are all-pervasive and implicit. In his analysis of Bill Forsyth's fim *Local Hero*, McArthur argues that Forsyth was not likely to have been aware of the 'unconscious discourse within which Scotland is a magical realm which transforms the stranger' (1993:101). He goes on: 'we tend to be written by the dominant Scottish narratives rather than ourselves writing stories about Scotland' (ibid.:102). Once more, these cultural discourses are linked to political projects: 'it has to be understood that the historically dominant narratives about Scotland can impede political advance and must therefore be confronted, deconstructed and replaced with new narratives' (ibid.: 104).

These are big claims, and the questions raised by Beveridge and Turnbull about the need to analyse the reception of these discourses is all the more urgently in need of an answer. Imputing the influence of a 'Scottish discursive unconscious' on both artists and consumers alike raises important questions about how we are to know this. We might take the view that the pastiche of heritage in Scotland is little different from post-modern cultural forms generally, and that how it is picked and mixed depends on consumers, but crucially on the institutions which act as intermediaries between Scottish cultural representations in the abstract and the actual images of Scotland available. This is a much bigger question than the scope of this book in which we are concerned with the heritage culture of Scotland. In the next chapter we will examine the mediation of the key heritage institutions, the Scottish Tourist Board, The National Trust for Scotland, and Historic Scotland.

Chapter 4

Manufacturing Scottish Heritage

In the previous chapter we showed how 'Scottish heritage' was part of a contested cultural and political agenda which lays down ways of imagining Scotland. In this chapter we will focus on those organisations who mediate and manufacture Scottish heritage, taking, as it were, the deep structure of heritage and laying it out for consumers. These 'gatekeepers' will have different, even competing, versions of heritage, and will mediate and amplify them in different ways. In the first chapter, we made the point that heritage is an 'industry' insofar as it has a product (or products), a manufacturing process, markets, and consumers. The organisations we deal with here operate as its 'entrepreneurs'.

Heritage in Scotland is an industry which is characterised by a high degree of diversity. Three bodies constitute the 'holy trinity' of Scottish heritage: the Scottish Tourist Board, Historic Scotland and the National Trust for Scotland. They work alongside each other, but have distinct aims and purposes, and quite different organisational cultures. They are set within a political and cultural framework which includes government departments and private operators. At the state level, the Scottish Office provides most of the funding for heritage dispensing it indirectly through its public agencies such as the Scottish Tourist Board which receives three-quarters of its budget from the Scottish Office, Historic Scotland (80 per cent), Scottish Museums Council (72 per cent), and Scottish Natural Heritage (100 per cent). Only the National Trust for Scotland does not receive funds directly from the state, although it is a major recipient of grant in aid from Historic Scotland for the upkeep of many of its properties. Further down the heritage chain, private and commercial

operators of 'stately homes', independent as well as local
authority museums, receive grants from state agencies like
Historic Scotland and the Scottish Museums Council. The heritage industry in Scotland has a strong 'voluntary sector' ethos
(in contrast, for example, to that in France with its historic
sense of national *patrimoine*), but it is clear that it would not
survive without public funds.

As we pointed out in Chapter 1, the British state has long
played a crucial role in the heritage industry. The National
Land Fund was established in 1946 by the Labour government
with £50 million which came into the Exchequer from the
sale of surplus war materials. The Chancellor, Hugh Dalton,
saw it as a fund for those Britons who had died for their ancestral nation during the Second World War. However, as Patrick
Wright points out, 'while the words were undoubtedly fine,
the reality was rather less forthcoming' (1985:45). Not once
in its lifetime was the National Land Fund used as an emergency or contingency fund to protect the heritage it claimed
to represent. The formalising of the state's support for heritage came in 1980 with the National Heritage Act which had
been planned by the Callaghan government, and was promul-
gated by the incoming Conservative administration in 1979
with all-party support.

Despite the open-ended definition of heritage which
National Heritage Memorial Fund adopted – 'We could no
more define the national heritage than we could define, say,
beauty or art . . . so we decided to let the national heritage
define itself' (cited in Hewison, 1987:136–7)) it is clear that
its managers had in mind works of art: paintings by Turner
and Constable; sculptures by Moore and Hepworth; buildings
like Chatsworth and Edinburgh Castle; 'great scenic areas, the
flora and fauna' (ibid.). The 1980 Act was basically a three-fold
measure: to allow the transfer of property defined as 'heritage' to the state in lieu of tax; to idemnify museums against
the costs of insurance; and to aid the establishment of the
National Heritage Fund (Wright, 1985).

The National Heritage Fund was important because it was
grafted on to what remained of the National Land Fund which
stood at £16.6 million by 1980 by means of an additional £5.5
million per year. Wright argues that the fund represented the
Thatcher government's attempt to capture the political rami-
fications of heritage:

[the fund] indicates . . . a generalised and everyday sense of the way things used to be, and in this respect stands as an early engagement with that anxious and vernacular sense of historical existence which Thatcher has deliberately gone on to make the ground of so many spuriously 'historical' gestures and pleas. (1985:46)

Hewison makes a similar point. He argues that while it refused to define the national heritage, the fund's first annual report made it clear that 'national heritage' is above all something which is under threat. The threats are vague but multiple – decay, decline, change – and that they were the same threats that were at the heart of Thatcher's more overtly political rhetoric (Hewison, 1991).

The National Heritage Act of 1983 was driven to be more explicit about national heritage insofar as it established the body 'English Heritage' to hold the state's properties in its care. Its first chairman was Lord Montagu, stately-home owner and author of the book *The Gilt and the Gingerbread: How to live in a Stately Home and Make Money* (1967). He was living proof that it was possible to do so. English Heritage acquired both the listed building and the responsibilities of the Ministry of Works in England. Its second chairman, the newspaper magnate Jocelyn Stevens took over in 1992, and almost immediately announced his plans to sell 200 or so less well-known sites to save some £90 million a year. His critics argued that the plan was only to keep sites with 'earning capacity' and to abandon financially unprofitable ones (*The Guardian*, 24 October 1992).

The very idea of creating a body called English Heritage under a National Heritage Act illustrates very nicely the usurpation and equation of the term 'national heritage' with English or Anglo-British heritage. In Scotland, state heritage remained in the hands of the Historic Buildings and Monuments directorate of the Scottish Development Department, and did not change its name to Historic Scotland until 1991 when it became an executive agency. (It eschewed the title 'Scottish Heritage' as being too resonant of its English counterpart.) The vocabulary of the 'nation' is problematic in Scotland, as it resonates a quite different and even conflicting 'national history', when so many of the key icons of Scottish history like Bannockburn were in opposition to English ones (Ash, 1990).

The Scottish semi-state operates differently north of the border. Here, state conservation, preservation and protection are discharged through the various departments and directorates of the Scottish Office. The Scottish Office Development Department is responsible for policy and functions affecting the physical development of Scotland – town and country planning, housing, roads and transport, water supplies and sewerage, control of air and river pollution, and building control, as well as for conservation. It is also responsible for the general policy on local government administration.

A year later, Scottish Natural Heritage was given similar status as a child of a marriage between the Countryside Commission for Scotland, and the Nature Conservancy Council. Its definition of heritage is quite explicit: 'the interaction of man and nature . . . flora and fauna, geology and physiology'. Its aim is 'to help people to enjoy Scotland's natural heritage responsibly, understand it more fully and use it wisely so that it can be sustained for future generations' (SNH, 1992). Although its remit refers to 'nature', the organisation is frequently misnamed as Scottish *National* Heritage, implying that it has wider responsibility for the built as well as the cultural inheritance of the country. It operates in an environment in which it liaises with bodies such as the National Farmers Union of Scotland, Scottish Landowners Federation, Scottish Wildlife Trust and Scottish Society for the Protection of Birds, as well as the National Trust for Scotland, which owns land as well as buildings in Scotland. Scottish National Heritage is an important player in the heritage game north of the border, but stands somewhat outwith the remit of the three key organisations primarily concerned with the built heritage of Scotland. It came into being after our study had begun.

Other aspects of Scotland's heritage which are managed by the state are the museums in Scotland, which fall under the Scottish Office Education Department. The national museums and galleries, such as the National Museum of Scotland and the National Library of Scotland, are funded directly through this department. Other museums come under the auspices of the Scottish Office via the Scottish Museums Council which is funded by the state as the main channel of support for Scotland's 300 or more local museums. The Council was formed in 1964 as an independent company by guarantee with charitable status, and provides finance, advice and other services for independent museum trusts, local authorities, development corporations, universities, regimental museums, and historic houses. Out of an income of over £800,000, it disbursed over £375,000 to eighty-three member museums in 1990-1. This compares with a mere £6,000 in 1975-6, a reflection of the growing importance of the heritage industry north of the Border.

The Industry Department for Scotland has responsibility for the Scottish Tourist Board which receives 80 per cent of its budget of £11 million from government. It is also responsible for the enterprise agencies, Scottish Enterprise and Highland Enterprise, which have an involvement in Scotland's heritage business via bodies like the Scottish Tourist Board. This is the national tourism agency for the country, and as such (and given the size of its budget) plays a crucial part in defining and promoting Scottish heritage. That is where we will begin in our review of the manufacturers of this heritage.

THE SCOTTISH TOURIST BOARD

In Scotland, heritage and tourism are inextricably linked. The Scottish Tourist Board is in many ways the central nervous system of the Scottish heritage industry. Until the late 1960s, there was in Britain no comprehensive government policy on tourism. National tourist boards did exist, but they were non-statutory and had little influence. The potential for tourism as a creator of wealth and jobs was highlighted by the dramatic growth in tourism to the UK after the Second World War. In 1946, there were 200,000 overseas trips to Britain; by 1969 these numbered 5.8 million (STB - Development, Objectives and Functions, 1991:1). The dramatic increase in overseas visitors signalled to the government the potential of tourism, and the Development of Tourism Act of 1969 established a statutory British Tourist Authority, as well as national tourist boards for England, Scotland and Wales. The Northern Ireland Tourist Board had already been formed under separate legislation in 1948. The new tourist boards were given 'responsibility for the promotions and development of tourism to and within Great Britain, and also to encourage the provision and improvement of tourist facilities and amenities' (STB, 1991:1). The specific remit of the Scottish Tourist Board was 'to attract holidaymakers to destinations in Scotland, to encourage the development of visitor facilities, and to coordinate tourism interests'. This included coordinating the activities of the thirty-five area tourist boards which had been established under the 1969 Act. By 1993, the government had indicated its intention to 'rationalise' these boards, and by implication, give more power to the centre.

Scottish tourism in the 1990s was calculated to be generating almost £2 billion annually for the Scottish economy, and was employing directly 180,000, making it by far the country's biggest employer. By 1990, the Scottish Tourist Board was spending around £26 million annually, made up of £10.6 million on promotion (75 per cent of which came from government grant in aid, and the rest from the private sector), and £15 million on capital expenditure (about 80 per cent in the private sector, and the rest from government). Government expenditure had increased by 1992 to £13.3 million, a rise in the STB's budget since 1979–80 of more than 30 per cent in real terms.

The Scottish Tourist Board places much higher priority on generating income and creating jobs than on conservation and preservation. It distinguishes itself from the two main heritage bodies, Historic Scotland and the National Trust for Scotland, by using a direct market analogy. It sees its job as persuading people to visit the 'shops' which are Historic Scotland and the National Trust for Scotland, whereafter it is up to these bodies to sell the 'goods on display'. In 1984, the organisation won the right to market Scotland overseas directly (hitherto it had to use the services of the British Tourist Authority), and it defines its priority markets as USA, Japan, Germany, France, and Scandinavia, closely followed by Canada, Netherlands, Belgium, Ireland, Australia, Switzerland and Italy. The USA is Scotland's most important overseas market generating income of more than £2 million, and to that end, the Scottish Tourist Board coordinates a network of around 400 travel agents with the title SCOTS (specialist counsellor on travel to Scotland). While overseas marketing is very important there are no financial resources to run general advertising campaigns overseas. The British Tourist Authority does this on its behalf, with the Scottish Tourist Board coordinating joint advertising campaigns with the British authority, the area tourist boards, and Highlands and Islands Enterprise. (Under the new government requirements, the Tourist Board has decanted a proportion of its staff to Inverness to work with this organisation.)

The UK market, however, remains the main one for Scotland, and the prime target is the 35- to 55-year-old married couples in the upper income groups (ABC1) holidaying without children. The Scottish Tourist Board has run regional campaigns in England, in the North, as well as in the South-East. Its campaign using advertising in the London Underground suggesting that London was somewhere to get out of, attracted press publicity and satisfaction at the Tourist Board itself. As well as television advertising, it uses full-page colour advertisements in the UK press. Other marketing devices include direct mailings, and participation in UK holiday exhibitions and travel trade events. In the early 1990s, the organisation's slogan is 'Scotland: One visit is never enough', and in the 1980s, it was 'Scotland's for me'.

The Scottish Tourist Board is organised into five divisions: marketing, visitor services, investment and planning (which includes sections on research, product development, development promotion, development projects), press and public relations, and finance and administration. Employing 120 people directly, it was headed until 1994 by Chief Executive, Tom Band, who joined the board from Historic Buildings and Monuments, and Chairman, Ian Grant, who came from the National Farmers Union of Scotland. The commercial ethos can be gauged from the priorities of the Board's press and publicity division (STB Development, Objectives and Functions, 1991): a) to ensure that the value of tourism to Scotland as a *wealth and job creator* is recognised; b) supporting Scottish Tourist Board divisions by *promoting their products and services*; c) introducing journalists to those within the *tourism industry* seeking to promote their area of service; and d) highlighting Scotland's unique identity and attraction as a tourism destination at home and abroad. It is clear then that the Scottish Tourist Board speaks the language of business, and that as the body responsible for coordinating tourism in Scotland, it does not have a special commitment to heritage as such. It is only one of many of its concerns, and is deemed important primarily as a means of attracting visitors to Scotland.

THE SCOTTISH TOURIST BOARD AND HERITAGE

We can gauge the Board's approach to heritage from two sources: the images it presents; and what it says about Scotland's heritage. Scottish Tourist Board advertising campaigns stress landscapes and locations. Its television projects recently include the 'talking eagles', in which two eagles fly down a Scottish loch discussing why there is no better place to be, and 'Mull early closing', in which a shopkeeper closes early in order to go fishing with friends. The latter also has a Gaelic version, and both are on offer in mainland Scotland. The STB has also exploited the poster industry under its campaign, 'One Visit is Never Enough'. The poster industry is a lucrative and important part of late twentieth-century tourism, indicating (or implying) the message of 'been there, done that', and posters become the accoutrements of travel like T-shirts and key rings.

The posters attempt to convey particular images of Scotland:

- *peopleless places – the landscape*: this is the stuff of Romantic representations with 'nature' presented as wild, rugged, barren, beautiful. The dominant colours are blues, browns, white. The lochs are deep, calm, and always brooding
- *majestic Scotland – castles, kilts, pipers*: Edinburgh Castle is the icon associated most strongly by tourists and by natives with Scotland
- *'everyday' Scotland*: the posters of post boxes and of curlers convey the everyday melting into the exotic. Strange games are played on ice by men in kilts, post boxes miniaturised in strange locations. Low and high heritage blur in the manner described by the French minister for culture 'it is no longer cold stones or of exhibits kept under glass in museum cabinets. It now includes the village wash-houses, the little country church, local songs and forms of speech, crafts and skills' (Hoyau, 1988:28).

The tourist brochures also convey the familiar and the quaint. The brochure for the UK market carries a photograph of a sailing dinghy on a loch. The blue-green motif of sky and water recurs throughout the brochure. Inside the front cover are two icons; one of Loch Katrine, the other of tartan clad children at Luss Highland Games. Carrying a brief account of key Scottish icons like the saltire, thistle, and gaelic language,

FIGURE 4 Representing Scotland

the brochure poses the question – why Scotland? It answers: the great outdoors, shopping facilities, whisky, golf, ceilidhs, castles and islands. The focus is on activities. Commerce, culture and heritage are all interwoven. Yet tartanry and rampant rhetoric are rather subdued. The STB's view is that English people, who are by far the most numerically significant, should not be put off by legendary anti-Englishness. This is a particular concern for Scottish tourism when 1993 figures showed a decline in visitors from south of the Border. Key words employed in the business of selling Scotland are 'romantic', 'mysterious' and 'friendly'. The image purveyed is of a Highland Scotland so much further away than it actually is. The perceived cultural difference between Scotland and England is judged to work in the Scottish Tourist Board's favour.

By contrast, the overseas brochure issued by the Board is strong on tartanry. The cover contains a picture of mountains, a loch, and hill walkers. The inside cover has two photographs, one of Blaven on the Isle of Skye, and the other of a ranger in Glen Nevis. The explanatory account of Scottish symbols is the same as for the UK brochure. The overseas edition, however, has a much longer section on Scotland itself: central themes highlight scenic Scotland, Scotland's rich heritage, Scotland in history, the quality of Scotland, all prime Scottish products. Throughout the brochure a wild, romantic past is continually hinted at through references to clans, to the Highland bagpipes which led them into battle. Celtic symbols and tartan abound. The cities of Edinburgh and Glasgow are contrasted. Edinburgh is a 'sophisticated city', 'a city of symmetry and grandeur', whose appeal 'lies in the blend of the old and the historic, symbolised by Castle and Old Town, with artistic excellence and quality, which both the New Town and cultural events like the Edinburgh Festival represent'. There are accompanying photographs of its 'inspiring' skyline silhouetted against a purple evening sky and its 'elegant' New Town. In the presentation of Glasgow 'culture' is the key word. The city offers 'a unique cultural experience' combining as it does 'commercial flair' and 'artistic heritage'. Glasgow is portrayed as a cosmopolitan city with 'friendly local people'.

The other insight into this Tourist Board's conception of heritage comes from a major report it commissioned in 1989

After a holiday in London you need a holiday.

SCOTLAND
One visit is never enough

What are you doing on the London Underground when you could be enjoying yourself in Scotland? So discover new horizons – for your free brochure call 0500 636 666 or call into the Scottish Tourist Board at 19 Cockspur Street, off Trafalgar Square.

FIGURE 5 Hitting the market: the Scottish Tourist Board's aggressive campaign on London Transport.

FIGURE 6 The Scottish Tourist Board's campaign in the 1980s.

from an associate member of the international consultants Arthur Young International. This report formed the basis of a publication 'Visitor Attractions: a development guide', aimed at entrepreneurs interested in setting up or developing visitor attractions, including heritage sites. The remit of the heritage study is worth reproducing in full because it indicates the Board's definition of heritage. Heritage attractions, it spells out:

are intrinsically related to the Scottish
- landscape
- history or
- way of life
can be presented in a way which will
- attract and satisfy visitors
- generate income and employment and
- help to conserve the features to which the attractions relate.

The key elements of this definition are that heritage attractions:
- must have core elements which are intrinsic to Scotland in some significant way
- *need to be concerned solely with history and the past* [our emphasis]
- must be linked directly to visitor use and economic benefit and to conservation. (STB 'Visitor Attractions')

This account is interesting for a number of reasons. First, it gives priority to commercial aspects ('generate income and employment', versus '*help to* conserve the features . . .'). Second, and more significantly, there is a curious contra-diction between the terms of reference for the Heritage Attractions Study commissioned by the Scottish Tourist Board's International and Planning Division, and the subsequent publication whose definition of heritage is spelled out above. Whereas one of the key elements in the above is that heritage attractions 'need to be concerned solely with history and the past' (see italics above), the terms of reference for the study itself says precisely the opposite: 'need *not* be concerned solely with history and the past'. We have been unable to find out how this *volte face* arose, but from the tenor of the consultants' report, it is plain that 'history and the past' are not deemed necessary in developing heritage attractions.

We can only surmise that in the final publication, its producer assumed that history and heritage were the same thing,
whereas the gist of the consultants' report was that the economic potential lay precisely in the *lack* of correspondence
between heritage and history.

The consultants' report, of course, cannot be taken as an *ex
cathedra* account of the Board's position on heritage, but it is
certainly indicative of its general approach. The consultants
were asked not simply to review the marketing of heritage in
Scotland, but to explore the outer reaches of heritage imagination to see where the boundaries between acceptability and
unacceptability lay. The consultants concluded that heritage
attractions formed a major but fragmented element of
Scotland's tourist industry; that there had been a significant
growth in provision and use in recent years; that 'heritage as
such is not a viable proposition' insofar as it does not have
stand-alone commercial viability (investment in a hotel was
reckoned to be able to generate two or three times the level of
operating profit of a heritage centre); that there should be
more liaison between the main agencies; and that one of the
main obstacles lay in the fact that the main players National
Trust for Scotland and Historic Scotland (then the Historic
Buildings and Monuments board) were too conservative in
their approach to heritage, being associated with 'traditional
type of property products', hence 'locking up' enormous
heritage assets away from independent heritage developers.

Scottish Tourist Board's consultants, Arthur Young International, were highly critical of the exploitation of heritage
sites in Scotland. Their views would probably be unacceptable
to bodies like the National Trust for Scotland and Historic
Scotland. For example, Bannockburn, the site of Robert the
Bruce's victory over the English army in 1314 is now in the
care of the Trust. The consultants judged it to lack the 'magic
of the real'. They proposed a 'battle experience' using multi-
image projection and special effects, with an 'exhibition
focused on the idea of nationhood, and Scotland's struggles,
led by the famous heroes like Wallace and Bruce, culminating
in the battle, and the emergence of the country as the oldest
nation state in Europe' (1989:82). It is highly improbable
whether the National Trust for Scotland would embark on such
a 'political' project in this manner, especially as Bannockburn

is an annual symbol of the Scottish National Party's march for Scottish Independence. In similar vein, the consultants argued that the Scottish Mining Museum which operates on two sites in Mid- and East Lothian is poorly located and 'lacks the underground experience'. It would be better they suggested if it were relocated closer to the main centres of population in the central belt of Scotland. The 'magic of the real' does not require an actual site to give it authenticity.

Taken together, heritage sites in Scotland number, according to the consultants, over 120, excluding the top thirty monuments and castles. Nevertheless, they judge that there are considerable gaps in the market for heritage which might be met with the following projects:

- *a Celtic/Pictish/Roman hill-fort experience*: 'possibly based on a hill farm in eastern Tayside'. As well as some loose historic link, such a project would fill a geographical market niche in this part of Scotland.

- *archaeological/history park ('archaepark' in heritage-speak)*: this would link together Bronze-Age, Roman and Viking experiences and structures. 'Visitors would progress through Scottish history on foot, or be transported – perhaps by bicycle or by themed pedal vehicles on a track or by horse-drawn wagon, possibly in part on water.' (STB/AYI, 1989:119). The purpose of this would be 'to get away from often dull and incomprehensible (to all but the experts) archaeological features, preserved or archaeological digs, HBM sites etc . . .' (ibid.:B23). Such a site would be 'accessible to the whole central Scotland day trip market'.

- *a hi-tech/innovation theme park*: there is a 'theme gap' in heritage in Scotland, the absence of any kind of centre dealing with scientific innovation, a *'Tomorrow's World'*-style of linking the past (Bell, Fleming, Watt, Simpson, Baird), the present (Silicon Glen, computers) and the future (artificial intelligence, biotechnology). It is a pity, these consultants conclude, that Edinburgh has invented a science festival when the bulk of the Scottish population is in the West of Scotland.

There are other ideas for heritage projects: a) a 'living memory' exhibition based on a UK rather than simply a Scottish experience, but sited in the West because 'the vernacular feel of the product strongly suggests Glasgow' and because it would fit in with that city's project to become a major tourist destination; and b) the 'Scotland in Fire and Ice Experience', telling the 'real (sic) story of Scotland's geological formation and its scenic sculpting' (STB/AYI, 1989:126). Are we to assume that these are simply 'creative ideas' to stimulate the consultants' sponsors about heritage? The fact that the Scottish Tourist Board included it in the remit perhaps implies that these ideas are the wider reaches of the heritage industry, but not by much. 'Living history' techniques, with the stress on 'the magic of the real', authenticity rather than history, historic enactments, actor role-playing and outdoor theatre are to be found in many other heritage projects and in other societies. Thinking the unthinkable out loud is frequently a device for testing the waters in the marketplace, especially if we remember that the development guide produced by the Tourist Board is aimed at developers and operators of what it calls 'heritage attractions'. We might think that we are looking at the Scottish heritage experience of the millenium. However, in 1994, a proposal was announced to open a £3m Neolithic heritage park near Oyne, a village of 200 people, in Aberdeenshire. The main attraction is to be a 900m² grass-covered dome, which will be approached by a time tunnel to put visitors in the pre-history mood using interactive displays, laser shows and video walls. The park itself will include mock Iron-Age houses, a Neolithic long house, and a Roman camp. The whole project is to be funded by the local council and Scottish Enterprise (*Scotland on Sunday*, 17 April 1994). About the same time Historic Scotland announced that its pre-historic hill fort and burial mound at Cairnpapple near Bathgate would not be open in the coming season as the number of visitors was unlikely to warrant it. Fiction, it seems, is more palatable, or profitable, than truth.

MANAGING THE STATE'S HERITAGE: HISTORIC SCOTLAND

Scotland has a rich legacy from the past – a heritage of monuments and buildings which bear silent witness to our proud history stretching back over 5000 years, which are a delight to us today and which we must carefully preserve for future generations.

(Historic Scotland, 1991:1)

In using these words in its first framework document, the Conservative Secretary of State for Scotland, Ian Lang, was setting the agenda for Historic Scotland to manage the nation's built heritage. If the Scottish Tourist Board treats heritage as a product, and uses the vocabulary of commerce, then Historic Scotland defines heritage much more as artefact, and speaks the vocabulary of technique. Historic Scotland, however, has, like British Rail, succumbed to business-speak by referring to its users as 'customers' ('We actively seek views from our customers and are investing more in training our staff in service delivery' *Raising the Standard for the Built Heritage*, leaflet GE1488/3/93).

Historic Scotland was set up as an executive agency by the government in 1991 as 'the government body which protects Scotland's built heritage and helps everyone to see and enjoy it' (SH's *Welcome* newsletter). It cares for (sic) over 330 properties which 'all portray Scotland's colourful and industrious past'. These vary from the Stone-Age village of Skara Brae on Orkney and the standing stones at Callanish on Lewis, from 'Border abbeys to Highland keeps, from west coast castles to east coast palaces' ('A Journey Through Time'). Caring for Scotland's 'wealth of prehistoric sites and historic buildings' and to 'keep them safe for future generations' is Historic Scotland's *raison d'etre.* This is a continuous process: 'as the scaffolding comes down on one property, it goes up again on another'.

All three bodies, Historic Scotland, English Heritage and CADW Wales, were products of the National Heritage Act 1983, an act which was fuelled by Mrs Thatcher's desire to make the organisations responsible for protecting traditional heritage more commercially minded. The properties in the care of Historic Scotland had been inherited from Historic Buildings and Monuments, and before that the Scottish Office of Works in 1827. Many of these properties had come into the hands of the state as far back as 1587 under the act of the Scottish parliament annexing former church properties.

Following the fashions of the 1990s, Historic Scotland set out its 'mission statement' as safeguarding the nation's built heritage, and promoting its understanding and enjoyment while making the best use of resources available. Under its chief executive, a lifelong civil servant, Historic Scotland has cautiously moved away from the language of the architectural historian and the civil service bureaucracy. It had inherited a guidebook vocabulary which made few concessions to the non-professional (the language of garderobes, and aumbries abounded). The incoming marketing director applied his press officer test: if there was something in a guidebook she did not understand, it was altered. The old title 'Historic Buildings and Monuments' (its public organisation had been called by the Monty Pythonesque title, 'Friends of Ancient Monuments') was altered to Historic Scotland. Apart from being shorter and easier to remember, Historic Scotland avoided sounding like a belated carbon-copy of English Heritage. Similarly in keeping with the new times, the defensively sounding 'warders' of properties became user-friendly 'custodians', swapping prison officers' garb for more informal tartan trews and jumpers.

The new-style custodians were ushered in along with:

> . . . the shop assistant who sells guidebooks and souvenirs, the mason who carves stone to repair 500 year old buildings, the historian who writes the guidebooks and the display boards, the archaeologist who recognises the secret of a bump in the ground, the architect who makes sure that buildings stand for future centuries and managers who keep the organisation running smoothly. (*Welcome*, Winter, 1992)

Changing from technical civil service mode to user-friendly executive agency is not likely to have been straightforward. Historic Scotland has a staff of about 600, some 100 fewer than in the mid-1980s, largely because some of its services, for example archaeology, have been contracted out. The requirement to popularise the work of the agency, and especially its guidebooks, seems to have caused tensions within the organisation between the popularisers and the conservation experts, largely architects and technical staff. Nevertheless, the limits of popularisation are recognised. The marketing director commented: 'We are not in the theme park business. Ours is a real heritage (sic) and not created. Although we feel visits can be enjoyed as well as being worthwhile, we should remember the dignity of the monuments. It would be quite wrong to change royal castles and palaces into theme parks' (Blair, 1989:83). As this quotation shows, the emphasis is very much on education rather than entertainment (or the hybrid, 'infotainment'), with free visits to sites for school parties, and the production of information packs aimed at primary school children and their teachers.

Historic Scotland has a budget of some £30 million (80 per cent from the state, and rest self-generated). It has virtually doubled since 1984, with running costs for 1993–4 at £12.7 million. These figures put it on a par with the Scottish Tourist Board. Visitors to Historic Scotland's seventy sites have risen in that period from 1.8 million per annum to 2.4 million, an increasing interest reflected in the 30,000 members of its 'Friends' organisation.

In line with its new image, Historic Scotland engaged the Faulds advertising agency of Edinburgh. The agency carried out a study in 1991 which made two important discoveries. Firstly, Historic Scotland attracted a very low level of awareness among the public compared with the National Trust for Scotland. While 82 per cent of those questioned had heard of the latter, only 28 per cent said the same for Historic Buildings and Monuments, and a paltry 6 per cent for Historic Scotland. Secondly, there was considerable potential interest among skilled manual workers and their families (the C2s in advertising parlance). The agency felt that there was a huge untapped market within Scotland, especially among those looking for a 'good day out'. Faulds' remit has been to make Historic Scotland more accessible to home-based Scots, especially to those from lower- middle- and upper-working-class families.

The popularising of Scottish heritage has focused on literature and advertising, both press and television. The 'Scotland' which is presented in the literature is clear-cut and action based. What kind of Scotland is it?

> Scotland is a land of castles. Mighty fortresses on rocky heights, isolated keeps, elegant homes for great families and grim strongholds set on towering sea cliffs.
>
> These were the stages on which the dynasties of Bruce, Douglas and Stewart played out their power struggles; where William Wallace fought for Scotland's independence, and Mary Queen of Scots fought for her life.
>
> In the great halls, great men discussed affairs of state against backdrops of regal splendour. Behind the scenes, whispered plots and counterplots were hatched, while in

the gloom of the dungeons, unfortunate wretches ended their lives in misery and despair.

Noble men and tyrants, kings and queens, lords and commoners all made their entrances and exits, and now only the stones remain to speak centuries of drama. (Historic Scotland, *The Popular Choice*, n.d.)

This pamphlet, with its revealing title *The Popular Choice*, is a long way from the technicalities of medieval ruins. The text continues with descriptions such as: 'ruthless political intrigue', 'buccaneering raids', 'wayward churchman', 'burning and looting', 'a rare sense of tranquility'. Its history is fairly nationalist and masculinist: the Jacobite Risings are not 'rebellions'. By contrast to 'the ruthlessness of the Hanoverian forces', the Highlanders were 'too loyal to take the gold offered for Bonnie Prince Charlie'; there is whisky-smuggling, harsh punishment for soldiers, and all in all, 'real stories for real men' (sic). The implicit message seems aimed at fathers taking young sons on boisterous days out at castles. This is backed up by the agency's own focus-group research: it shows that 'the 'stories' of the history of Scotland are of great interest to the audience. The message should use 'colour', fun and excitement rather than text-book style teaching. The research showed that in this there was less difference between AB social categories (managerial and administrative workers) and C2s (skilled manual workers). Whereas, as we might expect, nearly eight out of ten people in AB groups said they were very or quite interested in visiting historic sites, over six out of ten C2s indicated an interest, and as the agency pointed out, the latter group were nearly twice as large a group in the population compared with AB groups. Further, the C2s interest lay in 'history and stories' (41 per cent), and 'a love of history' (30 per cent). When prompted, 68 per cent agreed with the statement that 'it was important to learn about Scotland', and 53 per cent agreed with 'I enjoy the atmosphere'.

The research led to a series of television and newspaper advertisements, all designed to be witty and eyecatching. It ran the thirty-second television commercial 'Gargoyles' in the summer of 1991 to increase awareness of its activities. The script is presented in Figure 7, and the creative team for the agency were pleased with its impact. Follow-up research showed that 85 per cent of C2s liked the campaign, compared with 69 per cent of ABs. Apart from budgetary considerations, there were bounds of acceptability which the agency team felt they could not transgress. They had to ensure the dates were correct; not too much English-bashing; and murder was only an acceptable subject if it was 'long ago'. Historic Scotland's budget did not stretch to a 1992 campaign. Instead, the newspaper advertisements used cartoon drawing and commentary such as 'King comfortably enthroned at Linlithgow Palace', 'What kind of person carves his name on the wall of a 16th century abbey?' [answer: the architect]; and 'Waverley man finds Crown jewels in spare room' [Walter Scott's discovery of Scotland's Crown Jewels at Edinburgh Castle in 1818]. Examples of advertisements used in the popular press appear in Figures 8 and 9.

Historic Scotland appears to be protected by a broad nationalist discourse in Scotland which extends to the Conservative politicians who run the Scottish Office. So it would be hard to envisage a similar controversy to the one which engulfed English Heritage in 1992 when it proposed to sell off its less profitable assets even though Historic Scotland certainly has some. In fact only Edinburgh Castle, and to a far lesser extent Stirling Castle, are profitable in their own right. Also, given the weakness of the Tory party in Scotland, the Scottish Office would have found it very difficult to appoint a Conservative businessman to lead Historic Scotland in the way that it did south of the Border. Nevertheless, the organisation has found itself under attack for its interpretation of Scottish history. In late 1993, Allan Macinnes, the recently appointed Professor of History at Aberdeen University, criticised Historic Scotland for employing no general historian, and only a limited knowledge of Scottish history and of Scotland's place in Europe. In a letter to *The Herald*, he wrote:

> I have become increasingly concerned about its direction and application of funding as well as the diffusionist historical interpretation manifest in numerous guidebooks; by diffusionist I mean the wilful reluctance to accept that developments could have originated in and spread from Scotland to Europe rather than having flowed inevitably from England and France. (6 January 1994)

Professor Macinnes implied that there might well be internal debate in Historic Scotland about its interpretation of Scottish

VISUAL	AUDIO
Open on a long shot of a silhouetted castle	*Gargoyle 1*: Oh the stories we could tell . . .
Cut to a shot of two timeworn gargoyles on an old wall. They talk to camera.	*Gargoyle 2*: Aye, the battles . . .
Dissolve to the two gargoyles looking much newer. It is evening. Orange firelight flickers over their faces. They look from side to side in unison as if watching a tennis match as cannon balls fly back and forth.	*Gargoyle 1*: Advantage King James.
The second gargoyle nods.	
Cut to daytime. The two gargoyles are craning their heads forward to listen in to a whispered conversation.	*Gargoyle 1*: The intrigue . . . *SFX*: Whispering . . . 'Ssh walls have ears'
The two gargoyles immediately resume their normal position with expressions of innocence.	

FIGURE 7: Script of 'Gargoyles', Historic Scotland's 1991 television commercial.

history, and concluded his letter with the suggestion that the organisation be amalgamated with Scottish Natural Heritage.

Nevertheless, Historic Scotland has developed a strong domestic market aimed at exploiting a robust sense of Scotland's history. Unlike the National Trust for Scotland, it is far less dependent on its 'Friends' association for its source of revenue. It is quite willing to play a strong Scottish national card (speaking for example of Scotland's crown jewels as 'symbols of sovereignty', and commenting 'For a small nation jealous of its unique identity, the Honours are precious beyond

Cut to evening.	*Gargoyle 2*: And the romance . . .
	SFX: We hear a lute being strummed, a man's voice begins to serenade . . . 'My sweet lady love . . .'
The two gargoyles look at each other. They dodge out of the way as a torrent of water is thrown down past them onto the singer.	*SFX*: Giggling from above.
Dissolve to the gargoyles in situ on the south wall of the palace at Stirling Castle. Visitors wander around taking photos etc.	*MVO*: Historic Scotland protects the nation's historic properties. Visit one and enjoy a great day out.
Cut back to close up of the two gargoyles.	*Gargoyle 1*: Hey, they're going to take a photo.
They both make hideous faces as a flash bulb goes off.	
We dissolve to a square flagstone in a shaft of light. Dust blows across it to reveal the logo etched into it.	*MVO*: Historic Scotland. Where every stone has a story.

price' (*Welcome*, Summer 1993:9). It recognises that for over-seas visitors, 'The main reason tourists come to Scotland is heritage. Many British and American tourists feel that they have connections with some part of Scottish history and they want to experience it for themselves' (*Welcome*, Spring 1993:12). Nevertheless, it avoids the term 'heritage' as much as possible, because in the words of its chief executive, it is 'tacky and dated', and it evokes 'images of Camelot recon-structed off the M6'. Its user-friendly image is reflected in the title of its glossy quarterly newsletter to Friends, *Welcome*.

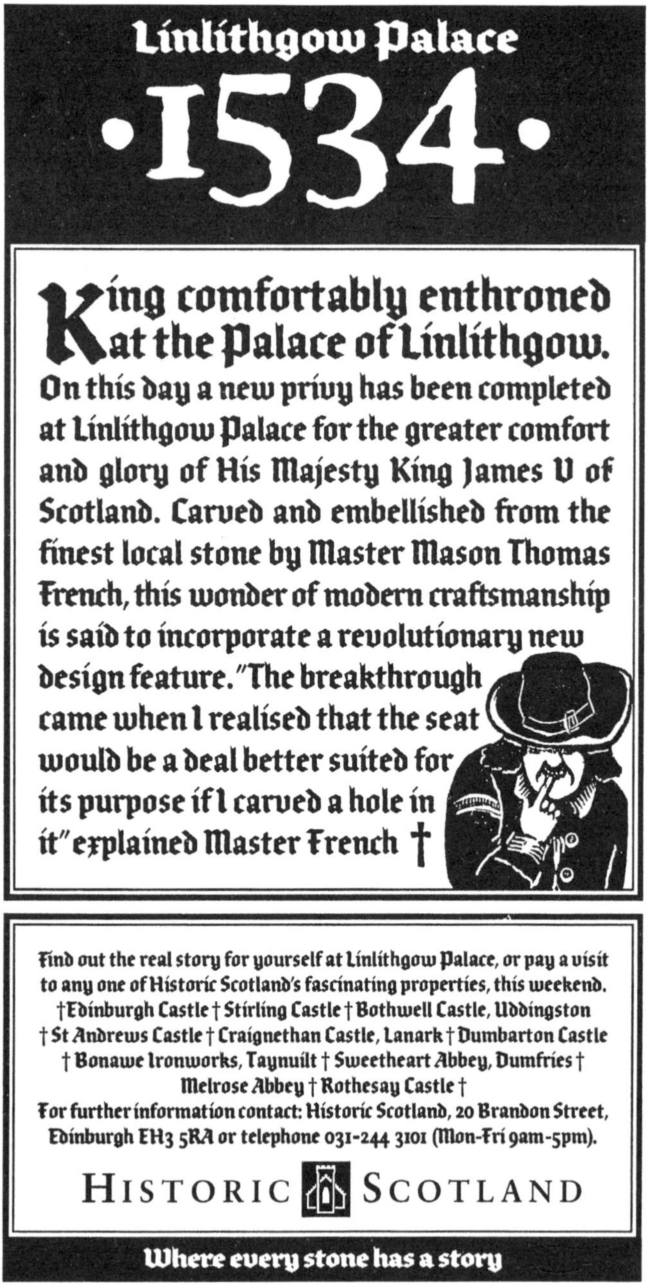

Linlithgow Palace

·1534·

King comfortably enthroned at the Palace of Linlithgow.

On this day a new privy has been completed at Linlithgow Palace for the greater comfort and glory of His Majesty King James V of Scotland. Carved and embellished from the finest local stone by Master Mason Thomas French, this wonder of modern craftsmanship is said to incorporate a revolutionary new design feature. "The breakthrough came when I realised that the seat would be a deal better suited for its purpose if I carved a hole in it" explained Master French †

Find out the real story for yourself at Linlithgow Palace, or pay a visit to any one of Historic Scotland's fascinating properties, this weekend.
†Edinburgh Castle † Stirling Castle † Bothwell Castle, Uddingston
† St Andrews Castle † Craignethan Castle, Lanark † Dumbarton Castle
† Bonawe Ironworks, Taynuilt † Sweetheart Abbey, Dumfries †
Melrose Abbey † Rothesay Castle †
For further information contact: Historic Scotland, 20 Brandon Street, Edinburgh EH3 5RA or telephone 031-244 3101 (Mon-Fri 9am-5pm).

HISTORIC 🏛 SCOTLAND

Where every stone has a story

FIGURE 8 Historic Scotland: a good day out.

FOR LOVERS OF HISTORY, A QUICK GEOGRAPHY LESSON.

You don't have to travel far to go back a long way in time. Scotland is full of historical interest. (Around 5000 years-worth at the last count.) Pictish stones, abbeys, castles, gardens and Royal palaces... you name it, there's sure to be one or the other on your doorstep. (As the attractions highlighted alongside confirm.)

For a more precise location and description of these and other Historic Scotland properties, phone for your free map that'll send you in the right direction for a great day out. The rest, as they say, HISTORIC  SCOTLAND will be history.

JUST BRING YOUR IMAGINATION

Historic Scotland, 20 Brandon Street, Edinburgh EH3 5RA. Phone 031-244 3101.

FOR YOUR FREE MAP OF PROPERTIES THROUGHOUT SCOTLAND, CALL FREE ON **0800 77 22 00**

FIGURE 9 Historic Scotland: popularising heritage.

The expected title *Heritage Scotland* has, ironically, been given to the same journal of the National Trust for Scotland, which conveys a quite different image of 'heritage', and it is to that organisation that we now turn.

NATION IN TRUST: THE NATIONAL TRUST FOR SCOTLAND

If the Scottish Tourist Board represents heritage as product, and Historic Scotland heritage as artefact, then the National Trust for Scotland interprets heritage as inheritance. Its vocabulary is that of organic order, and contrasts with the Tourist Board's language of commerce, and Historic Scotland's vocabulary of technique. For example, the chairman of the National Trust for Scotland's council commented in his forward to the 1993 annual report: '. . . our heritage – whether it be the built heritage or the heritage of countryside and wilderness – is part of the soul of the nation and we ignore the nation's soul at our peril' (NTS 62nd Annual Report, 1993:2). It is hard to imagine either the Scottish Tourist Board or Historic Scotland making a play to be keepers of the national soul. What makes this doubly odd is that the National Trust for Scotland is not an agency of government but a charitable 'trust' (in setting up the National Trust in England in 1895, Octavia Hill preferred the word 'trust' to 'company' in order to stress the benevolent aspect of the operation). It is this ethos of voluntarism which helps to give heritage in Britain its image of good works and service, although in terms of funding it is likely that the state is by far the major contributor.

Both the National Trust (which covers England, Wales and Northern Ireland) and the National Trust for Scotland are recognised by act of parliament. Although this study is about Scottish heritage, it is important to make three points about the relationship between the two organisations: a) the National Trust for Scotland was founded in 1931, some thirty-six years after the National Trust, which was deemed to be neglecting the Scottish interest; b) since 1943 there has been a policy of mutual representation on the boards of each trust; and c) although they share similar aims, their visions as to what constitutes heritage are somewhat different.

The National Trust is not only the most important voluntary conservation body in England, but also the largest institutional landowner, owning around 554,000 acres, much of it coastline and open country. It is the size of its landholdings which

helps to explain the significance of the furore in 1992 surrounding its threat to ban fox hunting on its lands. The
National Trust for Scotland has escaped this controversy not
only because fox hunting is far less common on a less hospi-
table terrain, but because it is a far smaller landowner, with
100,000 acres, mainly forest, mountain and moor.

The two organisations have also had quite different and
unpredictable histories. The National Trust was formed in
1895, but the impetus came earlier in the previous decade as
a result of the experiences of the Common Preservation
Society. This society was legally barred from acquiring land,
and could not purchase common rights because it did not
have corporate status. To rectify this, its solicitor, Robert
Hunter, proposed in 1884 the creation of a body which would
be incorporated under the Joint Stock Companies Act, and so
could buy and hold land 'for the benefit of the nation' (Wright,
1985:50). Hunter's idea was to have 'a land company formed
. . . with a view to the protection of the public interest in the
open spaces of the country' (ibid.). The National Trust was
formed by socially aware English intellectuals such as Octavia
Hill and Canon Hardwicke Rawnsley in the late nineteenth-
century, people who were concerned with preventing the
destruction and despoiling of the countryside. Its origins can
be traced back to the Commons, Open Spaces and Footpaths
Preservation Society founded in 1865. Hewison points out
that the original purpose of the Trust was therefore not the
protection of buildings or private property, but public access
to the countryside. It was Canon Rawnsley who spoke out in
1900 for unrestricted access to Stonehenge, a place where
'men's feet (sic) all up the ages have been as free as air to
come and go' (Wright, 1986:32). As Wright points out, the
ghosts of the National Trust founders must have raised an
eyebrow when travellers were turned away from this site
nearly a century later.

Thus, it was the natural landscape rather than the man-
made environment which people like Hill and Rawnsley were
concerned to protect. They both had connections with John
Ruskin, and it was his ideal of a wild, beautiful and untamed
nature that was the inspiration behind their work. However,
as Hewison argues, 'memory too had a capacity for moral
change, by acting as a reminder of former greatness and the
landscape could not be seen without its human associations'

(Hewison, 1987:36). Accordingly, when the Trust was finally registered with the Board of Trade in 1895, it was as 'The National Trust for Places of Historic Interest or Natural Beauty'.

Over time, the 'human associations' came to dominate, and the National Trust became firmly associated with the cult of the country house. In order to understand 'the peculiarly strong hold such places have on the British - though for once it seems more appropriate to say English - imagination' (Hewison, 1987:51-2), we have to look at what the country house represents and symbolises. Essentially, and importantly, Hewison argues, the Country House symbolises an unbroken continuity with the past:

> because there has been no foreign invasion, civil war or revolution since the seventeenth century, these houses both great and small represent a physical continuity which enables the same adaptability to change within a respect for precedent and tradition that has shaped the common law. With a garden, a park and a greater or lesser estate they enshrine the rural values that persist in a population that has been predominantly urban for more than a century . . . As the great celebration of the Country House at the National Gallery of Art in Washington in 1985-86 sought to demonstrate 'they have become as it were vessels of civilization.' (1987:52)

There were also more pragmatic reasons for the National Trust to increase its interest in the country house. In 1923, it asked the Chancellor of the Exchequer, without success, to grant tax concessions to owners of important country houses so as to keep the properties in reasonable repair. However, under the 1931 Finance Act, land or buildings given to the Trust could escape death duties. This made for a happy compromise: the National Trust gained considerable amounts of property while owners and their heirs could keep the rest of their estate intact. In 1937 the Act was extended to instances where the donor retained a life interest in the property. As a result, the Trust was able formally to launch its Country House Scheme, whether or not the owner lived on the premises. As Wright points out, the 'emphasis on continuity of place takes on an ancestral dimension . . . an already closed definition of the nation and history is linked to the present through an idea of genetic continuity' (Wright, 1986:34). Of course, the National Trust's interest in the welfare of English aristocrats is a far cry from the old ideal of unlimited access to land. As Hewison argues: 'In exchange for often quite limited rights of access to the public, the owner had been able to continue his life very much as before, without the financial burden of maintaining the house in which he lived' (Hewison, 1987:59).

The catalyst for forming in 1931 a separate National Trust for Scotland appeared two years earlier when the 500-acre Loch Dee estate in Galloway was offered to the Association for the Protection of Rural Scotland. But the association was not allowed to own land, and so there was a threat that the estate would pass to the English National Trust. The National Trust for Places of Historical Interest or Natural Beauty in Scotland was formed on 1 May, timed to coincide with the Finance Act of that year which made National Trust (and hence National Trust for Scotland) property exempt from death duties. In that year, Sir John Stirling Maxwell gave the Trust in Scotland its first property, Crookston Castle near Glasgow. By 1935, the Trust had become a statutory body enabling the council to declare Trust lands and buildings inalienable and able to be held by NTS in perpetuity.

From the outset, this organisation has had a strong aristocratic and landed domination of its council. Its first president was the Duke of Atholl (1932–42), who was succeeded by Sir John Stirling Maxwell (1944–54), its vice-president from 1932–43. (Maxwell was also Chairman of the Royal Commission on the Ancient and Historical Monuments of Scotland (RCAHMS), 1940–9.) No president followed until the Earl of Wemyss and March in 1968, serving until 1991 when the Marquess of Bute took over. (Wemyss also succeeded Maxwell as Chairman of RCAHMS, serving until 1985 when the Earl of Balcarres was appointed.) Chairmen of the NTS Council have all been male, and titled persons served for the first fifty years of the Trust's history: Sir Iain Colquhoun (1932–45), The Earl of Wemyss and March (1946–68), and the Marquess of Bute (1969–84). He was succeeded by W. M. Cuthbert (1985–9), and by R. C. Tyrell (1990–4). The chairman-designate of the Trust, Hamish Leslie Melville, is an Eton and Oxford-educated financier who owns an estate in Garve, Ross-shire.

Vice-presidents have also been drawn heavily from lairds and gentry. Only in more recent years have non-titled persons begun to appear on the council. Vice-presidents have been: the Earls of Crawford and Balcarres (1932–9; and 1946–75), Sir Iain Colquhoun (1946–8), The Earl of Elgin (1933–68), Sir David Russell (1951–5), Admiral Sir Angus Cunninghame Graham (1956–81, Major Michael Crichton-Stuart of Falkland (1958–74), Mr E. J. Ivory (1963 to the present), Mr J. Gibson CA (1963 to the present), Sir Robert Russell (1970–2), The Hon. Mrs Derick Gascoigne (1974–80), A. Kennedy CA (1976 to the present), The Duke of Atholl (1978 to the present), Mrs Denny OBE, DL (1982 to the present), A. S. Roger MBE, JP (1984 to the present), the Marquess of Bute (1985–93), Mrs Mackie (1989 to the present), and R. C. Tyrell (1990–4). The remarkable feature of this list is the overwhelming preponderance of the titled, the landed and the powerful. Only three women have been vice-presidents, and only from the late 1970s onwards.

Executive responsibilities have lain with the Secretary/Director of the Trust, and these have been long-serving in the main: Arthur Russell, Writer to the Signet, was Secretary and Treasurer in the first year (1932–3), and was succeeded by Captain Stevenson CVO, MC, FSA (Scot) (1933–46). The Liberal politician, Jo Grimond, was director for a year in 1947–8, and he was succeeded by the naturalist, Sir Jamie Stormonth Darling, from 1949 until 1983, when Lester Borley, who had been with the Scottish Tourist Board, took over until he retired in 1993 to be succeeded by retired Vice-Admiral Douglas Dow.

It is not surprising then that the National Trust for Scotland has a strongly patrician and paternalistic air. Male patricians run it; females service it. Of its army of volunteers, 95 per cent are women, who also serve as secretaries on the paid staff. Scottish aristocrats have also served on the board of the National Trust. The Marquess of Lothian continued on the English Trust after the Scottish Trust was formed in 1931, while the Marquess of Zetland was appointed chairman of the National Trust in 1932. Since 1943, there has been a policy of mutual representation on both organisations. In that year, Sir Iain Colquhoun, who in the words of the National Trust of Scotland's first historian, 'personified the romantic notion of the Scottish laird and soldier' (Prentice, 1971), was chairman of the council of that body and was also on the council of the English Trust, while Lady Charles Trevelyan of the National Trust was appointed to serve on the council of the Scottish Trust.

In a country like Scotland where the land question has been an integral part of its political agenda, it might seem to be a disadvantage in terms of its wider popularity for the Trust to be so dominated by lairds and gentry. The organisation has worked to offset this by stressing its ideology of stewardship and social responsibility. For example, the National Trust for Scotland places considerable store in its 'Little Houses' scheme, and while it is reluctant to make an explicit contrast with its English counterpart, it is not unhappy that observers draw the conclusion that its commitment is to much more than the Great Houses. The Trust presents an ethos of organic conservatism, of a society in which the laird's house and the little houses are integrated in an organic whole so that all have their part to play in the scheme of things. This does not mean, of course, that all mix freely. At the opening of the House of Dun in Tayside, one of the Trust's most recently opened properties, the local landowners were invited to a reception in the daytime, and 'the locals', as they were referred to by the NTS director, in the evening: there is a place for everyone. So in the words of the previous director, interviewed on the fiftieth anniversary of the Trust: 'We are a private organisation serving the public's needs. We are a loss leader for the leisure industry. People seem to like what the Trust stands for' (*The Scotsman*, 27 August 1991).

The other way of embedding itself in Scottish civil society is for the Trust to incorporate other groups on to its council. Hence, from the outset, its council had representative members from: the city councils of Edinburgh, Glasgow, Dundee, Aberdeen, Inverness, and Perth; the Association of County Councils of Scotland; the Convention of Royal Burghs; the Royal Society of Edinburgh; the Royal Scottish Academy; the Royal Scottish Geographical Society; the Royal Scottish Forestry Society; the Forestry Commission; the Scottish Land and Property Federation; the Highland and Agricultural Society of Scotland; the Royal Incorporation of Architects in Scotland; the Society of Antiquaries of Scotland; the Scottish Ecclesiological Society; the Botanical Society of Edinburgh; and the Association for the Preservation of Rural Scotland.

Later, it added the Town Planning Institute (Scotland) in the 1940s; the Scottish Mountaineering Club, Saltire Society and Scottish Civic Trust in the 1950s; the Nature Conservancy Council, District Councils' Association for Scotland, and the Scottish Georgian Society in the 1960s; the National Farmers' Union Scotland, Council for British Archaeology, An Comunn Gaidhealtach (the Gaelic Society), and Scottish Women's Rural Institute in the 1970s, together with representative members of the regional councils for Fife, Grampian, Highland and Tayside, and of the district councils for Ettrick and Lauderdale, Edinburgh, Glasgow and The Stewartry; and, finally, the Scottish Museums Council, The Mountaineering Club, Scottish Conservation Projects, and Scotland's Garden Scheme in the 1980s. Manifestly, there is technical assistance to be had from this representation, but it also provides considerable political and institutional clout when required.

The National Trust for Scotland's property portfolio is prudently mixed. Its work has been concerned with castles and great houses, alongside the 'little houses' which were originally the homes of merchants, burgesses and artisans, and 'built in the vernacular styles peculiar to the region in which they stand, and were as comely and native to Scotland as the towers and great houses from the barons and lairds' (Prentice, 1971:7). The Trust is keen to stress that historic and architectural worth is not the only consideration of importance in its conservation work. Lamb's House in Leith, for example, was restored in association with Edinburgh and Leith's Old People's Welfare Council to be used as a day centre for old people. In addition to buildings, the organisation owns 100,000 acres of land, notably gardens and estates, which are acquired for their historic or aesthetic value, such as Bannockburn, Fair Isle and St Kilda. It is significant that Scotland's two great battlefields, Bannockburn and Culloden, are run by this voluntary organisation and not directly by the state. These two major heritage icons of Scotland will be analysed, along with the third – Edinburgh Castle – in the final chapter.

The 1935 Confirmation Act gave the National Trust for Scotland a constitution which allowed great freedom of action, including power to 'maintain and manage or assist in the maintenance and management of lands as open spaces or places of public resort', and 'to make all such provision as may be beneficial for the management of the property or desirable for the comfort or convenience of persons resorting to or using such property'. The 1935 Housing Act also helped to give the Trust a social role by reclaiming derelict buildings. The 4th Marquess of Bute conceived the idea of listed buildings of historic or architectural interest, and provided the funds for an architect to make a national survey. These lists enabled local authorities to note buildings of merit, and after the Second World War, the Scottish Office took over responsibility for listed buildings based on the so-called Bute lists.

The 5th Marquess of Bute made possible the Trust's tenancy of its headquarters at 5 Charlotte Square in Edinburgh's New Town, and in the 1960s it came to own the north block of the square under National Land Fund procedures. Number 7 was converted into the Georgian House, one of the Trust's most visited properties; number 6 became Bute House, the official residence of the Secretary of State for Scotland; and a flat in number 7 was turned into a residence for the use by the Moderator of the General Assembly of the Church of Scotland. In this way, the Trust and its aristocratic begetters embedded themselves in the national institutions of Scotland. Whatever the Trust was, it could not be accused of being a patrician implant on Scottish soil. On the death of the 6th Marquess of Bute, who was president at the time, his obituary said simply: 'The Sixth Marquess of Bute: guardian of Scotland's natural and cultural heritage' (*The Scotsman*, 22 July 1993).

By 1993, the National Trust for Scotland had an income of nearly £15 million, made up of three main sources: membership subscriptions (22 per cent) (the Trust has 235,000 members); donations and legacies (18.5 per cent); and investment income (17 per cent) (63rd Annual Report, 1994). Grants (17 per cent), admissions (7 per cent), other income (11.5 per cent), trading company contribution (4 per cent), and rents (3 per cent) make up the rest. Support from government agencies, such as Historic Scotland and Scottish Natural Heritage stood in 1993 at £1.1 million. Income from membership at over £3.3 million is an important financial base for the Trust, as is the support of nearly a quarter of a million members who account for over 50 per cent of total visitor numbers. The Trust depends on legacies almost as much as on subscriptions, both for general purposes (in 1993 one such for over £200,000 was given), and for specific funds (including one over £200,000 for the purchase of the West Affric estate). What sort of image of Scottish heritage does the trust convey? In keeping with its patrician image, it is a traditional, 'respectable' one, eschewing any downmarket iconography of Scotland, as befits a gentry-led organisation. Its magazine, *Heritage Scotland*, is douce and worthy as this editorial by the director illustrates:

> We regularly read newspaper headlines denouncing the 'moral sickness' within our society. It is therefore important to all of us to know that somebody cares. It is also important to know that there are caring organisations like the National Trust for Scotland, which not only preserves and protects buildings and inanimate objects, but also cares for the people and the communities at its properties. *The trust is very conscious of its responsibilities in its role in the community. The Trust is, itself, a community but it is also part of a wider community which it seeks to serve through its duty to act 'for the benefit of the nation'* [our emphasis]. (Summer 1993, 10,2:10)

The Trust operates within a model of society which is an organic conservative one. It does not speak the vocabulary of the marketplace, as does the Scottish Tourist Board, nor that of technical expertise, as does Historic Scotland. Its appeal can be gauged from its own magazine and its ethos. It carries advertisements for the following: backache relief, elderly people's pets, walking shoes, Ordnance Survey maps, tartan chairs, guide dogs for the blind, Aga cookers, solid wood furniture, conservatories, Saab and Volkswagen cars, fireside companion sets, educational holidays in Samarkand, Saga holidays for the over-sixties ('Over 60 and the world at your feet'). Scottish Nuclear values the NTS's douce image sufficiently to take prominent advertising in the Trust's magazine. What is projected is an up-market image of Scotland in which pursuits and objects are tastefully presented. We will see how closely its life membership articulates its image in Chapters 6 and 7 when we focus on the consumption of Scottish heritage.

The National Trust for Scotland is not without sources of opposition. Conflicts have arisen over its handling of land in Glencoe and Ben Lawers. For example it has a dilemma over

FIGURE 10 Festive Edwardian evening at Fyvie Castle, December 1991.

FIGURE 11 Reconstructing history: the Sealed Knot Society re-enact the Battle of Fyvie, August 1993.

whether or not to adhere strictly to the letter of the so-called Unna Rules laid down by Percy Unna who left the Trust tracts of land in Glencoe on the understanding that the wilderness should be kept wild and free from visitor centres and the like. The Trust's estates in the western Highlands have also raised questions over its conservation policy: that is, the balance between conservation and development. However, what is remarkable is that, given the social composition of the Trust's hierarchs, and its conservative image, so little controversy has been generated over its image of heritage. This seems to be the result of cautious anticipation, and powerful allies.

CONCLUSION

In this chapter we have focused on the key agencies involved in Scottish heritage. Each has their own carefully constructed rhetoric and vocabulary. Whereas the Scottish Tourist Board is closest to a market conception of heritage and the vocabulary of commerce ('Scotland's For Me!'), Historic Scotland forefronts the heritage of artefacts ('Don't believe it when they tell you stones can't speak'), while concentrating on technical expertise. As we have seen, the National Trust for Scotland employs the language of Conservative nationalism ('our heritage is part of the soul of the nation'). In the next chapter we will see how private social and economic interests have mobilised the heritage of the 'stately home' in Scotland as a solution to political and cultural issues.

Chapter 5

Status and Heritage

An examination of heritage sites in the Scottish Borders reveals an apparent conundrum. Why, in this most historic part of Scotland, does the National Trust for Scotland have so few properties? In the central borders, the Trust can offer only four attractions – a reconstructed printing works (Robert Smail's at Innerleithen), a waterfall (The Grey Mare's Tail), Priorwood Garden at Melrose, and Turret House museum at Kelso. By contrast, Historic Scotland has its illustrious abbey ruins at Jedburgh, Dryburgh, Melrose and Kelso, as well as a few other minor attractions. The answer to our puzzle is not that the borderlands are bereft of heritage, but that the key ones are in private hands. They are the great stately homes of those whom Checkland called the 'mighty magnates' of Scotland. Here is the private face of heritage.

HERITAGE ON THE BORDER

The border country is the site of some of the most important heritage monuments of Scotland – the castles and abbeys which were fought over and on in the course of Scotland's wars with England. It also contains some of the country's best farming and grazing lands, and as a consequence the largest estates in Scotland. John McEwen's work on landownership showed the extent of this domination. The biggest landowner in Scotland, as well as a major landowner in England, the Duke of Buccleuch owns 277,000 acres, including substantial holdings in the Borders – over 60,00 acres in Roxburgh, and nearly 30,000 acres in Selkirkshire. The Duke of Roxburghe owns 96,000 acres, and more modest holdings are in the hands of the Earl of Wemyss and March (44,000), Lord Haddington (who owns 5,200 acres in Roxburgh, and 9,200 in Berwickshire), Lord Lauderdale (8,100 acres in Berwickshire) and Lord Home (5,500 acres also in Berwickshire). By 1970, fully 44 per cent of land in East Lothian and 55 per cent in Berwickshire were parcelled up in estates of more than 1,000 acres (Callander, 1987:88).

What is more important for our purposes is that these estates contain some of the finest stately homes in the country, and these form some of its prime heritage attractions. From East to West, the country houses lie across the Border country, from the Earl of Wemyss and March's Gosford House in East Lothian, Lord Binning's Mellerstain, and Douglas-Home's The Hirsel in Berwickshire, the Duke of Roxburghe's Floors Castle near Kelso, Maxwell-Stuart's Traquair House in Peeblesshire, and above all, Buccleuch's two estates, Bowhill near Selkirk, and Drumlanrig Castle in Dumfriesshire. All are an integral part of the stately home business, and help to form one of the most lucrative tourist trails in the country. Their public access is, however, of recent provenance.

The oldest and most illustrious heritage creation belongs to Walter Scott's descendents at Abbotsford which was opened to the public only one year (1833) after its founder's death. It was not until 1956 that Traquair House was also opened by the radical and Jacobite Maxwell-Stuart who claimed it as the oldest continually inhabited house in Scotland. The bulk of these border stately homes welcomed fee-paying tourists in the 1970s. In 1975 while *Brideshead Revisited* was under production for television, Bowhill, the Borders home of the Buccleuchs, was opened to the public, followed in 1976 by Drumlanrig Castle in the western Borders. Floors Castle, the ancestral home of the Duke and Duchess of Roxburghe followed in 1978, having been opened only once a year previously for charity events. Other stately Border homes soon followed: Mellerstain, the home of Lord and Lady Binning, and Manderston, owned by Adrian Palmer, the descendent of the trader with Russia in hemp and herring in the 1860s. Manderston is especially interesting because it is a nice illustration of the process described by the historian Martin Wiener (1985) through which the bourgeoisie sought to become culturally assimilated into the gentry by the purchase of a landed estate.

By the late 1970s, at the point at which the heritage industry was created in its modern form, the Border landowners were in a prime position to exploit their heritage potential.

Why should this be? The assistant factor at Floors Castle pointed out that the 'high maintenance costs of the castle were a primary reason for opening Floors to the public in order that the revenue from the castle could help to defray these costs' (estimated at £100,000 a year). There is much in this, but we shall argue later in this chapter that there is a more fundamental socio-political reason for this investment.

The running of estates as businesses cannot be avoided in the 1990s. Analysis of the Buccleuch Estates, for example, which includes its stately homes projects as well as the management of land, indicates the scale of the enterprise. The 1990 company accounts lodged with the Registrar of Companies reveal a turnover of just under £5 million, 12 per cent of which is profit pre-tax (£605,000). The Estate has a staff of just under 300, and a wage bill of over £2.5 million per annum. The total assets less current liabilities of Buccleuch Estates stood at over £15 million. The Buccleuchs had been among the first to take advantage of new business practices, incorporating their company as Buccleuch Estates Limited in 1923 for these purposes:

> to purchase and acquire and take over from John Charles, Duke of Bucleuch and Queensberry KT certain estates in all counties of Edinburgh, Roxburgh, Selkirk and Dumfries . . . to carry on the business of managing and developing the said estates and other properties and assets . . . to carry on all or any of the trades and businesses of farmers, horse breeders and dealers, sylviculturists . . . raisers . . . forestry work . . . hotel keepers . . . livery stable keepers . . . dealers in objets d'arts and articles of virtue . . . to construct roads, railways, tramways, reservoirs, to build waterworks, harbours, gasworks . . . to open, develop, work quairies, mines, springs, natural deposits . . . sporting and fishing rights. (Register of Companies, SC 12615)

The development of the heritage potential of its houses fits into this portfolio, with both Bowhill and Drumlanrig open to the public, and Buccleuch's third 'home' at Dalkeith leased first to the computer company ICL, and since the mid-1980s to a consortium of the University of Wisconsin for use as a teaching establishment. (Dalkeith House had an early introduction to the heritage business, being the temporary home of George IV when he was persuaded to visit Scotland in 1822 by Walter Scott. See John Prebble's account, *The King's Jaunt,* 1988.)

We have less information from public sources about the Duke of Roxburghe's foray into heritage, although the Floors Stud Company was established in 1951. By the 1990s, Floors Castle was being offered as a site for corporate entertainment. The 10th Duke had inherited the title in 1974, and manages the 56,000-acre estate, along with its twenty-two bedroom hotel located near the castle gates. In 1988 and 1990 the castle had been the site for major promotions of Borders knitwear and textiles. The 1992 venture was geared to the corporate sector under the following rubric:

> With a roofscape studded with pepperpot domes and spires and an idyllic setting overlooking the River Tweed, one of the great salmon rivers of Scotland, it is hardly surprising that it inspired Sir Walter Scott to describe it as 'altogether a kingdom for Oberon and Titania'.

(The Walter Scott seal of approval, it seems, is a vital ingredient of stately homes heritage. The Earl of Strathmore has also invoked the novelist in his brochure on Glamis Castle in Angus, while the Buccleuchs have an in-built claim on Scott who saw in the Duke of his day his kinsman and 'clan chief'.)

Roxburghe's monetisation of heritage can be gauged from the charges and fees for the hire of Floors:

Location fees
Dining-room   from £500
All state rooms   from £750

Daytime rate
Morning coffee, buffet lunch,afternoon tea, castle guide-book & service charge   £44 (per person)

Evening rate
Four-course gala dinner castle guide-book & service charge   £44 (per person)

Fireworks
Dependent on requirements: e.g. five-minute finale with special effects & musical soundtrack   from £1850

Musical entertainment
Pipers   from £50
Highland dancers (minimum of 3),   from £75
(each)
Toastmasters   from £75
Pianists & Clarsach players   from £120
Classical trio/quartet   from £300
Regimental pipe band   from £600

Clay-pigeon shooting
(minimum of 15 participants)
Full day per head   £100

Private barbecues & picnics
Barbecues (minimum of eight people)   £22 (per
person)
Picnics (minimum of eight people)   £15 (per
person)

Off-road vehicles, fly-fishing, archery, hovercraft
driving, croquet etc. also available. (from *The
Scotsman*, 9 April 1992)

The commoditisation of Floors Castle was part of a broader
initiative undertaken by stately-home owners in the Borders in
conjunction with the local tourist board under the banner
'Scotland's Border Heritage' which brought together the owners of thirteen castles, historic houses and gardens with a
current turnover of £8 million per year. The heritage potential
of the venture was not lost on the director of the Scottish
Borders Tourist Board, who commented: 'In an area better
known for its inter-family feuding, it is nice to see the Scotts,
the Kerrs and the Homes co-operating for their own benefit'
(*The Scotsman*, 12 March 1992).

HERITAGE AND THE LANDED ELITE

The conventional way of explaining the capture of heritage
for commercial purposes by the owners of the stately-homes
industry is that this has become an economic necessity in a
modern world which is not of their financial and ideological
making. There is truth in this, but we will argue that there is
more to it than that. Let us begin with a more general account
of the changing fortunes of the aristocracy in Britain, and

FIGURE 12 The laird at home: Colonel William Gordon of Fyvie,
by Pomeo Batoni.

with the important work of David Cannadine *The Decline and
Fall of the British Aristocracy*, published in 1990.

Cannadine's thesis is straightforward, and reflected in the
title of his book. In the 1870s, he argues:

> These patricians were still the most wealthy, the most
> powerful and the most glamorous people in the country,

FIGURE 13 The laird at home: the 10th Duke of Roxburghe,
by Howard Morgan.

corporately – and understandibly – conscious of themselves as God's elect. But during the 100 years that
followed, their wealth withered, their power faded, their
glamour tarnished, and their collective sense of identity
and purpose gradually but inexorably weakened.
(1990:2)

He emphasises that his is a work of British rather than
simply English history, and he traces the interlocking élites of
Scotland, England, Ireland and Wales. Landowners were particularly dominant in late nineteenth-century Scotland and
Ireland, where 93 per cent and 78 per cent respectively of
land was held in estates of more than 1,000 acres, in contrast
to 56 per cent in England and 61 per cent in Wales. In 1880,
four of the top ten great British landowners were Scottish –
Buccleuch, Bute, Sutherland and Hamilton – and nine of the
top twenty-nine had Scottish estates. Land agitation against
the landed classes was a feature of the late nineteenth-century
Celtic countries, whereas 'the social fabric of rural England
was never subjected to the same degree of stress' (ibid.:60).

In Ireland and Wales as a result of religious and political
agitation, the landowners virtually disappeared, whereas in

Scotland and England they did not. The implication of this, of course, is that the landowners had a particular grip on Scotland, given that they started out from a much higher ownership base even than in England. This economic domination was reflected in political control at the local level. Whereas in 1892 two-thirds of conveners of Scottish county councils were local landowners, seven were peers and five were also lord-lieutenants. As late as 1940, a half of conveners were local landowners, seven were peers and ten were also lord-lieutenants (ibid.:161).

Historians seem well agreed that landowners have been unusually powerful in Scotland. In Timperley's words: 'Power and landownership have been synonymous in Scotland from time immemorial' (1980:137). Loretta Timperley's own pioneering work on landownership patterns in 1771 shows that 'the overall control of Scotland's land by the great landlords was most complete in the Borders at around 65 per cent, and up the east coast, at between 40 per cent and 50 per cent (Callander, 1987:48). (She defines 'great landlords' as owning more than £2000 Scots.) The exceptions, she argues, were in the west and central regions where the great landlords never owned more than 35 per cent of land. Most of the wealthiest estates were owned by titled families, eighty-one out of the 123 wealthiest estates.

The 1871 official enquiry into landownership in Britain was designed to show that land was far more equitably distributed than radical critics made out (Cannadine, 1990). What it actually revealed was a pattern of landownership in Britain and Ireland more concentrated and monopolistic than in almost any other European country (Cannadine, 1990:55). In Scotland, as Callander points out: 'The 1,500 largest landowners . . . had held over 90 per cent of the country in 1872, and this had only dropped a percentage point or two thirty years later' (1987:78-9). The twentieth century saw some reduction in the area held by larger estates, an increase in the number of small owners, and the expansion of land owned by the state and public agencies like the Forestry Commission.

Scotland is fortunate in that several individuals notably Roger Millman (1970), John McEwen (1977), Loretta Timperley (1980) and Robin Callander (1987) have regarded the 'land question' as an important public issue, as well as one worthy of academic attention. Despite some reduction in the

number of very large estates over 20,000 acres, 'the traditional estate survived with a fair degree of constancy during the
period 1872 to 1970' (Callander, 1987:81), even although
there was a turnover in ownership. The average proportion of
Scotland's counties taking the form of estates of more than
1,000 acres fell from 93 per cent in 1872 to 63 per cent in
1970. Inevitably, some erosion of concentration occured too
at the local level. Lord Lauderdale's holdings in Berwickshire
in 1872 had totalled some 24,700 acres, and a century later
stood at just over 8000 acres. Similarly, the Earl of
Haddington's landholding had dwindled from 14,300 acres to
9,200 acres over the same period. Nevertheless, as Callander
comments, it is the stability rather than change in landownership which is striking: 'In 1970 three-quarters of all privately
owned land in Scotland was still held in estates of 1,000 acres
or more, half in estates of 5000 acres or more, and one-third
in estates of 20,000 or more' (1987:92).

Callander's view is that the apparently higher rate of estate
turnover in recent decades is simply the result of a small number, mostly owned by absentee landowners, changing hands
more frequently, and he concludes that 'the present pattern of
landownership in Scotland still matches closely the earlier
pattern stretching back through the last nine centuries'
(ibid.:131). He quotes the comment made by Sir John Sinclair
that 'in no country in Europe are the rights of proprietors so
well defined and so carefully protected' (ibid.:136).

By and large historians have viewed Scottish landowners as
'in an even more powerful position than those in England'
(Checkland, 1984:56). The mighty magnates like Buccleuch,
Argyll, Bute, Atholl, Sutherland and Roxburghe who owned
vast tracts of the Scottish countryside as well as some urban
land belonged to a rentier class which made its money from
its substantial stakes in land, and was then able to translate
its economic power into social domination. By the late nineteenth century, social welfare administration remained in
their hands:

> The administration of nineteenth century welfare in
> Scotland was domianted not by new forces, the new
> wealth, the industrial capitalist that ruthlessly exploited
> the natural and labour resources around them, but by an
> older set, one that looked to an earlier, seemingly golden

period. Scottish government meant the laird, who as was said by Skelton, sought the quietness of the country life but instead 'lamented the encroachment of Morningside suburbia'. (*Scots Pictorial*, 1897:434, quoted by Ian Levitt, 1989)

The gentry were also marked off from the bourgeoisie by their commitment to the country rather than the town, and in cultural terms they diluted their Scottishness by sending their sons to English or English-style 'public schools'. The historian Roy Campbell has pointed out the propensity of large proprietors to educate their sons in this way based on

> the belief that intellectually and culturally Scotland could not offer the wider horizon for the life of an educated and cultured gentleman. It led as a direct consequence to the need to speak and write in a langauge most easily understood by cultured society, and that was not to be found in Scotland for many. (Campbell, 1985:103).

In religious terms too, the landed élite were marked off from the population at large. While some like the Argyll family played a key role in Scottish Presbyterianism, others like Strathmore retained a commitment to Episcopalian protestantism, while others like the Lothians remained recusant Catholics. Whereas in England the established Church played a key role in defining the status of 'the gentleman' and in legitimating their social and cultural ascendancy (Scott, 1991), in Scotland the lairds could not count on the unequivocal support of the Kirk.

In political terms too the lairds were marked out as different. They had provided the leadership of the Conservative Party and had contributed to its somewhat reactionary image right down until the 1890s (Fry, 1987). Even after the issue of Irish Home Rule had split the Liberals, there were important social differences between the Conservatives and the new dissident Liberal Unionists. In the 1895 intake of Scottish MPs, for example, nine of those calling themselves Conservatives were landowners, seven were businessmen, and one came from the professions. In contrast, nine Liberal Unionists were businessmen, two were professionals, and only three described themselves as landowners. In contrast to the aggressive market orientation of Liberal-Unionism, Toryism was, in

Ian Hutchison's words, the creed of 'lairds and law agents' (1986:200).

Scottish and English landed families were also united by complex marriage patterns as even a cursory glance at Debrett's Peerage or Burke's Peerage will reveal. Landed estates were inherited or purchased on both sides of the border. The Duke of Buccleuch, for example, also holds the title of the Earl of Doncaster and Baron Tynedale, a seventeenth-century English title. The Duke of Sutherland is also the Marquis of Stafford, Viscount Brackley and Earl of Ellesmere. One particularly famous but short-lived union was the marriage between the 5th Duke of Westminster's daughter and the 10th Duke of Roxburghe in 1974, which 'inextricably welded two of the greatest bank balances in the world' (Winchester, 1982:99). The marriage of the Duke of Westminster's 'most beautiful daughter Jane to one of the most eligible young men in Britain' was 'almost too good to be fair' (ibid.:99). At the time of his marriage, Guy Roxburghe was 'a slim soldier with the Blues and Royals'. His seat was 'the enchanting Floors Castle set in an island of 80,000 acres in the Borders', and he had been left more than £2,000,000 by his father. Winchester's comment about the match being too good to be fair had a prophetic ring to it, and the marriage was dissolved in 1990.

Another area of common ground is that, while no longer forming the wealth élite *tout court*, Scottish lairds and English lords are still well represented among the wealthy. In 1988, for example, 20 per cent of the richest hundred individuals in Britain were members of the nobility (*The Money Magazine*, 1988:20). Of these, eight had Scottish titles: in descending order of wealth, Buccleuch (£309m), Atholl (£143m), Seafield (£120m), Argyll (£87m), Sutherland (£83m), Roxburghe (£72m), Cawdor (£57m), and Stair (£54m).

THE DECLINE OF THE LANDED ELITE?

What has brought about the relative decline in the power of the landed élite, and what is the significance, if any, of their foray into the heritage business? Cannadine's account is fairly straightforward. The loss of material and economic power, most notably through the long fall in land prices since the 1880s, meant that at the local level the prestige and status of the landed élite deteriorated, while at the national level its political power both in the House of Lords as well as the Commons suffered. Between 1912 and 1920 the land agents Knight, Frank and Rutley alone reckoned to have sold 1.6m Scottish acres, one-twelfth of the land area of the whole country (Cannadine, 1990: 109). More generally, in the period pre- and post-First World War, one-quarter of the land of England was sold, as well as one-third of Wales and of Scotland. This was also the period in which the landed estates sold off many art treasures which they had acquired from relatively impoverished continental aristocrats. Their wealth and their power now passed in turn to a new class of rich plutocrats (Cannadine, ibid.:112).

By the 1980s, comments Cannadine, 'the old landed order had effectively ceased to be an economically definable class at all' (ibid.:638). Just as the old aristocracy ceased to dominate the land as this new plutocracy translated their new wealth into old forms of prestige, so the landed classes took up new forms of money-making. The Buccleuchs, the largest landowners in Scotland, were no exception:

> Even a ducal family as broad-acred and illustrious as the Buccleuchs had become unprecedently involved in the City and big business by the inter-war years. In a family as rich as the Buccleuchs, it was the younger sons who took to business: the Duke himself and the heir to the title [the Earl of Dalkeith] remained essentially full-time landowners. (ibid.:417)

In Cannadine's view, the last 100 years saw the decline of the landed aristocracy as a social class: 'The fact remains that the traditional landed class has ceased to exist as the unchallenged and supreme elite in which wealth, status and power are highly correlated, and are underpinned by territorial pre-eminence' (ibid.:693). It is important to underline the concepts Cannadine uses to account for the decline of the aristocracy. His first task is to consider their financial resources; secondly, how that wealth was translated into social prestige and status; and finally, how powerful this class was and is as a ruling or governing elite. To summarise his position, he sees their economic base as a class challenged in such a way that they were progressively unable to translate wealth into social prestige and political power. And almost automatically their social position declined.

How does heritage figure in this account? At the height of their power, the landed grandees dominated the construction and preservation of 'national culture'. They became the cultural trustees of the nation, serving on the boards of museums, galleries, the National Trust, the Fine Arts Commission, and so on. We have noted in the previous chapter, for example, the extent of patrician domination of the National Trust for Scotland. They have also occupied positions of social prestige in academe, serving as chancellors of the older universities. As their power declined, so did their occupancy of these élite positions, observes Cannadine. Their increasing marginality confined them to the cultural fringes, notably as custodians of heritage, where they operated 'as the self-styled and self-promoting guardians of what they like to call the national heritage' (ibid.:639). Estates were sold (Sutherland's shrank from 1.3m acres in 1880 to a mere 138,000 in 1976). New taxes stretched them. Even the establishing of a National Heritage Memorial Fund in 1980 was, comments Cannadine, a sign of weakness insofar as it recognised country houses as relics rather than assets. The fund and its agents, notably the National Trust, were 'undertakers, embalming these once great power houses for posterity' (ibid.:655). Even the great families like the Buccleuchs and the Roxburghes had by the 1970s 'capitulated' (sic) to the stately homes business. This new role invented for themselves as the self-appointed guardians of 'national heritage' becomes little more than a sleight of hand to retain a semblance of public acceptability, according to Cannadine. In his words, 'The lions of yesteryear have become the unicorns of today' (ibid.:708).

POWER TRANSFORMED, NOT ENDED

It would be perverse to dispute the broad sweep of Cannadine's argument that the aristocracy in particular and the landed élite in general have lost power. It might seem, however, that his way of understanding power predisposes him to expect their demise, to predict in other words the end rather than the transformation of their power. Much of this depends on how we define the aristocracy in theoretical terms. We think that there is much mileage in seeing them as a status group rather than a social class as such. It is interesting, though slightly misleading, to note that Cannadine employs Max Weber's analytical model to explain their changing fortunes. If we use Weber's concept of status group rather than class, we are able to explain how the landed élite tried to define and control the boundaries of the group, to allow entry to those with new sources of power, and to exclude others. Above all, such a perspective allows us to focus on aspects of lifestyle, on the social rather than on the economic means of control and boundary maintenance. In this way we can see aspects of social consumption, beliefs and lifestyle not as the inevitable outcomes of economic processes, but as relatively autonomous from class position. If we approach the landed élite from this viewpoint, we are better able, for example, to explain why 'aristocratic values' survive. To do this we must set out more clearly what we mean by 'status'.

In strictly ideal-typical terms, status groups for Weber were distinct from social classes:

> In contrast to the purely economically determined 'class situation', we wish to designate as 'status situation' every typical component of the life of men that is determined by a specific, positive or negative, social estimation of honour. This honour may be connected with any quality shared by a plurality, and of course it can be knit to a class situation: class distinctions are linked in the most varied ways with status distinctions. Property as such is not always recognised as a status qualification, but in the long run it is, and with extraordinary regularity. (Weber, 1978:932)

Weber is making the point here that 'property' in its economic sense – its capacity to generate income – also has status overtones. In our kind of society, we frequently confuse economic class and social status although they are analytically distinct. In fact, said Weber, there are three potential dimensions of power to be considered, economic, social and political, and these in turn are expressed as social types – classes, status groups and political parties or organisations. Weber was showing that societies could theoretically be stratified in different and quite complex ways. Hence, depending on which dimension(s) was dominant and how it related to the others, we would not expect societies to be identical in their power structures. While, for example, the economic dimension of power will predominate in capitalist societies, how it is mixed with other dimensions will reflect in large part the historical legacy. Power structures will be differently configured in Britain and the USA despite both being 'capitalist' societies.

To return to our analysis of lairds, the point is that while status groups frequently have economic dimensions, it is possible for the propertied and the propertyless to belong to the same status group. The 'clan' would be an obvious instance of such a group. However, the disparity of wealth in the long run tends to make this status group quite unstable, as its members may have materially little in common. A specific lifestyle is normally expected from members of a status group, and because members are peculiarly dependent on social acceptance by other members, it is thus that social order is maintained. What often appear to be the trivia of social life – matters of dress, decorum, diet and ritual – are central to it because these become the means of social control. In Barnes' words:

> A distinct style of life is not an accidental consequence of how members are able to live, given their position in a hierarchy of consumption privileges. It is nearer the mark to think of the need for exclusivity and distinctiveness having to be met through consumption. (1992:11)

In this way, matters of economic activity are derived from social interaction through the group, and not vice versa. The emphasis placed upon defining social intercourse by means of inter-marriage, shared leisure pursuits and educational experiences have to be understood in this context. That is why Weber was interested in Indian castes as powerful/powerless status groups from which economic opportunities followed. Similarly, Weber pointed to the landed aristocrats, the Junkers of late nineteenth- and early twentieth-century Prussia as an example of a status group who were unable to control social and economic access to power.

In strictly theoretical terms, then, classes and status groups are not the same thing. In Weber's words:

> We have seen . . . that the market and its processes knows no personal distinctions: 'functional' interests dominate it. It knows nothing of honour. The status order means precisely the reverse: stratification in terms of honour and styles of life peculiar to status groups as such. (1978:936)

This excursus into the realms of Weberian sociology provides a valuable antidote to a sort of crude class theory in which economic interests preordain social and political privileges. The point to be made here is that status groups, and the social honour which derives from them as a means of social control, have the theoretical capacity to be independent of class interests. To reinforce this important point, consider this comment by the Weberian scholar, Randall Collins:

> Weber tends to speak of classes and status groups as antithetical phenomena. For example, he speaks of status group-based monopolies as characteristic of traditional societies, where they act as irrational constraints on the market. Thus in many feudal and patrimonial societies, the hereditary appropriation or exclusion of groups from military, landowning, mercantile or other occupations is a phenomenon antithetical to rationalised capitalism. (1986:128)

The point being made here is not that status groups do not care about money. Far from it. They seek to control access to money-making very precisely, but not in ways which are determined by the 'market'. How successful they are in doing this will determine whether or not they succeed as a status group. The problem in market or capitalist societies is that such principles and procedures do not sit at all well with the new economic order. As Frank Parkin has pointed out: 'The political driving force of individualist doctrines arose in part from the opposition of the emergent middle classes to aristocratic pretensions and exclusiveness centred around the notion of descent' (1979:64).

Parkin distills from Weber's writings the concept of 'social closure', a process whereby social collectivities seek to maximise their rewards by restricting access to resources and opportunities to a narrow circle of eligible people. Hence, ruling groups succeed where they gain monopolistic control over valued resources such as land, esoteric knowledge, or arms. In the case of aristocratic domination and reproduction, this is most obviously done via the lineage system. The capacity to capture for one's peers and descendents exclusive social privilege marks out the essence of status group domination. Where status groups cannot maintain such dominance or else make adjustments to share power with new competitors, they go to the wall, as in the case of the Prussian Junkers.

In other situations closer to home such as the landed élites of Britain, there was a more or less successful adjustment to the new order, although there was nonetheless a gradual loss of distinctiveness and privilege. It is this process of adjustment between aristocracy and bourgeoisie which Marx referred to as the 'antiquated compromise' between the old and new social orders. In more recent years, this 'compromise' has generated a considerable debate about the surviving 'cultural' power of the aristocracy vis à vis capitalism more generally. Its best-known proponent, the historian Martin Wiener, has argued that Britain never became a thoroughly capitalist society in terms of its dominant values at all, and that the new class simply accommodated to the values and life style of the old. This thesis has generated its own debate among historians about the relationship between material and cultural forms of power in nineteenth-century Britain (see, for example, Collins and Robbins, 1990).

UNDERSTANDING SCOTTISH LAIRDS

If we consider landowners in general as a status group rather than as a class *per se*, then we can begin to chart their continuous struggle to hold the line of social privilege. Without denying that they have used their property assets as productive resources, it seems that their social behaviour can be better understood within the framework we have outlined. For example, concern with the lifestyle of the 'gentleman', with the proper ways of behaving, with 'noblesse oblige', and correctness of rituals and beliefs does reveal the principles of status honour rather than class advantage.

None of this is to deny that landowners have been and are concerned with money making. Cannadine's study shows just how successful the landed élite has been in retaining economic privilege. While it is true that the old patrician class no longer forms the wealthy élite, the landed élite are still well represented among the wealthy. The standard practice in the modern period has been for new money and old wealth to conjoin. The pattern of astute inter-marriage has been a well remarked feature of the last couple of centuries (Scott and Hughes, 1980:218–21).

The Buccleuchs are unsual insofar as they belong to the top stratum of aristocratic grandees rather than run of the mill lairds. They do indicate, however, the way the wind is blowing. As we have seen they were among the first to embark on the stately homes business in the 1970s, and all three 'homes' are part of their heritage portfolio. At the level of small-scale heritage, the Buccleuchs have been active in local and national politics. The activity and involvement of Border lairds in local and parliamentary affairs is a tradition which goes back to the thirteenth century. After the Second World War, this tradition began to die. In the General Election of 1950, Lord William Scott of Buccleuch lost his seat in Roxburgh and Selkirk to the Liberal candidate. The present Duke was a Conservative MP for an urban Edinburgh seat in the 1970s, while his son, the Earl of Dalkeith, has twice failed in the 1980s to win that party's nomination for a Borders seat in the new-model Thatcherite Tory party.

However, at the local level, landed hegemony lasted much longer. Between the years 1900 and 1975 when local government was reformed, the Dukes of Buccleuch and of Roxburghe between them held the convenership of Roxburgh County Council for forty-three years. The Border landowners could also exercise their influence indirectly through the offices of Sheriff Depute (held once by Walter Scott), Commissioners of Supply, Lords Lieutenancies, and as Justices in the Commission of the Peace. By 1975, the year that Roxburgh County Council was abolished, the Duke of Buccleuch opened Bowhill to the public.

The stately-home heritage industry, at least in the context of the Scottish Borders, is not simply an economic device to make great houses pay their way. Likewise, the move into heritage by the likes of Buccleuch and Roxburghe is not just an attempt to fill up their time following the end of Empire. One key to understanding why they became eminent Scottish heritage entrepreneurs lies in their exit from local politics in 1975. Stripped of their political function, the stately-home industry represented a way of securing their economic future as well as a means of legitimising their privileged position.

THE POWER OF THE LAIRD

The term 'laird' in Scotland is suitably ambiguous. Deriving from the old Scots word 'laverd' – a lord – it refers, according to the Scots Dictionary, to: (a) a prince or chief; (b) the landlord of a landed property or an estate; (c) the chief of a Highland clan; (d) 'chiefly of lesser landowners, a landowner holding directly to the Crown, and so entitled to come to parliament (till the eighteenth century), but not a lord of parliament'; (e) an owner of property in general, including a house owner. This ambiguity conveys an important ideological resource for landowners in a society which frequently has been very hostile to them. While the ambiguity presents us with analytical problems, it does operate at the ideological level as a device in the legitimation of power. In similar vein, at a British level the term 'aristocracy' emerged from the early nineteenth century as a status description glossing over the legal distinctions between the peerage and the wider class of landowners. As John Scott has pointed out: 'The language of class came to use "aristocracy" to describe the social category rooted in power in the power bloc of the old society. The word "gentleman" remained in use to describe its individual members' (1991:59).

This is not to imply that lairds and aristocrats are the same social category, or that 'laird' implies an undifferentiated mass of landowners. It is something of an umbrella term which binds the small landowner to the mighty lord for ideological purposes. In his apologia for the 'lowland laird', for example, James Fergusson, writing in 1949, commented:

> They should be remembered not as picturesque antiquities, but for what they did. They cared for the land and their dependents with as much thought as does the modern state and often with more discrimination. To them too, Scotland owes all its finest woodlands, a quantity of noble architecture, and collections great and small, of pictures, books and furniture which have made the Scottish country house a living and harmonious example of our culture at its best. (1949:23)

These are interesting grounds on which to pitch a defence, because they convey the very modern sense of legitimacy – that the lairds are the keepers of Scotland's heritage – which is the central part of our argument. As such, the lairds have been able to diffuse much of the hostility towards them in the last quarter of the twentieth century. Fergusson's account was written in the context of the social change ushered in by the post-war welfare state, and under the continuing shadow of the powerful attack by Tom Johnston, *Our Scots Noble Families*, published in 1911. This book caught the tide of hostility towards the landed élite in Scotland which had been

such a central feature of both Liberal politics of the nineteenth century and Labour's politics in the early twentieth.
Fergusson's adoption of the term 'laird' allowed him to present landowners in a much more attractive, and above all
Scottish, light. He could elide the social divisions between the
great landlords and the 'bonnet lairds' by implying a high
degree of homogamy:

> Class distinctions were never strong in Scotland. Earls'
> families intermarried with knights', the small laird wed-
> ded the daughter of the great, and the great laird might
> choose his bride from the daughter of the prosperous
> burgess – while that burgess himself might be the son or
> grandson of some cadet of a noble house. (1949:14)

Of course, this claim is not easily validated, but that is not
its purpose. It is to ground the laird firmly in the Scottish
tradition, not as some alien, anglicised imposition (post the
Unions of Scotland and England, crowns and parliaments, in
1603 and 1707), but as part of the fabric of Scotland's social
structure. Three factors made for a 'kinship' of feeling which
in 1949 at any rate Fergusson judged to be far from dead.
This kinship arose 'partly from the feudal relationship which
bound the laird's Jock to the laird as it bound Harden to
Buccleuch, and Buccleuch to the king.' Secondly, it also
derived in Fergusson's view 'partly from a common simplicity
of life and manners'; and thirdly, 'perhaps partly from a community of race, since the Norman strain was assimilated in the
Scottish nobility instead of overlaying society with an alien
aristocracy, as happened in England' (ibid.:24).

We do not need to concern ourselves here with the accu-
racy of this statement, we need merely observe that Fergusson
was alluding to older controversies on either side of the
Border: in England to the myth of the indigenous Saxon
oppressed by the Norman yoke (MacDougall, 1982), and
North of the Border to the Bruce–Wallace controversy. The
preference for the 'proletarian' Wallace over the 'aristocratic'
Bruce had long figured in arguments about the 'true Scotland'
(Ash, 1990). Tom Johnston, for example, had denounced the
Scottish aristocracy on the grounds, more polemical than
analytical, that three-quarters of them were 'descendents of
foreign freebooters who forcibly took possession of our land
after the Norman Conquest of 1066' (1911:ix). Again, 'Bruce,

a Norman, convinced our forefathers that his fight against the English was for Scottish freedom, and lo, when the invading hosts were driven back, the Bruce handed our common fields to his fellow Normans' (ibid.: viii).

The ideological purposes of the claim is clear, namely, to discredit the 'Scottishness' of the landed élite. Both Johnston in 1911 and then Fergusson nearly forty years later were engaged in a war of legitimacy for and against the lairds. Johnston sought to portray them as a cynical bunch of foreign freebooters, while Fergusson claimed them as the indigenous creators of modern Scotland. He describes how the Lowland lairds were important in setting up the Kirk, in transforming agriculture as Improvers of the land, in encouraging learning and developing politics at both the local and national levels. Fergusson's aim in writing the 1949 book was not simply to give them a further stay of execution in a post-war world, but to prolong their active life. He argued that:

> the spirit that once vitalised that responsibility must not perish; it must be directed into other channels, into con- scientious service of the land itself, and into the innu- merable committees, from those of a county council downwards, through which local government is carried on. It is in this sphere that the traditions of the old lairds must be kept alive and renewed. (1949:26–7)

Fergusson's predictions were largely fulfilled. From this period until the reorganisation of local government in 1975, the energies of the lairds were funnelled into county councils and committees. As we have indicated, nowhere was this more the case than in the Borders where the Dukes of Buccleuch and Roxburghe dominated the convenerships of the council of Roxburgh. The reorganisation of local govern- ment in the 1970s and the consequent removal of Border lairds from positions of direct political power meant that new channels of influence had to be found. The 'spirit' of the lairds which Fergusson had extolled in the threatening days of the late 1940s found new avenues for wealth creation and cultural legitimacy. With considerable irony this involved converting the history with which Tom Johnston had tried to convict them into a commodity whereby they could save themselves. It was, in short, the capture of heritage.

The conventional wisdom about the stately-home industry

is that it is largely a financial device to maintain the great houses by state and voluntary means. There is clearly truth in this, but not the whole of it. The inclusion of the word 'home' helps to evoke the private as well as the public domains, just as 'house' describes the family and its name as well as its relationship to its property – titles, residences, heirlooms and land. The word 'seat', for example, clearly implies residence. But many lairds have their homes elsewhere, often in London. Nevertheless, as Wright points out, the symbolism of 'home' has been used to romanticise the patriarchal family, to idolise domestic drudgery, and to vaunt a national heritage of 'stately homes' (1985:11).

This fusion of public and private is nicely captured in the following comment about Floors Castle, the seat of the Duke of Roxburghe: 'First and foremost, Floors Castle is a private family home', declared the duke as he entertained a group of writers in his state room to explain his plans to open up the castle to a much wider audience' (*The Scotsman*, 9 April 1992). The point here is not that there is a contradiction in trying to combine the private and the public domains, but that it is precisely their fusion which has to be achieved to make a 'successful' stately home. That is why careful attention is paid to personalising the heritage, leaving family pictures and bric-a-brac in strategic places to convey to the visitor a sense of intimacy and awe, that it is a privilege to see inside the home. This inner sanctum is largely what visitors pay to see, something which museums do not convey. It is also the case that rarely are the private apartments on show, or that the family lives there for much of the time. The Historic Houses Association, formed in 1973 by the owners of historic houses, points out that visitors to properties enjoy looking at photographs of the family as much as they enjoy the art treasures. Similarly, the iconography of being ushered into a cavernous 'sitting room' equipped with a single-bar electric fire of dubious vintage carries the dual meaning of intimacy as well as a suitable degree of penury which is, of course, put a little to rights by the modest entrance fee for the privilege of access.

The stately-home heritage industry allows the lairds to insinuate their own history into that of the Scottish and British nations. While having distinct identities as Scottish lairds – 'authenticated' by family names, crests, mottos, tartans and clans – they have much in common with great landowners

South of the Border. It is not uncommon to find a Scottish
laird owning land in England, and vice-versa. The Duke of
Buccleuch has a considerable estate at Boughton in Northamp-
tonshire; the Earl of Rosebery, he of Mentmore fame, holds
lands in Scotland as well as England. Baron Mowbray owns
two estates in northern England, plus a 'sizeable chunk' of
shooting and fishing country near Forfar (Winchester,
1982:191). The Duke of Westminster in addition to owning
much of central London has holdings in Durham, Shropshire,
Cheshire, Lincolnshire, Norfolk, Merioneth, Surrey, West-
moreland, as well as Sutherland and Wester Ross.

Stately-home guidebooks provide the ideal format for this
interweaving, with their manicured family trees, tracing family antecedents back in genealogical time to the great figures
of Scottish and English history. If the nation's history can be
told through the medium of the family biography, then one
cannot be destroyed without the other. The family and the
country become united. Hence, heritage techniques allowing
the retelling of myth, like the myth which justifies the massive
landholdings of the Buccleuchs. Scott of 'Buck-Cleugh' saving
King Kenneth of Scotland from the fury of a wounded stag or
buck would seem a more romantic justification than a purely
etymological one describing a local geological feature (a
cleugh is a ravine or gorge in Scots), and somewhat more
noble than a more likely account which credits the lands as
reward for military services in the Netherlands under the
Prince of Orange in 1606 (Debrett's Peerage and Baronetage,
1990:174).

In this official account, the public and private histories are
elided. The Duke of Buccleuch 'owns' the land around Ettrick
Forest because they were bestowed upon his ancestors in
return for services to Robert the Bruce [Scottish credentials]
in the fourteenth century. At the same time, the Duke is, in
the words of the Buccleuch guidebook, only 'a life trustee
dedicated to the constant improvement of a vital asset to the
benefit of everyone concerned, as well as further generations
of his own family, on whom the responsibility for future
progress rests'. The guidebook, then, is not simply a guide to
the layout of the family property, but a chronological narrative
of how the dynasty came to occupy the positions it holds. It
continues:

Once the links in the chain of continuity are broken, through the irreversible process of the break-up of estates, the merits of multiple land-use are lost forever. The advantage of continuity spanning many generations apply just as much to the families of those who occupy let farms and estate employees. On Buccleuch estates some family partnerships between landlord and tenant go back possibly as far as the 12th century. (n.d.:23)

Thus, the ideology of land and landownership is intricately connected and interwoven with a theory of history in a vernacular and informal sense, and with a theory of everyday life. The Buccleuchs are able to exploit the ambiguity of the term 'nation'. While their works of art are part of the British 'national' heritage, their connections with Bruce and with Douglas (the family name associated with Drumlanrig in the western borders) make their Scottish credentials abundantly clear. The Buccleuchs and their fellow landed proprietors see themselves as champions of 'history' rather than as captains of a heritage industry. In this regard, Sir Walter Scott played a crucial role not simply in 'heritagising' Scotland, but in weaving into the 'story' of Scotland the Buccleuchs whom he vested with the (inauthentic) honour of being his own 'clan chief'. Whereas those who had access to the trappings of a Highland culture could play the clan chief, Scott was investing his own lowland namesake with the title too. To do so may have made poor history, but good politics, as we can see from this comment from the Duchess of Erroll, writing as Hereditary Lord High Constable of Scotland in 1968:

In too many countries the great historic families are separated from thre mass of people, but in Scotland we have been fortunate in that the pride of Name has never depended on wealth and rank, and in that the clan tradition has always prevented class barriers from arising to divide our proud nation . . . We are all one family of Scots, the branches of that family being the clans and Names, and the Chief of Chiefs our Queen. (Bain, 1968:7)

CONCLUSION

Heritage is a word which, by its own self-definition, cannot be defined. It is also something that is, in this definition, always in danger of being lost or under threat. The Historic Houses

Association declared their aim as follows: 'to safeguard and secure private heritage for the benefit of future generations and the nation'. To this day the Association maintains that families are always the best people to care for an historic property because it is more natural to do so if your ancestors and their spirits have lived and died there. In the words of the first, and financially most successful, chairman of English Heritage, 'we belong to our possessions rather than our possessions belonging to us. To us, they are not our wealth, but heirlooms, over which we have a sacred trust' (Cannadine, 1990:694). Says Cannadine:

> The moral is clear. If the guardians of the national heritage behave thus responsibly and altruistically, the government in turn has a duty to ensure that these great houses and collections should remain intact, and that their owners should be allowed to continue the residential and custodial role which fulfils their own most deeply felt desires, and realises their forebears' most ardent and altrusitic ambitions. (ibid.:694)

In a country where the lairds and the land question have a salience in politics of some significance, and in the context of Scotland's place in the British state being questioned as never before, Scotland's lairds appear to have succeeded in converting their own and the nation's history into commodities whereby they can save themselves.

Chapter 6

Consuming Heritage

In the last quarter of the twentieth century there has been a revolution in leisure. Men and women now have more leisure time than at any point in history. The average British male in full-time employment has on average nearly forty-six hours of free time each week, fourteen hours more than a woman (1992–3 data). Put differently, men have more than ten hours free time per weekend day, and five hours in every normal weekday. Women have eight hours and three hours respectively because they spend more time looking after children, cleaning, cooking and shopping. This increase in leisure time has taken place largely in the last thirty years. Between 1961 and 1988, the normal basic weekly hours worked by full-time manual employees fell from nearly forty-three hours per week to just under thirty-nine hours (*Social Trends*, 20, 1990).

The increase in leisure time is reflected in changing patterns of consumption. Leisure services accounted for 7.5 per cent of average household expenditure, and spending on leisure goods about 5 per cent in 1988–9 (*Cultural Trends in Scotland*, 1992, PSI). Taking holidays into account, the average household spent nearly 17 per cent of its weekly budget on leisure items in 1992. It is spending on average over £11 per week on holidays, an increase in real terms of nearly half since 1986. About a quarter of adults took two or more holidays in 1992, more than three times the proportion twenty-five years previous (*Social Trends*, 24, 1994).

What are the implications of increased leisure for the consumption of heritage? More people visit historic buildings, sites or towns as part of their social and cultural activities than go to the cinema (*Social Trends*, 20, 1990). The 1980s also saw an exponential growth in the consumption of state-funded heritage. The total UK attendance at national museums rose by 25 per cent, from 22.6 million in 1982 to 28.2 million a decade later. The numbers attending the Scottish national museums showed an even steeper increase of over 50 per cent between 1982 and 1992. A succession of surveys has indicated the demand for heritage in its different forms. The 1988/9 General Household Survey reported that 28 million people in the UK had visited a 'built heritage' site during the 1988/9 period, 10 million had gone to a castle or ancient monument, 9 million to a stately home, and 9 million to a cathedral or church, spending a total of £143 million in the process. Nor is this simply a native activity. Foreign visitors, especially from North America, cite 'visiting heritage sites' as by far the most important feature of their visit to the UK (*Cultural Trends*, 15, 1992), with the largest proportion – 37 per cent – highlighting visits to heritage sites, followed by 30 per cent visiting heritage exhibits such as museums. Consuming the performing arts comes a poor third at 19 per cent. In similar vein, overseas visitors account for a substantial proportion of all visitors to historic buildings. Thirty five per cent of all visitors to UK heritage sites comes from overseas, and this figure rises to 46 per cent in Scotland, compared with only 25 per cent in Wales. Heritage in Scotland is a major dollar (and yen) earner.

Visits to sites run by Historic Buildings and Monuments in Scotland rose rapidly during the 1980s, with an overall increase of 32 per cent in the number of visitors between 1984/5 and 1989/90. However, the annual growth rate in 1989/90 which had been 11 per cent, stood at 7 per cent the following year, and had fallen back in 1991/2 by 8 per cent. This general trend seems to have been common to the UK as a whole. The 1993 editor of *Cultural Trends* commented: 'looking back with hindsight from the vantage point of the beginning of the new century, it might well be observed that the middle years of the 1990s marked the end of a period of virtually unbroken growth in government funding of the arts' (1993:39).

The amount of public investment in heritage has grown significantly as a result of increased demand. Whereas in 1985/6, £103 million was spent by the state on museums and galleries, by 1993/4 it had risen to £213 million, doubling in only seven years and an increase in real terms of 150 per cent (*Cultural Trends*, 19, 1993). In Scotland, central government expenditure on the arts and cultural industries rose in real terms from £39.8 million in 1985/6 to £46.2 million in 1989/90. Local government expenditure on libraries, museums and galleries represented £15 per head of the population, some £77 million (1.6 per cent of all services provided by local authorities in Scotland). The budget for the National Museums of Scotland rose in real terms by 250 per cent between 1986/7 and 1992/3; for the National Galleries of Scotland by 200 per cent in the same period, while the Scottish Museums Council received a 120 per cent increase in its budget. In total, central government spending on heritage doubled in real terms, from £8.28 million in 1986/7, to £25.5 million in 1992/3 (*Cultural Trends in Scotland*, 1992). By 1991/2, central government grant in aid per visitor stood at £11.60 in Scotland, £2 more than in the rest of the UK.

In terms of consumption, heritage is proportionately more important North of the Border than in the UK generally. Edinburgh Castle attracts around 1 million visitors a year which places it in third place in the UK behind the Tower of London, and St Paul's Cathedral. The annual visitors survey which is carried out for the Scottish Tourist Board since 1982 records 'visitor attractions' which are defined as:

> a permanently established excursion destination, a primary purpose of which is to allow public access for entertainment, interest or education, rather than being principally a retail outlet or a venue for sporting, theatrical or film performances. It must be open to the public for published periods each year, and should be capable of attracting tourists or day visitors as well as local residents. (Association of Scottish Visitor Attractions, 1992:1)

The number of visits to heritage attractions in Scotland is over six times the size of the population. These totalled 31.5 million in 1992, in a country of only 5 million people, albeit this figure includes visitors from the rest of the UK and from overseas. Despite the fact that there had been a decrease of 14 per cent in the number of visits since 1991, this is a staggering figure for such a small country. It is also significant that twelve out of the top twenty 'visitor attractions' requiring paid admission are heritage sites, attracting 64 per cent of visitors to the top twenty. Prominent among these are the three main castles in the care of Historic Scotland - Edinburgh (1 million), Stirling (260,000) and Urquhart on Loch Ness (170,000) - as well as the main National Trust properties - Culzean Castle and grounds (350,000), Glencoe (160,000), Inverewe Gardens (130,000), Crathes Castle (130,000) and Culloden (124,000). If Falkland Palace and Threave are included, seven of the Trust's sites account for 1 million visitors, compared with 1.4 million for the three Historic Scotland castles.

Visitors to heritage sites are overwhelmingly middle class. A survey of visitors to National Trust for Scotland properties in 1983, conducted by a market research company for the Trust, indicated that over three-quarters were middle class, with professional and managerial groups representing 40 per cent of all visitors. A mere 3 per cent of visitors came from the manual working class. Plainly, heritage-going is by and large a middle-class pastime. In the UK as a whole, twice as many members of the non-manual social classes (14 per cent) as manual workers (7 per cent) visit heritage sites, a differential leading some social analysts to conclude: 'It is not the nation which consumes "culture" but overwhelmingly the middle classes. The role of the working class in this selective process is to subsidise the maintenance of the "national" heritage' (Clarke and Critcher, 1985). Others argue that while a class differential in the consumption of 'culture' is to be expected, such a focus ignores the substantial use of museums and galleries by the manual working class. Attendance at Glasgow museums, for example, doubled between 1982 and 1989, and the market for museums and galleries has more skilled, semi-skilled and unskilled manual consumers (30 per cent in Glasgow, and 47 per cent in Liverpool) than theatre and concert audiences (J. Myerscough, quoted in Ambrose and Runyard, 1991). And whereas there were only 900 museums in the UK in 1963, this figure had risen to more than 2500 by 1989, a rate of opening of more than fifty a year (*Social Trends*, 20, 1990). Scotland has 20.3 local authority museum facilities per 1 million population, compared with 12 in the North of England, and 17.9 in Yorkshire and Humberside (Ambrose and Runyard, 1991).

UNDERSTANDING CONSUMPTION

How are we to make general sociological sense of this scale of cultural consumption? It is fair to say that sociologists have traditionally neglected consumption, preferring to focus on production as the key generative arena for the emergence of dominant social relations in contemporary societies (Miller, 1987). The two main orthodox paradigms of sociology, structural-functionalism and Marxism, have had little time or understanding for consumption, seeing it from their different points of view as secondary and derivative of the process of economic production. Of the classical sociological writers, only Max Weber has made lifestyle a central feature of his sociological account. As we saw in the last chapter, Weber attributed to social status the theoretical capacity to generate social interests alongside those of social class and organisational power. Being able to 'capture' a key aspect of lifestyle is not merely the expression of material interests but also has the capacity to shape them.

It is this capacity of cultural goods to shape social relations independently of class relations which has generated interest in the sociological significance of leisure. Few sociologists claim that it is possible anymore to 'read off' lifestyle from material circumstances in any straightforward way, which makes the comment by Clarke and Critcher above somewhat dated. While we accept that some forms of culture are hegemonic in their effect – insinuating specific class cultures as surrogates for 'national' ones – both the changing shape of the class structure as well as the lack of fit between cultural and material capital makes the study of leisure in general and heritage in particular especially interesting. As Abercrombie points out: 'The shift from producer to consumer means that the capacity to determine the form, nature and quality of goods and services has moved from the former to the latter. This represents a profound change in social relationships' (Keat and Abercrombie, 1991:172). He argues that producers are losing much of their social position and with it a concomitant loss of authority to determine the form and content of production and consumption. 'It is a change from social organisation dominated by a relatively small and well-structured group of producers to one consisting of a more diffuse and much larger assembly of consumers' (ibid.:173). This decline in the 'culture of production' has a number of interconnected effects. Leisure patterns are no longer simply derived from workplace cultures. We might think here of the patterns of non work activity described in studies of 'solidaristic' work communities like mining villages (Dennis et al., 1969), and the alternative, more open-ended, and unpredictable forms practised by 'Affluent Workers' in car plants in the 1960s (Goldthorpe et al., 1969). Within producer organisations themselves there has been a power shift away from the technical-producer sphere to the marketing-consumer sphere.

Another manifestation of the shift from producer to consumer culture relates to the erosion of the distinction between 'high culture' and 'popular culture' (Keat and Abercrombie, 1991:183). The ability of high-culture to set the agenda and to define the criteria of cultural excellence has been eroded. The revival of market liberalism as both political practice and ideology since the 1970s is in part a reflection of this cultural pluralism. As Russell Keat has pointed out, there is a relationship between subjectivist theories of values on the one hand, and free market criteria on the other. In other words, in giving supremacy to the concept of 'consumer sovereignty', 'there are no further objective or authoritative criteria by reference to which their own opinions and preferences can be assessed' (Keat and Abercrombie, 1991:228).

How are we to relate this rediscovery of consumption to our understanding of heritage? In Chapter 4, we outlined the tensions between the different 'producers' of heritage in Scotland, most notably the market-led consumerist concept of heritage employed by the Scottish Tourist Board, and the high-culturalist conservative one embedded in the National Trust for Scotland. A glimpse of this tension can be had from contrasting comments made by representatives of these bodies. In 1994 the Scottish Tourist Board appointed a new overseas marketing director who previously worked for the British Tourist Board in foreign markets. He commented: 'The first time I heard the Cairngorms [mountain range] described as a product, I thought it was a disaster, but in marketing jargon, that's what it is' (*The Scotsman*, 2 April 1994). Contrast this view of heritage with that enunciated in the same month by the recently appointed director of the National Trust for Scotland:

> One of the enduring characteristics of the Trust has been described as 'perseverance', and whilst we may be regarded as having one foot in the past, we must also have an eye to the future in upholding standards, values

and traditions which are important to the whole society. The Trust can be depended upon to 'persevere' as it preserves.' (*Heritage Scotland* 11,1 1994:12)

We can see here a contrast between a view of heritage as a product which is defined by the market, and heritage as a wider and deeper set of social and cultural values which have to be revered and protected. 'Consuming' heritage, then, can refer to both sets of values – market and sacred. Heritage then has to be reduced to consumable commodities, to bite-size products, even if they turn out to be mountain ranges. On the other hand, heritage is much closer to *patrimoine*, to a deeply embedded set of social and cultural values which have custodians rather than consumers. The tension here is between 'sacred' values and market values. Our study of life members of the National Trust for Scotland set out to identify which perspective dominated among these self-defined heritage consumers.

In this regard, we find the distinction we introduced in Chapter 2 between 'economic' and 'cultural' capital particularly helpful. In his account of contemporary tourism, John Urry employs Pierre Bourdieu's concept of *habitus* (1984) to make sense of an economy of 'cultural goods', and a 'cultural economy' with its own logic, currency and rate of convertibility into economic capital. This economy of cultural goods evolves 'taste' as an economic and social construction in such a way that some groups may rank highly on economic capital but low on cultural capital (industrialists, for example) while others like teachers have high amounts of cultural capital but relatively little of material or economic capital (Featherstone, 1988).

Bourdieu's concept of *habitus* is not simply a description of a cultural locale; it refers to a system of classification and cultural ordering manifest in distinctive cultural practices, thereby giving it a dynamic and enabling role in determining social action (Lee, 1993). Just as economic relations can be quantified in terms of economic capital, so, too, do cultural relations express differential levels of cultural capital. These competences are mainly acquired through education, which, while correlated with amounts of material wealth, are not automatically derived from them. In this regard, income *per se* is not a good predictor of lifestyles and cultural consumption.

'Taste' is neither the outcome of 'natural' disposition, nor the automatic expression of class power. The growth in social groups whose power resides in their capture of levels of cultural capital rather than in their ownership of the conventional means of material production is the corollary of this. Cultural goods become symbolic utilities, valuable not for their inherent properties, but as objective vehicles for demonstrating the interpretive skills of consumers. Hence, the consumption of high cultural commodities like opera have a wider social significance than simply the capacity to pay for an expensive ticket.

The 'production' of taste is closely linked to the changing nature of the material production process itself. The shift away from the uniformity and standardisation of production towards a more diversified system has its analogue in the sphere of consumption. Cultural products and events are themselves commodified, and become part of the 'enterprise culture' (Keat and Abercrombie, 1991). Bourdieu links this new cultural economy with the growth of the 'service class' which is differentiated into the 'new bourgeoisie', those service- and white-collar workers concerned with the production of symbolic goods and services who have relatively high amounts of economic and cultural capital, and the 'new petty bourgeoisie', the lower echelons of the service class. This petty bourgeois stratum is involved mainly in the presentation and representation of cultural goods (such as marketing, sales and PR), and in those organisations providing symbolic goods and services (media, journalism and so on).

The difficulty in defining precisely where the divide between these two strata lies, and, indeed, between the class as a whole and other social classes, is not a conceptual failure, according to this canon, but a reflection of the opacity and fluidity of the social formation as a whole in the late twentieth century. The substantial increase in the size of the service class reflects the centrality of symbolic work, the commodification of culture (in the media and advertising industries, for example), and the loosening of the tight relationship between cultural and economic capital (Urry, 1990). Heritage, and the creation and consumption of the 'authentic', become key identifiers of this class as well as the more traditional bourgeoisie, with its commitment to high culture.

In this chapter and the next, we will focus particularly on one key group of heritage consumers, the life members of the National Trust for Scotland, a group who are self-defined as key consumers of heritage. While our study is not designed to test out the validity of the service class thesis, we will be able to examine in considerable detail both the patterns of heritage consumption as well as its symbolic significance in the lifestyles of this group. We will be able to see whether or not key groups of 'cultural capitalists' figure prominently, and the ways in which heritage connects with social and political values.

CONSUMING NATIONAL HERITAGE

What kind of people become life members of the National Trust for Scotland? We set out to interview a random sample of life members from the lists held by the Trust. Our survey generated 97 respondents, a 72 per cent response rate of those approached. Technical details are available in the appendix. In social terms, life members are overwhelmingly middle class, specifically from the professional classes (80 per cent), with teachers being the most common occupational group. Thirty-five per cent of NTS life members in our survey were or had been teachers. If we include those who have or had spouses who were teachers, this figure rises to 45 per cent of our sample. Further, if we take into account the occupational backgrounds of their families of origin, over half (52 per cent) of our respondents were either teachers themselves, had parents who were teachers, or were married to teachers. This is a remarkable preponderance from one occupational group. In contrast, 14 per cent of respondents are or had been civil servants, administrators or managers (rising to 26 per cent if spouses are included). Eighteen per cent are or had been self-employed (25 per cent including spouses).

In sum, life members of the National Trust for Scotland are drawn overwhelmingly from professional backgrounds, and especially from teaching. Indeed, 57 per cent of respondents are or have been professionals, a figure which rises to 67 per cent if we include spouses and parents. There is, then, clear evidence to support the view that heritage has a particular appeal to those with high degrees of 'cultural' capital. As regards occupational histories, job or professional stability is the norm, with only 35 per cent having changed career. One-third had been in the same job since leaving school, and 31 per cent had changed job but within the same profession.

As regards men in the sample, 28 per cent had spouses in professional employment, 22 per cent had spouses who were either retired (virtually all of these had been in professional jobs), and the same proportion who had been or were house-wives. Women life members, on the other hand, tended to have spouses in professional occupations, whether they were still working (82 per cent), or whether they had retired (80 per cent). Both male and female respondents came from similar social origins, with 40 per cent of men and 50 per cent of women with fathers in professional occupations when respondents had left school. Similar patterns appeared for their respective spouses, with 44 per cent and 48 per cent of men and women respondents indicating that their spouse's fathers had been in professional occupations.

Life members in our sample are highly educated, with 82 per cent staying on after reaching school leaving age (78 per cent of men and 86 per cent of women). Further, the majority (57 per cent) received higher education at degree or post-graduate level (59 per cent of men and 55 per cent of women). Only 25 per cent had received no further education (28 per cent of men and 22 per cent of women).

Despite the fact that over half of our sample of respondents were no longer in employment, income levels were high, with 57 per cent having household incomes of more than £20,000 in the previous financial year. Only 10 per cent had a house-hold income of less than £10,000, and 20 per cent earned more than £40,000.

In short, life members, based on the sample interviewed, are drawn from highly educated, professional backgrounds both in terms of their own occupational patterns and those of their spouses, as well as the families of origin of both respondents and their partners. Given the age structure of the group – the mean age was 59 – it is unsurprising that only 43 per cent were currently in employment (virtually all full-time), with the rest retired. Despite this they tend to have above average incomes. Only two were unemployed, and only one respondent in the whole sample had a manual occupation.

How are we to read the social background of our respon-

dents? We are able to identify a solidly bourgeois and conservative stratum in which cultural capital matters. While
entrepreneurial strata are under-represented, those from professional, and especially educational, backgrounds are most
conspicuous. We shall explore the meanings of heritage for
these groups more fully in the next chapter, but first it is
necessary to describe how they use their life membership of
the National Trust for Scotland.

Most of those we interviewed had been life members for some
considerable time (an average of sixteen years), ranging from
a minimum of four to a maximum of forty-eight years, virtually the lifetime of the Trust itself. Somewhat surprisingly, half
had joined directly as life members, with the same proportion
having come in as ordinary members, before transferring to
life membership. Of this latter group, the average (median)
had joined twenty-five years previously, and most (85 per
cent) had been members continuously since joining.

Financial considerations seem to have played an important
part among reasons for joining the Trust, with 24 per cent
attracted by the savings in annual membership fees, and 19
per cent by the bargain package available when they joined.
However, the largest proportion – 29 per cent – gave their
interest in the aims of the National Trust for Scotland as their
main reason for joining when they did. As we shall see later,
we should not make too much of the distinction between
monetary and non-monetary considerations as they are not
competing interests.

Joining Associations

Just over one-third (35 per cent) of life members interviewed
are also members of other national heritage bodies such as
Historic Scotland, the Architectural Historical Society of
Scotland, and Scottish Civic Trust. Of these, Historic Scotland
was by far the most significant, with 56 per cent of our
respondents being members of that body also, on average (the
mean time span) for six years. A higher number (38 per cent)
belong to local heritage associations, and such activity seems
to fit into a broader commitment to local organisations,
reflecting the embeddedness of the local middle class. Over

two-thirds (69 per cent) were members of locally-based groups ranging from church associations (30 per cent), to local architectural societies (25 per cent), to conservation groups (22 per cent), and to round table or women's guilds (21 per cent). What we observe here is the rich associational activity of local professional and middle-class people with fairly extensive commitments to their local communities. This conclusion is reinforced by their patterns of membership of leisure groups. Sixty-one per cent were active in recreational groups, 42 per cent in sports clubs, and 23 per cent belonged to craft or hobby groups. Similarly, just under half (42 per cent) were members of local interest groups, councils or committees.

This broad pattern of social involvement is also reflected in support for charities. Nearly nine out of ten respondents (89 per cent) regularly supported charities, mainly aimed at human welfare (80 per cent) but also animal welfare (23 per cent). Support was mainly in the form of financial donations (27 per cent make regular contributions, 22 per cent occasional ones, and 17 per cent make covenants), while 21 per cent actively participated in some other way, 13 per cent, for example, collected for charity.

In similar vein, one-third of respondents supported social and political causes, with 17 per cent belonging to social organisations like Amnesty International and Greenpeace. Fifteen per cent were members of political parties, with the Conservative Party the most popular (11 per cent), though both the Liberal Democrats and Labour also had a few members among our respondents. The political predilections of National Trust for Scotland life members will be discussed in detail in the next chapter in the context of the cultural and political meanings associated with heritage.

The professional and associational character of the sample is also reflected in the high membership of work related organisations (62 per cent), mainly professional (65 per cent) rather than trades unions (30 per cent). The associational histories of life members reveal a rich pattern. The general picture from our sample shows quite clearly that we are dealing with a group of people who are organisationally active, especially in locally-based organisations, across a wide spectrum of interests from politics to charities to local interest

groups. Our aim is to understand how their heritage activities
and interests fits into this broader pattern.

Heritage Activities

Life members are active consumers of the National Trust for
Scotland. On average, members had visited four Trust properties in the last year, with a minimum of one visit and a
maximum of twenty-three. By far the most popular site was
the Culloden Centre, visited by as many as half of the life members in the sample. This was almost twice as popular as the
next site, Culzean Castle on the Ayrshire coast. Other popular
sites visited in the last twelve months were Crathes Castle and
Falkland Palace (by 16 per cent each), the House of Dun near
Brechin (14 per cent), Gladstone's Land (12 per cent) and the
Georgian House (11 per cent), both in Edinburgh, as well as
Kellie Castle in Fife (11 per cent).

The majority (59 per cent) of life members regarded the
previous year's visiting pattern as typical. Of those who considered their visit pattern untypical, nearly three-quarters (72
per cent) thought they had visited fewer properties than
previously, and only one-fifth said they had visited more than
usual. A significant minority (41 per cent) had visited an
English National Trust property, and it was clear that the
attractions of using the National Trust for Scotland card South
of the Border were considerable. Fully three-quarters had
done so, with one-quarter on a regular basis.

Visiting heritage sites was not simply confined to trips to
Trust properties. Two-thirds of life members had visited
non-Trust sites, on average two in the last twelve months. The
range was quite broad, with around one-third visiting none,
and one member visiting as many as nine non-Trust heritage
sites in the previous year. What is striking, however, is that
many life members claim to attach little or no importance to
visiting heritage sites. As many as 41 per cent answered in this
way, but, on the other hand, 23 per cent placed it as important or very important in their leisure activities. This does suggest that life membership does not in itself guarantee a great
deal of heritage visiting, but that for some it is a central life
interest. Those who rate heritage visits as an important part of
their leisure activities are more likely to belong to local historical or architectural societies, and to have visited National

Trust properties in England, Wales or Northern Ireland. The importance they attach to heritage is not a function of the length of time they have been members of the National Trust for Scotland. They are, however, more likely than other members to visit more trust properties, and more frequently.

As well as asking about which properties life members visited, we were interested in which ones they preferred. These are by no means the same thing. For example, while the Culloden battlefield was the most visited, only one life member in the whole sample rated it as a favourite. On the other hand, Culzean Castle was a favourite with 28 per cent of our sample. No other property came anywhere near that rating. Falkland Palace, the castles at Craigievar, Brodick and Brodie, and the Georgian House in Edinburgh were mentioned by around 8 or 9 per cent of life members. The attractions of these places are based on their setting and scenery (rated by nearly 30 per cent), and on the gardens themselves (just under 25 per cent), rather than on the symbolic significance of the properties.

The preference for more traditional icons like castles and large houses was also reflected in members' preference for heritage generally. While 30 per cent confined their preference for heritage sites to those owned by the Trust, for the rest, castles (28 per cent) and stately homes (22 per cent) were much preferred.

On average, life members in our sample visited the same heritage property about three times, mainly in the company of others – family and friends. It is clear, then, that using heritage in this way is part of a broader social activity, rather than something individuals do on their own. This is especially true when it comes to entertaining visitors from abroad or South of the Border. Fully 69 per cent had taken overseas visitors to a National Trust for Scotland property, often to more than one. A similar proportion (65 per cent) had entertained English visitors in this way, again visiting more than one property. This pattern is reinforced by the high levels of satisfaction which our respondents claimed on behalf of their visitors. Nearly all reported favourable reactions by their guests, helping, one imagines, to reinforce this pattern of entertainment. Using NTS properties to entertain visitors might help to explain why Culloden is the most visited site in our sample, even though few claim it as a favourite. It is, perhaps, being used for external consumption rather than indigenous enjoyment.

As an indication of their approach to heritage, we asked our respondents to describe to us any books about Scotland's heritage which they might recommend to anyone wishing to find out more about it. Three-quarters said they could do so. What they had in mind were, in the main, guidebooks (35 per cent, with 15 per cent mentioning the Trust's own guide). If we include guides along with other texts, this figure rises to 65 per cent of our sample. Only 22 per cent mentioned works of non-fiction alone. We might infer from these findings that life members have a fairly 'practical' and conservative view of reading matter on the subject of heritage.

Heritage and Leisure

How does the consumption of heritage fit into broader leisure patterns, in particular, holidays? Nearly nine respondents out of every ten (86 per cent) have had a holiday in the last twelve months and fully 56 per cent have had more than one. Three-quarters of those who had taken a holiday described it as a fairly typical one, suggesting once more a rather conservative disposition among our respondents. By and large, heritage was not a central organising theme for vacations. Only 21 per cent said that they regularly organised their holidays around heritage visits, while 36 per cent never did so. Even if we include those who occasionally visited heritage sites when they are on holiday, only 38 per cent could be said to link holidays with heritage in any meaningful way. Not even those who claimed that heritage was an important part of their leisure were inclined to organise holidays mainly around visits to sites.

A minority, 42 per cent, tended to take holidays in Scotland, and 35 per cent never did so. Those who holiday in Scotland did so because they 'like the country' (55 per cent), or because it was convenient (13 per cent). The attractions of going abroad were much more important to those who did not holiday in Scotland (55 per cent). Nine out of ten respondents claimed to visit a heritage property when they are on holiday, but only a little over half (52 per cent) make it a regular feature. Once more, we can see that being a life member of the Trust does not necessarily mean that visiting heritage sites is a predictable central life interest. There is considerable variation among members in their attachment to and use of heritage as a leisure activity. This can vary from the opportunistic use of heritage, as, in the words of one respondent: 'If they [heritage sites] are there, we'll visit, but we won't go out of our way.' For another, heritage as a central leisure interest: 'It's central. We always do this. For example, we went to Rome, Florence and Venice to see the buildings. We organise our holidays around heritage.'

Life membership of the National Trust for Scotland is overwhelmingly seen as good value for money (92 per cent). However, asking about value for money drew out some ambivalence among our respondents, as if we were inferring that financial considerations were the main rationale for membership. Eighty-two per cent agreed with the statement that value for money was not what membership was about, including 46 per cent who stressed that they were keen supporters of the Trust. Many, like these respondents, saw the financial considerations as irrelevant:

> 'Value for money is a poor way in which to view heritage.'

> 'Membership goes beyond value for money; it's important to support the trust.'

> 'It's general interest really, rather than it being a "good deal".'

> 'Being a member goes beyond just value for money.'

More commonly, however, there is recognition that both go together. In the words of one respondent:

> 'It's important to keep our heritage. The NTS needs every penny. Members should get involved and help out.'

Managing Heritage

Given that the National Trust for Scotland is a voluntary organisation, how did its life members see the relationship between the different bodies involved in heritage, that is, the state, local government, private owners and voluntary organisations themselves? By and large, our respondents thought that heritage should remain in the hands of voluntary bodies like the Trust. Just under half, 47 per cent, were happy with this arrangement, while 37 per cent thought that the state should be more involved, especially with regard to funding. A further 14 per cent thought that a judicious mix of the two was most appropriate.

The philosophy of voluntarism can be gauged from the following comments:

> 'Generally speaking, voluntary organisations work fairly well, people are more enthusiastic. Governments bring in restrictive forces.'

> 'If the state did more, there would be a loss of enthusiasm. State activity is poorly organised, and does not encourage voluntary activity.'

> 'If the NTS can sustain itself, then this is better because of the standard of maintenance of its properties. State control would be more distant, and destroy the spirit of involvement.'

> 'It should stay in voluntary hands; people take more personal interest in things if it's voluntary.'

> 'It is good that it is voluntary, because you need the enthusiasm, but it needs to be well-funded.'

> 'In France there is very little voluntary heritage. It is left to the state. But only voluntary work carries the commitment. It is a great asset to have organisations of this sort [NTS], and to show politicians the way.'

> 'Once the state gets its hands on it, it's a problem. It's better in the hands of enthusiasts, although the financial considerations could be a problem. We want people who are proud of heritage and want it to survive.'

Others, just over one-third, wanted a stronger role for the state:

> 'The state should be more active, after all, much of our heritage goes abroad, and only the state can prevent this.'

> 'The state should do more. It's important that it is kept. Voluntary organisations dwindle and don't keep it up.'

Nevertheless, a more common response was to value the balance between state and voluntary bodies:

'The balance is not far wrong. The state should provide the context, and the voluntary sector should run it.'

'A balance is essential – voluntary contributions on a local basis, but the state on the general level.'

'The state will have to take a more active role for financial reasons. I slightly regret this because voluntary effort gets people involved.'

'The state can do more in funding; volunteers can only do so much. But the state shouldn't get too involved, because it is less efficient.'

'I prefer the voluntary approach, but the state should support it. The state can be clumsy, and voluntary organisations have more enthusiasm.'

This preference for voluntary activity was also reflected in support for the private owners of heritage properties. Twenty-five per cent thought that they should have a greater say in heritage, and only 6 per cent less involvement. Twenty-three per cent thought that the balance was about right, and 19 per cent thought it too difficult to generalise. Twenty-seven per cent had no opinion on the subject. Those who regard heritage as important in their leisure patterns were more likely to want less involvement from private owners in running heritage, although they were just as committed to the 'voluntary' principle as those less committed to heritage as a leisure pastime.

Those who supported greater private involvement expressed views similar to this respondent:

'It must depend on the private owner. They can do a good job of restoring the property. Owners take great care, on the whole. You need a private passion to manage a place.'

On the other hand, those who wanted their role diminished did so not because of ideological reasons, but largely because they were felt to be unduly restrictive having received public funds:

'Private owners should play their part. I'm all in favour of government grants to them but there should be a quid pro quo, and I'm afraid there isn't. If people get grants, then it should be publicly known and the building open to the public. There simply isn't enough access to the public.'

'Private owners should play a lesser role. Why should they get public money without more commitment to the public?'

Nevertheless, this comment tended to be more typical:

'It is their homes, after all, and they are struggling, so they should be helped to maintain their properties, so the state should help. But on the whole the balance is right.'

On the other hand, there was a fairly strong feeling that local government should be more involved, but with certain provisos. Fully 58 per cent wanted greater involvement, and only 18 per cent less, largely because of the potential for political bias and control. Nevertheless, this commitment to local government involvement in heritage was part of a broader belief in the virtues of localism which we touched on in discussing the associational activities of life members in their local communities. These observations were not untypical:

'Local government is already quite involved, but I feel they could do more. Local people should be encouraged to be active.'

'It is so important that local people are made aware of their heritage.'

'Local government should have a greater role in protecting local heritage. They have a better grasp than central government.'

'Heritage is very much a local affair. It's better to work on this scale.'

'Local government should take heritage as part of wider tourism, and promote local sites.'

'It's very important for people to be active on a local level.'

'It is important to be active on a small scale, to let local people be aware of their heritage.'

Broadly speaking, there was suspicion about the motives of local politicians:

> 'Many of these people [in local government] are philistines. They shouldn't be allowed to get their hands on heritage. I don't trust them. They're not always people of taste. Look at our area - you can't really get involved unless you're political.'

> 'It could be a good source of income, but there are too many strings. The ethos would change from voluntary ownership, and it would be subject to the pet views of local politicians.'

> 'No. It contains too many little tinpot businessmen with special axes to grind.'

In broad terms, then, life members were committed to voluntarism and localism in the running of heritage, preferring the personal commitment of individuals to state direction. Nevertheless, there was recognition that state funding is necessary and inevitable, while local government should play an enabling role by using planning controls as well as local grants. Our respondents think, however, that the prime role in heritage should, remain in the hands of local volunteers and bodies like the National Trust for Scotland.

CONCLUSION

In this chapter, we have introduced the sample of life members of the National Trust for Scotland whose meanings and motivations for their involvement we will explore in the next chapter. We have here a group of people whose financial commitment to heritage is reflected in their life membership which, in 1993, cost £460. It is clear, however, that their commitment is not simply a financial one, reflected in the numbers who decry the purely monetary significance of becoming life members of the National Trust for Scotland.

The key to their involvement in heritage appears to lie in their occupational backgrounds. We have seen that the professions, especially teaching, are disproportionately represented. What is the significance of this? By and large the social power of these groups derives from the high amounts of 'cultural capital' they have available to them. The post-war years saw a major increase in rates of social mobility achieved largely through improvements in educational opportunity. Data from studies of inter-generational social mobility show that in both Scotland, England and Wales a substantial proportion of the service class has been drawn from manual working-class backgrounds. In Scotland, for example, fully one-third of the top service class – higher grade professionals, managers and the self-employed – had fathers who were in manual occupations (McCrone, 1992:109). Cultural capital in the form of educational qualifications has been the key means of social mobility for such people. It is clear that they have also turned this cultural means into a leisure pursuit. Hence, we can consider it both a means of social production and of cultural consumption.

It is also clear that for many of the life members, heritage is a central 'enthusiasm', the dedication of leisure time to involvement in some activity (Keat and Abercrombie, 1991:179). As Abercrombie points out: 'All such enthusiasms invariably involve the accumulation of expert knowledge, the deployment of skill built up over time, the expenditure of considerable amounts of time and money, and often, the involvement with others in clubs and societies' (ibid.).

Membership of the National Trust for Scotland does not simply involve periodic and passive consumption of heritage sites. There is a rich network of local activity groups, travel outings, and active participation in heritage conservation through voluntary labour. What is available to life members is a co-ordinated lifestyle achieved through association with an essentially conservative organisation. The ethos of the Trust evokes high culture, described by Keat and Abercrombie as follows: 'High culture concerns set the cultural agenda, define the criteria of aesthetic excellence and, more importantly, determine the appropriate modes of cultural response on the part of consumers' (1991:183). It is unsurprising, therefore, that the commodification of heritage has made few inroads into the National Trust for Scotland and its life members. The comment of the Trust's director that 'it is reassuring to think of the National Trust for Scotland as being a timeless organisation upholding traditional values' (*Heritage Scotland*, 11,1, 1994:12) would seem to strike a chord with life members. Just what heritage means to them, and how it fits into their worldview, will be the theme of the next chapter.

Chapter 7

The Meaning of Heritage

Given the rapid growth in the the heritage industry which we have outlined in the last chapter, we could be forgiven for thinking that, like many products, heritage has a fairly shallow and tenuous hold on those who are its customers. In this chapter we will examine what lies behind heritage, this apparent 'emigration from the present' (Rojek, 1993:165), in the minds of members of the National Trust for Scotland. Given the rather pejorative meaning given to 'the heritage industry' by writers such as Robert Hewison, we might imagine that it has little resonance for these 'consumers'. On the contrary. In this chapter we will show that heritage is a highly meaningful part of the vocabulary of life members of the National Trust for Scotland, but that is often expressed in unexpected ways.

Our review also allows us to explore the political message of heritage. We saw in earlier chapters how the Thatcher government of the early 1980s sought to capture the concept of the 'national heritage' for its party. Mobilising a fairly unproblematic discourse of English/British heritage for political purposes was always likely to be less successful North of the Border. Indeed, one might be tempted to argue that the growing interest in heritage generally would have quite different resonances in the context of the relative political success of the Scottish National Party in the last two decades. It seems at least possible that the growth in political nationalism is closely connected with a developing sense of cultural nationalism. Would we, then, be correct in inferring that the rise of cultural nationalism in the form of heritage is the analogue of political nationalism?

In this chapter we will explore these two hypotheses, namely, that heritage in general is merely a marketing device and has little resonance for our sample of life members of the

National Trust for Scotland; and that if heritage does have a resonance, it correlates with the fortunes of political nationalism in general, and the Scottish National Party in particular. As we will discover, neither hypotheses is supported by our evidence. We will show that 'heritage' is a concept which resonates strongly for our respondents. We might even say that if the National Trust for Scotland did not exist, they would seek out an alternative vehicle for their heritage aspirations. Our data also show that while they have a strong and coherent sense of heritage both at a personal and a national/Scottish level, life members do not translate this cultural commitment into a political one in any simple way.

THE MEANING AND IMPORTANCE OF HERITAGE

In order to gauge the significance of heritage as a concept, we asked a series of five open-ended questions which allowed respondents to set their own terms of understanding. These questions were:

> We hear quite a lot these days about 'heritage'. Can you tell me what you understand by the term?
>
> Do you think that there is a distinction between 'heritage' and 'history'?
>
> As a life member of NTS, you obviously care about heritage. Can you tell me why you consider heritage to be important?
>
> How would you describe Scotland's heritage in particular?
>
> Are there any important differences between heritage in Scotland and in England?

Let us examine each of these dimensions in turn.

What is 'Heritage'?

From the outset it was clear that 'heritage' was not some alien concept interjected by the interviewer. It was part of the normal vocabulary of Trust life members. Only 5 per cent saw it as having negative connotations: a retired architect, for example, said: 'It's a bit of a cliché; it means what you want it to mean. The essential character of a place is seen in heritage, but it can be modern. It makes a statement.' Virtually everyone else used it freely and positively in discussion. The most common usage (mentioned by 63 per cent of our respondents) was in the context of 'history' or 'past lives', with 44 per cent defining it as 'tangible history'. (Because the question 'What is heritage?' was deliberately open-ended, more than one response is possible, and as a consequence, the percentages do not add up to 100 per cent). Only 35 per cent spoke of it in a more orthodox way as 'preservation' or 'conservation', and the same percentage (35 per cent) used it in a proto-political manner as nationhood culture.

In very general terms, there are two broad senses of heritage which emerge from our interviews. One stresses the physical artefacts – buildings, even landscapes. The other is much closer to the French word *patrimoine* – possession of a much broader legacy of culture and values, what we might call 'inheritance'. Of course, this is not a hard and fast distinction but we were able to distinguish these discrete versions of heritage. Let us examine them in turn. On the one hand, there are those who see heritage in the fairly straightforward terms of buildings and artefacts. Here is a sample of comments:

> 'Heritage is a handy shorthand term attached to some odd artefacts. It gives people a sense of ownership.'

> 'Historical buildings which need to be preserved.'

> 'It's the buildings and artefacts of the past, down through the centuries.'

> 'I tend to think of buildings rather than natural sites.'

Others broaden out their definition to include landscapes as well. For example:

> 'It's places as well as buildings, literature and art, landscapes and forestry – all of that.'

> 'It's the buildings and the countryside which need to be preserved.'

> 'The qualities and features of the physical landscape we have inherited, and which we have the duty to maintain.'

Defining heritage in terms of physical characteristics is fairly predictable. What is far less so is the capacity of respondents to 'read' behind the artefacts to a deeper set of values. Take these comments as instances:

'Heritage is about what's handed down from previous generations in terms of history and culture. It's exemplified by buildings, their contents, and the landscape.'

'It's the material representation of how things used to be.'

'The visible material history, culture and roots of my being. The fascination of the past that is all around us. I want to pass it on to my grandchildren.'

'It's really very broad. For example, my son is learning the pipes, and heritage includes culture – life and music, and art – it's much deeper than buildings.'

'The lifestyle of people in days gone by, but also how their lives affect ours. It's broader than buildings, extending to ways of living. It's part of our inheritance.'

The key word here is 'inheritance'. This broadening of heritage to include the cultural, and the personal, lies firmly behind the commitment to heritage. Let us take some more examples to elaborate the point:

'Quite simply, it's our birthright.'

'Heritage is part of our cultural identity and should be preserved.'

'It's living history, presenting something of the past of an area and its people. The past is not just buildings, but a way of life.'

'It's the tangible legacy of the past. We need to understand how our forefathers lived, and what their values were. It gives us continuity with our predecessors.'

'It's part of the history and the folklore of the country. It includes its art and countryside.'

'It's the whole of what has gone before, lifestyles throughout the ages, what we have inherited from our forebears. It's not just stately homes, but dry stone dykes. I'm a believer in posterity, the past, present and future running together.'

'A lot of it's gut feeling. I travel the world but I know that this is where my forebears came from; I know about their lives through heritage. It's a living thing.'

'It's partly the visible remains of our history, our inheritance from the past in the widest term.'

'It's the past, what you pass on to your children so that they know what their ancestors did and thought. It's really our inheritance.'

'It's important to learn lessons from the past. Heritage is about how we have developed, the sense of continuity.'

'It's important to preserve the past. It's your inheritance and gives you a sense of belonging to your country.'

It became quite plain in our discussions of heritage with our respondents that the concept is a natural part of their vocabulary. It represents much more than a collection of physical artefacts. It becomes a tangible link with a set of values, crucial to a sense of identity. Some make the connection to 'national' aspects of heritage quite explicitly. For example:

'It's all aspects of human life which contribute to make Scotland what it is.'

'It means a distinct national character.'

'Preserving what happened years ago for young Scots in the future. If you're Scots, it's something to be proud of.'

'It's our past, the upkeep of what we have. It's not necessarily maintaining the status quo, but of retaining Scottish values, the countryside and the architecture.'

'I'm Scottish all the way through. Heritage relates to Scottish buildings, customs, traditions, everything relating to our country.'

We have already pointed out that only a minority – around one-third – translate heritage into national-political terms. Nevertheless, as we shall see later, our respondents do articulate a strong sense of Scottishness though by no means one which translates straightforwardly into political terms.

All in all, we encountered few difficulties in raising the term 'heritage' with the life members we interviewed. It was important, then, to develop with our respondents this sense of heritage, and its meanings. The first way of getting at these meanings was to ask them to discuss, and if possible, to distinguish between heritage and history, to describe for us what they understand by Scotland's heritage in particular, and how it might differ, if at all, from heritage in England.

History and Heritage

Just as 'heritage' was a term which fitted easily into our respondents' vocabulary, so they had little difficulty distinguishing between history and heritage. Three-quarters thought that there was a distinction, and only 20 per cent that there was not, the two being too closely aligned. The distinction for those who saw it has various dimensions. At its most simple it is the difference between artefacts (heritage) and events (history). Thus:

> 'Heritage is things that are left - artefacts; history refers to events and processes.'

> 'History is what people did; heritage is more tangible, such as the built environment.'

> 'History is a form of verbal/written interpretation of the past; heritage is much more tangible.'

> 'History is something you read about in books; heritage is something you go and visit.'

> 'History is events and stories; heritage is buildings mainly, and you can read the story through the buildings.'

Even in these comments we can see that heritage is frequently seen as more 'alive', more 'personal' and more connected to people's lives than 'history'. To elaborate:

> 'Heritage is everything that's gone before - it's broader than history, which is things that have happened - events, if you like.'

> 'History is the bare facts. Heritage is more the meat and the bones, it looks at ordinary people.'

> 'Heritage makes history come alive.'

> 'Heritage is the living manifestation of history.'

> 'Heritage is an in-built thing, almost an attitude of people, their culture and way of life - like Burns's poetry; history on the other hand, is based on recordable facts - battles, kings and queens.'

'History is a clinical representation of the past, whereas heritage physically links you with the past.'

'Heritage is literature, culture, everything; history is facts, dates, events.'

'History is events and people; heritage is part of our culture in the widest sense.'

In other words, the distinction between heritage and history is not simply objects on the one hand, and events on the other, but between the present and the past, or rather the way the past relates to and informs the present. This is clearly evoked through buildings and artefacts, but it represents a much broader, connected process which appears to be more relevant to people's immediate lives. Thus:

'History is dead; heritage is ongoing and living.'

'History is a clinical representation of the past, whereas heritage physically links you with the past.'

'History is all-encompassing; heritage is more selective, and in some ways more contemporary.'

'Heritage always seems more alive. It's homes and families - human beings - our inherited culture. History on the other hand is rather dry - it's books and events.'

'Heritage is the interest in what is; history is more the background to how things came about.'

The distinction between history and heritage is, in many ways then, as much about the distinction between the past and the present. History, especially with a capital 'H' - high history - is deemed, as the following comments suggest, to be remote and over:

'History refers to political issues, battles and people, that is, things that happened. Heritage refers to the way people lived. This is much more interesting.'

'History is just about the 'past'. It's not necessarily a personal thing - it's not connected to you. Heritage on the other hand is *your* past, *your* personal details. It includes personal anecdotes and stories as well as buildings.'

There are some respondents who invert the significance of

history and heritage, but the connections between the past and the present remain. For instance:

> 'Heritage in the form of artefacts is very important, but they're not the whole story; it's the inheritance of our culture too. History on the other hand, is more about the complexity of society – events and processes.'

and again,

> 'Heritage is often restricted to the artefacts, arts and crafts – it runs the risk of being twee. History is more interpretive, to do with the motives and processes. It's a bigger concept, both conceptually and politically.'

> 'History is more about tradition, sayings and stories. Heritage is mainly solid things like buildings, landscapes, sites with historical connotations.'

The overwhelming view of our respondents, then, is that heritage rather than history is the more relevant, meaningful and connected with their own lives. It is this connectedness which allows so many to be sure of the distinction they make between the two, and which helps to explain the undoubted significance of heritage today.

The National Trust for Scotland and Heritage

Having asked our respondents to talk about the relationship between heritage and history in abstract terms, we then related this to their membership of the Trust by asking them to tell us why heritage was important. Here we were asking them to focus on their membership of a specific organisation, but it soon became obvious that once more we were tapping some deep and complex issues. It also became clear why heritage was more meaningful than history, namely, because it connects more intimately with everyday life.

It was striking that so many chose to answer this question in terms of their own conception of heritage rather than defining it in terms of what the NTS did. What was also noticeable was that respondents articulated a deeply personal sense of heritage rather than choosing to answer the question in terms of a specifically Scottish, that is, national, dimension. Fully 50 per cent answered this question in terms of their *own* need to give an account of their personal history, while 22 per cent spoke in more orthodox ways of protecting and conserving the national past. What we begin to see is a deeply conservative sense of heritage, of strong lines of continuity being drawn between the respondents themselves, their predecessors and their children. Here are some comments which make the point:

'Unless you know your roots, you don't know who you are.'

'The past has made us.'

'It's what we've inherited; it's living, and quite personal.'

'It's difficult to imagine life if you allowed the past to be wiped out. It provides enrichment to life.'

'Human beings especially children need a sense of history.'

'We are the products of our past. To understand yourself socially you must see what has gone before you.'

'We are all products of the past, and we can only understand the present by knowing what's gone before.'

'Heritage gives you an insight into yourself and your values, what you've come from.'

'It's a legacy, an inheritance, how life today grew out of previous days, and it puts you in touch with the past.'

'It's what we have inherited, and it connects us with our ancestors.'

'It is essential for people to know what's gone before. It develops a sense of respect for the past, and helps put life in perspective.'

'The love of history for different reasons; it's important to know where you've come from.'

'It gives you a sense of roots, what you've come from.'

This overpowering and insistent sense of continuity between themselves and the past epitomised in heritage allowed our respondents to draw moral implications for current society, and especially its offspring:

'There is a duty on all of us to take care of the past to provide continuity for our children.'

'It should be there for future generations. Whether these generations will come, troubles me.'

'I feel we are custodians and I believe in the continuity of history. I'm very anti-revolutionary.'

'It's a very important educational resource, and it gives one knowledge of ancestors.'

'It's to make sure that the younger generation has more advantages than its forebears had.'

'Recent history is very important. We enjoy it and we hope that these things will still be there for our children so as to give people an idea of how their forebears lived.'

Heritage too allows a contrast with life as it purported to be.

'Because the pace of life today is frenetic, and more gets lost, it's important to preserve and maintain what's gone before. It's easy to say that what's gone before has gone, but you need to know what you've come from.'

'It's necessary to have some kind of balance to today's speed, and there is a useful and tangible contrast in beautiful old buildings. The whole scene is relaxing, and helps to take away the stress.'

Heritage is to most of our respondents an intensely personal matter, which allows them to express their deeply held values, and their concerns about the direction and pace of social and cultural change. The appeal and the skill of the National Trust for Scotland is to give expression, implicitly and explicitly, to these sentiments. Compare, for example, the observations of our respondents with comments made by the Trust's director in his editorial for its magazine *Heritage Scotland*:

We live in an age when certain standards which ought to be timeless seem to have been turned on their head – both at an individual human level and in terms of corporate behaviour.

That is why it is reassuring to think of the National Trust for Scotland as being a timeless organisation

> upholding traditional values but without acquiring a rep-
> utation as a rigid patriarch with a quaint and fuddy-duddy
> outlook.' (Spring 1994, 11, 1:12)

The ethos and culture of the National Trust for Scotland
seems to be clearly in tune with the mood of its members.
Both share an implicit set of social and cultural values which
emphasise continuity, conservatism and roots. That is why the
question about the importance of heritage to members of the
Trust elicits a strong sense of 'personal history' (50 per cent),
and a sense of continuity (33 per cent), rather than a more
conventional sense of nationhood (22 per cent). Given the
powerful image of Scotland which permeates heritage North
of the Border, this is an intriguing finding. Far fewer of our
respondents than we might expect connected this question
about the importance of heritage with an explicitly Scottish,
national, dimension. As we shall see later, this apparent
absence of nationalism is not unconnected to a strongly conservative (and ostensibly unpolitical) view of Scotland, from a
group of people who are conservative in every sense of the
word. Those who did connect heritage with Scottish nationalism as such do so in the following terms:

> 'It is important to pass on Scotland's heritage in its vari-
> ous forms to succeeding generations.'

> 'Heritage is bound up with Scottish culture and identity.'

> 'If we lost our buildings we would lose a lot, that's why
> NTS tries to protect Scotland's heritage. But it's more
> than buildings, it's the preservation of the national out-
> look of the Scots, the need, if you like, to protect our
> moral fibre.'

> 'It's to maintain a national vision. People need to know
> their roots.'

> 'So that Scotland should keep its place in the world; its
> heritage could be under threat.'

More generally, however, it was common to find heritage connected with a broad sense of nationalism:

> 'At an emotional level, it's pride in your country, you try
> to learn about your past and its history. We must preserve
> the main elements, and we need to avoid sweeping away
> what we have inherited, to preserve the best of the past.'

'It is good to preserve the national identity. It also helps to preserve the countryside, our natural heritage.'

'If heritage isn't preserved, a country starts to lack identity. Heritage needs to be passed on to children.'

All in all, it is clear that the term 'heritage' is a cue for articulating a deeper and broader set of social values, a world-view which is both conservative and personal, in which the past has distinct lessons for the future, and in which there are distinct fears that not simply the icons of the past will be lost, but the signposts for the future.

Scotland's Heritage

Focusing more specifically on Scotland's heritage, we then asked our respondents to describe its main characteristics. By and large, they focus on physical characteristics rather than cultural ones, but as we shall see, this distinction is more often apparent than real. For example, the most mentioned characteristics of Scotland's heritage are the country's scenery (mentioned by 30 per cent), its geography (25 per cent), and its monuments, especially its castles (23 per cent). Other non-physical characteristics are its culture of perseverance and hardship (18 per cent), its language and culture (16 per cent), the specific heritage of Highland clans and the Highland Clearances (10 per cent), as well as its folklore (5 per cent). Our respondents have little difficulty in articulating a distinctive heritage for Scotland, frequently intertwining landscape and history as these comments make plain:

'It's highly influenced by its geography, the sense of persecution, the Covenanters and Highland Clearances, for example.'

'Features which are specific to Scotland such as the buildings which reflect the climate and environment. It's rugged. It also has links with Europe, unlike England which is rather insular.'

This too is a feature of our respondents' description of Scotland's heritage – the contrast, implicit or explicit, with England. Thus:

'Scotland was a family-oriented society, with close-knit communities, unlike England.'

'Scotland's heritage is significant because there is still time to do something, to preserve it, whilst in England there isn't.'

'Being a smaller country, we're more aware of our general heritage. Scottish buildings are different. For example, there are more ruins, and there are the battles with England.'

'Our history such as the clan system has some bearing on our lives. Culloden, for example, was a tragedy for the whole of Scotland. In the Central Belt there was a drift from the Highlands. Given the history of the Clearances, the bitterness against the English is understandable.'

In this regard, Scotland's people are seen as an important part of the heritage, and in particular at the intersection between landscape and culture:

'I think in terms of the toughness and resilience of Scottish people. Scots are very enterprising.'

'Scotland is fascinating. It's always been on the margins, and we've had to struggle to survive. So that has made us keener to leave our mark and conquer the natural elements.'

'The spirit of perseverence over hardship.'

'Scotland's character and its people. The country is less populous and more rugged. This appears in the character of the people – tough and down to earth.'

'Rugged buildings – there's a distinct hardy feeling to the buildings and the people. Heritage charts the history of the ordinary people.'

More abstractly, some identify Scotland's heritage directly in the social values of its people:

'There's a strong element of melancholy. We have suffered with conflict with our larger neighbour.'

'It's quite sad – people were often oppressed by the English, but there is a strong folk-mythic element.'

'The landscape, the history of its peoples. It's been far from happy, tragic really.'

We see, then, that what starts out as a distinction between physical and cultural aspects of Scotland's heritage turns into something much more complex. Social values and physical landscapes are interwoven into the picture of heritage, and frequently in contrast to that of its southern neighbour. This, of course, presents some difficulties for our fairly conservative (and Conservative) sample. It was not uncommon as a result to find an explicit denial of the connection between heritage and politics, one which recognises that at least in the last two decades the idea of 'Scotland' has become highly and conventionally politicised:

> 'Well it's not political, it's not the SNP! I don't like them but I think of myself as a Scottish patriot.'

> 'Being Scottish born, I stick up for Scotland, but the British should stick together. We should regard ourselves as British. We need to work to preserve Scottish heritage, though.'

> 'It reflects Scotland's austerity and the richness of England. Scots tend to dwell on battles unduly. We are a great nation together [Scotland and England]. We shouldn't split up into separate states.'

To develop the point of comparison between Scotland and England, we asked our respondents to point out the important differences, if any, between heritage in the two countries. Most (62 per cent) judge there to be a distinct difference, with only 35 per cent denying that there is one. With regard to those who see a difference, the reasons are mainly cultural (50 per cent), and less attributable to geography (only 17 per cent). England's heritage is characterised as consisting of grander houses (mentioned by 27 per cent), on a larger scale generally (18 per cent), and reflecting greater wealth (18 per cent). On the other hand, Scotland's heritage is deemed to be more 'democratic' (26 per cent), more varied (22 per cent), and on a smaller and more intimate scale (11 per cent). These themes emerge in comments such as:

> 'In England it's stately homes, and the riches of the upper classes. In Scotland heritage is more identifiable. The people who founded NTS were more socially aware and so they were concerned about the lives and the houses of other than the gentry.'

'England is a bigger country, but in England there are more stately homes. They're museums, really.'

'In Scotland, it's associated with the Clearances, the '45, the Jacobites. In England, it's stately homes, Tudors, Windsor – with an aristocratic focus.'

'English heritage is wealthier in terms of the stately homes, for example,'

Related to the presence of stately homes is the generally greater wealth attributed to England:

'England is wealthier. There are more grand houses, and country manors.'

'English heritage has a stronger sense of wealth, and it's also a larger scale.'

'English heritage is more about powerful people, the landed gentry.'

This theme of greater wealth is also connected with characteristics of the class systems of the two countries:

'English heritage is less democratic.'

'English heritage has a strong sense of its roots in feudalism, while Scottish heritage is more democratic.'

'English heritage has a much stronger class bias in heritage, that sense of inheritance.'

And more explicitly on differences in social values as such:

'Scotland's heritage like its people is hardy, and illustrates the intelligence of Scots people.'

'There is a different cultural heritage, a different background. The attitudes are different, the thinking is different. Our educational standards are higher. It's the English voices you hear in these parts these days, but our culture has firmer (if quieter) roots.'

'Scots are not so voluble, they're more reticent, even dour. Unlike England. We have a better sense of humour, though. England in general is different – there are more people, so it's crowded.'

'There is greater interest in life abroad because Scotland

was and is a small country. England was rather inward looking.'

The physical differences in heritage between the two countries are acknowledged, but, as we have seen, these are frequently judged to be expressive of more fundamental social and cultural values:

> 'The [English] NT has more of a focus on property, whereas in Scotland NTS view land as a very important commodity.'

> 'England is more quaintly rural – the village green imagery. Scottish heritage conjures up harsher images in terms of the physical environment.'

Here, then, we have a comprehensive picture of heritage in Scotland. Despite the fact that our respondents are socially and politically conservative, they consider themselves Scottish, and have a highly developed sense of the differences in heritage between the two countries. These differences are not simply reflections of England's and Scotland's different geographies and landscapes, but of deeper social values. Heritage touches, for them, a deeper stream of social consciousness, and helps to explain its salience in late twentieth-century society.

National Identity

The relationship between heritage and people's own sense of national identity was a key part of this study from the outset. We wanted to find out how an interest in Scottish heritage, defined by life membership of the National Trust for Scotland, is connected with our respondents' sense of nationality – whether, for example, they feel more Scottish because of their involvement in Scottish heritage. To examine this, we used a question to tap aspects of nationality, which allowed us to make comparisons between our sample and the population as a whole.

The question we used was: 'We are interested to know how people living in Scotland see themselves in terms of their nationality. Which of these statements best describes how you regard yourself?' Bearing in mind the sample size of less than 100, we should not draw too many conclusions from the data themselves. It is helpful to see these in comparative perspective.

	NTS members (%)	People living in Scotland* (%)	Conservative supporters* (%)
Scottish not British	8	32	18
More Scottish than British	45	29	17
Equally Scottish and British	34	29	44
More British than Scottish	10	3	6
British not Scottish	4	6	15

* ICM/*The Scotsman*, 1992.

It is plain from these data that most of our respondents claimed dual identity, but that nearly four times as many gave priority to being Scottish (53 per cent in categories 1 and 2) as to being British (only 14 per cent in categories 4 and 5). This priority given to Scottishness cuts across the political affiliations of life members, with fully 42 per cent of Conservative voters in our sample claiming to be Scottish rather than or more than British. While it is true that Conservatives are more likely than others in our sample to give precedence to being British (24 per cent compared with 15 per cent), it is the claim to be Scottish rather than British which characterises the Trust life members we interviewed.

(a) Scottish not British

On the whole, those who say they are Scottish and not British stressed their strong sense of nationality. For example:

'I've had family roots in the country for nine centuries, and I feel that Scotland can take pride in being a nation.'

'I feel a strong sense of belonging.'

'I take pride in my Scottish heritage. I feel a Scottish identity, and I've been conscious of this from childhood, and from my parents. I particularly feel this when I'm abroad.'

'I was born in Scotland, and I've always been interested in Scottish culture, and I think Scotland gets a raw deal.'

(b) Scottish more than British

Those in the second category, namely, those who give priority to being Scottish but retain a secondary sense of Britishness,

were divided into two categories. On the one hand, there
were those who emphasised their strong sense of Scottish
identity in a way which, in their comments, is virtually indis-
tinguishable from those who said they were Scottish and not
British:

>'Perhaps because of the way I was brought up to view
>history as part of identity.'

>'Scotland is a country, and I've always seen myself as
>Scottish.'

>'I worked in England since 1938 until 1956, and now and
>again I would get upset at the assumption that Scotland
>didn't matter, such as using England for Britain. I always
>wanted to get back to Scotland and it took me nearly
>twenty years.'

>'I'm Scottish. It's a country in its own right, and hence I
>feel very Scottish'.

>'Scottish people are culturally very different to the other
>people who make up Britain.'

On the other hand, there are those who give priority to
being Scottish but assert an overt sense of Britishness, often
linking it to a political statement:

>'I'm not nationalistic. I believe in the British Union.'

>'I subscribe to the British Union, but I'm still Scottish.'

>'I'm very proud of being a Scot, although I know I am
>British. I'm not a Nationalist, but being Scottish is very
>important.'

>'I think of myself as Scottish and British, but primarily
>more Scottish than British, but I don't want separation.'

>'The British Isles are four countries, each are separate
>nationalities, but I don't believe in separation, I believe
>in the Union.'

>'My father's people came from England, but I don't
>approve of Scotland breaking away from England.'

(c) Equally Scottish and British

Those who feel equally Scottish and British tend, as we might expect, to assert their Britishness, almost taking being Scottish for granted.

> 'What a ridiculous question! I'm Scottish and I live in Britain.'

> 'I feel Scottish but wouldn't like to live in an independent nation.'

> 'I'm not a Scottish nationalist if that's what you mean.'

> 'I don't want a Scottish parliament, but I still feel Scottish. Here in the Borders we live with our neighbours, so we can't afford to hate the English.'

> 'I'm definitely not more British than Scottish, but I'm not a Scot. Nat. The world is getting smaller, and what happens in Yugoslavia is a portent of nationalism.'

Being equally Scottish and British also permits those who were born outwith Scotland but who have lived here for a considerable time to claim a measure of Scottishness. For example:

> 'I was born in England, but I've lived in Scotland for the past forty years.'

> 'Though I was born in England, I've lived here long enough so I've become Scottish, I suppose.'

> 'I can't really qualify as Scottish, but I identify as a Scot. I don't feel English or British really, and I've lived in Ireland.'

(d) British more than Scottish/not Scottish

Those who gave priority to being British asserted a stronger unionism than the others, but these were in a distinct minority in the sample (a mere 13 per cent):

> 'I would hate to be governed by the Scots.'

> 'I feel more British than anything. My three grandparents were from all parts of Britain, including Welsh and Irish.'

> 'We are citizens of Britain, but we're still Scottish. We've got to work together; Scotland couldn't be independent financially.'

'I don't like all this dividing up, it could end up like Cyprus.'

It is clear that behind the fairly unequivocal statements about national identity, there is some complex reasoning which balances the different arguments. It is noticeable that Scottishness is a characteristic much more taken for granted than Britishness, which is more closely associated with an overtly political, that is to say, unionist, stance. It is as if respondents feel they have to explain why they claim British identity whereas Scottishness is the norm. We shall examine this issue in the following section in which we focus more overtly on political attitudes and behaviour.

POLITICS AND HERITAGE

In this final section we will examine more explicitly the relationships between political behaviour and attitudes and views about heritage. Our argument has been that heritage is treated as a deeply personal rather than a political characteristic. It comes as no surprise that life members of the National Trust for Scotland are from our evidence, both culturally and politically conservative. In answer to the question, 'If there were a General Election tomorrow, which political party would you vote for?' answers were as follows (Voting patterns at the 1992 General Election in Scotland for the population as a whole are given for comparison):

	NTS life members (%)	Scotland 1992 (%)
Conservative	40.6	25.7
Liberal Democrat	26.0	13.1
Labour	10.4	39.0
SNP	4.2	21.5
Don't know/would not vote	18.8	N/A

We can conclude there is virtually no connection in our sample between being a Nationalist and a commitment to Scottish heritage, if we accept that life membership of the Trust is evidence of the latter. Fully 62 per cent had always voted for the party they mentioned, with the largest number citing their general commitment to its policies, or because they agreed with its ideology. The minority (35 per cent) who intend to change their vote largely do so because they are disillusioned with their traditional party.

The general conservative tenor of our respondents' views can be gauged from the following comments which stress the link between conservatism and tradition. All are Conservative voters.

> 'They [the Conservative party] have a love of the past and tradition.'

> 'I've been brought up with and continue to believe in their ideals. And Conservatives value tradition.'

> 'I have a strong philosophical belief in Conservatism. The accumulated beliefs of the past are more likely to be right than the passing fads.'

> 'I'm not a political person. We've always been Tory here.'

> 'We were brought up in the country, and farmers were aye Tory. Our parents voted that way, and so did we.'

Our respondents have fairly strong views about what the political parties stand for. As we might expect, the Conservative Party attracts the most favourable comments (46 per cent, to 23 per cent which were negative), with the Liberal Democrats not far behind (43 per cent and 20 per cent respectively). While Labour is viewed fairly negatively (40 per cent to 20 per cent who gave it positive mentions), the greatest opprobrium is reserved for the Scottish National Party who attract negative comments from 45 per cent of our sample, and positive ones from only 15 per cent. These data show that it is this party rather than Labour which draws the greatest degree of disapproval from our sample, which is interesting, given the plausible association between cultural and political nationalism. It is as if our respondents feel the need to deny the political implications of their commitment to 'Scottish heritage'.

The dominant motifs of the parties reflect these attitudes. The Conservatives are deemed to stand for 'individualism and self-help' (18 per cent), 'free enterprise' (18 per cent), and 'tradition and the status quo' (13 per cent). Liberal Democrats for 'consensus' (30 per cent), 'idealism' (18 per cent), 'sound social politics' (15 per cent), and, somewhat negatively, 'people who can't make their minds up' (by 15 per cent). Attitudes to Labour tend to be much more negative: 'equality' (24 per cent), 'state intervention' (16 per cent), and 'working-class interests' (16 per cent). The Scottish National Party stands for 'putting Scotland first' (20 per cent), 'independence from Westminster' (also 20 per cent), and 'destructive nationalism' (17 per cent).

The dissociation of politics from heritage is further reinforced by the responses to the question: 'Which political party in your opinion is most concerned about heritage?' Few of our respondents think that any party is more concerned about heritage than their political rivals. Thirty-two per cent think that none of the parties is particularly concerned, 23 per cent that the Conservatives are, and the same proportion could not say. Those who think parties do make a difference most frequently do so based simply on their own experience. Those who think it makes no difference argue that this is because heritage has very little political pay-off for the parties.

These comments give a flavour of the responses:

> 'The Tories are letting stuff go down the drain, and I can't see that Labour would be able to give it a priority. But none of the parties can really be trusted on heritage.' (Conservative voter)

> 'I would hope the Tories were, believing in the need to preserve the past, because they are the people who have tended to own the properties, and now need help to maintain them.' (Conservative voter)

> 'They [Labour] care for the people and the people are the heritage.' (Labour voter)

> 'Labour – I've lobbied with Labour councillors on heritage projects.' (Liberal Democrat voter)

> 'The SNP because they are the only ones concerned about *Scottish* heritage.' (SNP voter)

> 'LibDems – because they think a bit better. The Tories are influenced by the landed gentry to preserve the land for themselves.' (Liberal Democrat voter)

> 'The SNP – it makes a point of supporting heritage, as a method of making political capital.' (Conservative voter)

The lack of interest in heritage by the political parties is largely explained as an empirical issue ('None of them seem to bother' – indicated by 50 per cent of those with a view) or because other issues are deemed to be more important.

In this chapter we have tried to show how life members of the National Trust for Scotland define heritage and articulate it with a sense of history, national identity and political behaviour. It is an inevitable part of this analytical process that we have 'sliced up' our interview data to draw out the different elements. It is also important, however, that we 'reconnect' these elements to show how they hang together in the accounts of key individuals. We will do this by producing cameos of particular respondents to show just how heritage figures in their lives and perceptions, and to give a flavour as to how a concern with heritage enmeshes with other attitudes.

The first respondent, Mr L, a fifty-year-old entrepreneur living on the East coast of Scotland, is a good example of someone for whom heritage is a central life interest. He has been a life member of the Trust for twelve years without having been an ordinary member beforehand. He is not particularly active in local heritage groups as such, but has used his family capital to restore old buildings and sailing ships associated with the family firm. He is also a member of the local Chamber of Commerce, Burgess of Guild and Enterprise Trust.

What does heritage mean to him? 'It's the rekindling of the past. My family were involved in shipbuilding locally. Heritage means looking at the past and preserving it, not just the buildings but the whole culture. It carries its own sense of heritage.'

Why is heritage important? 'My own family were shipbuilders, and I grew up with a facination for ships, especially old ones. I restored trawlers and sailing ships, and then became interested in buildings. It really developed from there. If I see a building in ruins, I visualise what it might look like after it's restored.'

Heritage is more interesting to Mr L than history: 'History is concerned with issues, battles and people – things that happened, if you like. heritage refers to the way people lived. This is much more interesting.'

Heritage is also a central part of his life style and leisure patterns: 'It's central. We went to Rome, Venice, Florence to see the buildings. We organise our holidays around heritage.'

Mr L sees himself as 'more Scottish than British' but, he says, 'I don't want separation.'

Nevertheless, he has an enthusiastic sense of Scotland's heritage: 'Scotland is fascinating. It's always been on the margins and we've had to struggle to survive. So that has made us keener to leave our mark and conquer nature.'

Its heritage contrast with England's: 'Ours is very different. Scotland is very much at the frontier of survival, and that's reflected in the types of buildings – towers and fortified houses. England was the power in the land, and rather complacent.'

Mr L is a Conservative voter, but not a particularly active one: 'I traditionally have been, but I'm not very enthusiastic.'

The second account is that of Miss F, a senior partner in a firm of solicitors in the North of Scotland. She has been a life member of the Trust for seventeen years, and joined through a concern to preserve the Culloden battlesite near Inverness. She is a member of local heritage associations, and is active in local politics, having held office in the Conservative party at national level. She remains committed to that party because 'There's less dogma and more scope for individual opinion.' She considers herself equally Scottish and British, and puts 'British' because of the UK especially when abroad. Nevertheless, she expresses a strong sense of Scottish heritage: 'It's more nationalistic and vernacular, influenced by the climate and economics. We are quite proud of who we are.'

Miss F sees a strong need to protect land in Scotland: 'In Scotland we have a major land issue. Land is being sold to non-British or non-Scottish people, and it is questionable whether we should be allowing this. Maybe we should adopt Jersey rules that you have to be born here. At the moment there are a number of middle-eastern gentlemen buying large chunks of Scotland who don't stay for long. It's also the Danes, and in the 1970s it was the Dutch.'

In general terms, heritage for Miss F represents 'buildings and artefacts of the past, down through the centuries'.

The third cameo study is that of a retired teacher, Miss J, who became a life member of the Trust on her retirement, having been an ordinary member for thirty years. She is also an active member of Historic Scotland and various local antiquarian societies. She lives in the Scottish Borders and is especially active in the local branch of the Trust. Miss J tends to look out for heritage sites while on holiday, a reflection of her strong commitment to heritage generally: 'Things about our country need preserving for the next generation, and we have a duty to preserve them for those to come.' She sees an important distinction between heritage and history: 'History is more theoretical. It studies what has happened in the past, and it's not really concerned about what remains, merely what happened then. Heritage on the other hand is primarily concerned with conservation. it's more personal.'

Particularly important to her is the need to protect heritage: 'There's a need to preserve the past, we have feelings of nostalgia for the past, and we're horrified to find them destroyed. You can destroy the past with concrete especially by commercialisation.'

Miss J gives priority to being Scottish: 'I taught in Germany and objected to being called English. I feel very Scottish.' Politically, she is a Liberal 'because they seem more intellectual and middle of the way'. What about the SNP? 'I'm not very fond of the leader of the SNP. I feel Scottish but I feel independence would be a step backward. We're not strong enough to be financially independent.'

The final cameo is of Mr B, a musician and composer in his forties who lives in the West of Scotland. He has been a life member of the Trust for fifteen years largely because his family had contacts with it. He is not a member of other heritage groups, and tends to visit Trust properties with friends.

He articulates a strong connection between cultural and political nationalism. Heritage is important because: 'Heritage is bound up with Scottish culture and identity'. And heritage means 'all aspects of human life which contribute to make Scotland what it is'. Scotland's heritage, he believes, reflects the fact that it is a small nation, and it differs from English heritage insofar as 'English heritage has a strong sense of roots in feudalism; Scottish heritage is more democratic'.

He considers himself to be Scottish not British because 'my family roots are in this country for nine centuries, and I feel that Scotland can take pride in being a nation.' He intends to vote SNP at the next election.

CONCLUSION

We began this chapter by setting out two plausible assumptions to be examined. The first of these, that heritage was largely an institutional imposition which had no deep significance for life members in our sample, was not sustained. Heritage is not a trivial issue foisted on them unwittingly or unwillingly. The majority of our respondents could readily distinguish heritage from history, and through that distinction conveyed a strong sense of lineage and inheritance. The objects of heritage appear to them to have the power to confer identity, and act as vehicles for bringing the past into the present, in such a way that the histories of ancestors or mythological events become an intimate part of their present identity. In other words, heritage has an identity-conferring status, not simply (or even) in collective and national terms, but in individual and personal ones.

The second hypothesis we set out to examine was the putative link between politics and heritage. In Scotland in the last thirty years there has been a revival of both cultural and political nationalism, and it seemed to us plausible at the outset that this was to be expressed in and through heritage. However, it was clear that people in our sample were undoubtedly Conservative and that the Scottish National Party made little headway among this group. Indeed, the group's antipathy was reserved for the nationalist party and its seeming capture of the Scottish issue. Our respondents see themselves as Scots first and foremost, and point to major differences between Scottish and English heritage. Conservatives in our sample are twice as likely to acknowledge this as not. Clearly their political identity does not deny their cultural or national one. In the final chapter we will explore this apparent conundrum by relating it to a broader and older conception of Scottishness, and show how in many respects heritage is the key to unlock it.

Chapter 8

Heritage in a Stateless Nation

In this book we have tried to show that the heritage industry in Scotland is deeply rooted, and that it has much raw material to play with. Selling 'Scotland' is a multimillion-pound industry with major players in the private and public sectors. All conspire in different ways to turn Scotland's heritage to advantage. At the same time there is considerable ambivalence about the Scottish heritage industry and the iconography at its disposal. As we have seen in Chapter 3, there is suspicion that much of what passes for heritage is fabricated, and further, that it has a negative psychological effect on Scots by confining them to stereotypes of themselves which are judged to have adverse political consequences. In orthodox nationalist circles, for example, much of what is passed off as Scottish culture – tartanry and tourism – is judged to be *ersatz* and debilitating. The judgement is that just as sporting images of Scotland generate 'ninety-minute nationalists', so the heritage and tourist industries have created music-hall Scots and short-bread-tin images of Scotland.

The nub of our argument in this book has been that heritage is significant in Scotland because it rests on a national and cultural dimension. Heritage is a reflection of nationalism in its widest sense. It may not, and frequently does not, carry political overtones, as the observations of life members of the National Trust for Scotland make clear. You do not have to be a Scottish nationalist to be a cultural nationalist although, as we will argue later in this chapter, it has become increasingly more difficult to separate the cultural and political realms in modern Scotland.

We will elaborate our argument in full for the connection

between heritage, nationalism and identity later in this final chapter. First, it is necessary to explore the significance of three key heritage icons of Scotland, Edinburgh Castle, Bannockburn and Culloden. The selection of these for discussion requires some explanation. Edinburgh Castle is by far the most visited heritage site in Scotland, and has come to 'stand for' Scotland in much national iconography. The other two sites encapsulate the battle iconography of the country, and have become sites of pilgrimage as much as tourism. Their geographical significance is also important. Culloden 'represents' Highland Scotland, while Bannockburn, the site of Scotland's national independence, is on the cusp of Lowland and Highland Scotland. Edinburgh, as the southern, national capital, completes the iconographic triangle. We will try to show that each of these icons cannot be read simply, but carry multiple 'gazes', to use Urry's term. In other words, there are different ways of viewing these icons these 'terrains of power' (Cosgrove, 1994) – and in many ways it is the conflict between the gazes which is most interesting.

EDINBURGH CASTLE

Edinburgh Castle[1] is the only one of the three sites which is owned directly by the state under the auspices of Historic Scotland. The others are run by the National Trust for Scotland in its role as voluntary guardian of Scotland's heritage. The Castle is described simply in Historic Scotland's guide as follows:

> In the centre of Edinburgh. This most famous of Scottish castles has a complex building history. The oldest part dates from the Norman period; there is a Great Hall built by James IV; the Half Moon battery was built by the Regent Morton in the late 16th century; the Scottish national War memorial was formed after the First World War. The castle houses the crown jewels (Honours) of Scotland and the famous 15th century gun Mons Meg. (*A Visitor's Guide to Scotland's Heritage*:11)

Edinburgh Castle has been a refuge, a fortress, a seat of government. It has been a centre for the Scottish arts, a prison, a barracks, the home of royalty, a hospital. It has even been parade ground and army headquarters. Now it is a tourist site. Undoubtedly the best-known icon for Edinburgh as well as for

FIGURE 14 Edinburgh Castle, Scotland's icon.

Scotland, it captures the country in a singular way. This famil-
iarity helps to sell a range of products, and it is by far the
central tourist attraction of Scotland with just under 1 million
visitors a year. Tourists flock to 'do' the castle because they are
told that it conveys the essence of the place.

It is, however, a complex icon. Castles are highly potent

symbols of power and place. Occupying commanding sites, they symbolise authority, and frequently embody struggles for power. Nor is this simply a pre-modern phenomenon when power actually resided within the castle (and had to be defended). When the Communist regime fell in Czechoslovakia in 1989, the rallying cry of the crowd was 'Havel to the Castle!'. Havel was a reference to the leading dissident who was to become president. His entry into the Castle potently represented the overthrow of the old regime. Edinburgh Castle does not have the same evocations for Scottish nationalists, although since the Castle authorities, that is to say, the British army, installed in 1992 a bigger flagpole from which to fly an even bigger Union Flag, there has been adverse comment in the press about this uniquely Scottish icon appearing to give undue political support to the British Union.

Other controversies have helped to reveal the Castle's meanings. In 1986, for example, an architectural firm was commissioned to carry out a feasibility study into the improvement of tourist facilities there. This uncovered a deeper controversy about 'the great castle debate' which had been running in and through the local press for some time. In the early 1970s Liberal councillors had identified a possible conflict between the needs of tourists and those of the army stationed there. The complaint was that too much of the castle was inaccessible to the public, and that the requirements of the two groups did not mix. The 1980s saw proposals about improving access to the Castle, remodelling the Esplanade, separating tourist and army access, and restoring facilities (like a tearoom) after an absence of some years (the previous one having been damaged by a bomb planted by persons unknown). The consultants' report unleashed considerable opposition, especially to the idea that a largely hidden, semi-submerged escalator be built to give access from a bus park. The Secretary of State for Scotland who had commissioned the report expressed concern that the proposals 'may prove to be controversial, or unaffordable, or both' (*Edinburgh Evening News*, 15 July 1986). The local newspaper which had campaigned for improvements thought that the scheme 'envisages more dramatic change than [we] have campaigned for', and letter-writers to its columns tended to agree with one correspondent who commented: If visitors wish to go to Edinburgh's most prominent building, as they have done for hundreds of years, what is to hinder them walking up to the castle from the Royal Mile?' (*Edinburgh Evening News*, 30 July 1986). (Visitors had only been encouraged to visit the castle since the 'discovery' of the crown jewels by Walter Scott in 1818.)

The outcome of this report was that little was done, apart from building a tearoom and shop within the Castle precincts (itself a controversial act). It is likely that it was not the cost which prevented this, but the fact that the Castle was a latent symbol, and when the conflict was crystalised between the 'army' and 'tourists', it was the latter who became the 'other'. It may seem strange that the military representatives of the British state would be preferred in this way, but it is important to remember the role of the Scottish soldier in both imperial history and Scottish consciousness (reinforced by the annual military tattoo). In the last resort, it is not the army which is the alien, but the tourist. This is reinforced by the fact that the Castle is not only the site of military museums, but also the Scottish War Memorial. It is possible to visit the Memorial without paying to see the Castle, although this is frequently viewed with suspicion by the warders who guard admission, and it is not uncommon for visitors to the War Memorial to be escorted to and from the site lest they slip into the other, paying, mode of 'tourist'.

For most Scots, the Edinburgh Castle remains a latent symbol which does not need to be thought of overmuch, except when it becomes the object of controversy. Neither is its significance static. At the time of the 'improvements' debacle in 1986, the Castle authorities (the army administration) refused to allow a concert on the Esplanade by the singer Rod Stewart. By the early 1990s this policy had been reversed so that the Gaelic rock group Runrig were regular performers, as were other groups. (In 1994 Runrig were also permitted to play at Stirling Castle, another army barracks/tourist attraction.) Scots do not labour over details of their castle. It is as if it has been objectified, decontextualised, and has come to exist as an end in itself. This does not mean that the Castle is emptied of meaning. For Scots it is historically grounded and connects them to the powerful myth of the past. Through the medium of tourism it is also experienced by the vast numbers who visit it each year under the tourist gaze. When discussions take place about improving the Castle for tourists, then the issue of who the Castle belongs to is raised. The 1980s' feasibility study activated local/Scot versus foreign/tourist gazes. It remains to be seen under what conditions a Scottish 'gaze' versus a British one might emerge. In 1994 it seemed more likely that the oppositional force would become a proposal to 'privatise' the Castle which emanated from within the British Treasury.

BANNOCKBURN[2]

It comes perhaps as a surprise to discover that the site of Scotland's most significant battle is in the care of a voluntary organisation, the National Trust for Scotland, rather than that of the state. It is even more surprising to discover its importance to Ian Lang, the Conservative Secretary of State for Scotland. In a newspaper series which asked prominent people to identify and explain at which event they would have liked to have been a 'fly on the wall', Lang said: 'I would have liked to have been on the field of Bannockburn on 23–24 June 1314, to see the most decisive battle in Scottish history: the victory of Robert the Bruce's Scots over Edward II's English army' (*The Scotsman*, 27 November 1993).

These phenomena may well strike many people as surprising because we expect the state to be in direct control of its politically sacred sites (think of the battlegrounds of France or the United States), and we are surprised that a prominent Unionist should associate himself so strongly with a sacred nationalist place. On reflection we should not be surprised, given the separation of the cultural and political domains in Scotland, and the evidence from our survey of National Trust for Scotland life members that, at least, historically it has been possible to be both culturally nationalist and politically Conservative.

The Bannockburn battlefield is described in the Trust's guide as follows:

> The Bannockburn heritage centre is situated at one of the most important historic sites in Scotland. On the battlefield nearby, in June 1314, King Robert the Bruce routed the forces of King Edward II to win freedom for the Scots from English domination. A few yards from the Centre is the famous Borestone site which by tradition was Bruce's command post before the battle. This site is enclosed by the Rotunda focusing on the approach route

of the English army to its objective – Stirling Castle. The
Rotunda was inaugurated by her Majesty the Queen in
June 1964, when she also unveiled the equestrian statue
of Bruce by Pilkington Jackson which was presented to
the Trust.

The guidebook goes on to observe that the Earl of Elgin, the
head of the Bruce family, helped to raise funds in 1930 to purchase 58 acres around the site, which was extended 30 years
later. The heritage centre is visited by nearly 60,000 people a
year (around half of those visiting Culloden near Inverness),
although there is no count of the numbers visiting the memorial itself which is free (the local district council estimates
that around 250,000 make the visit annually). Bannockburn is
surrounded by post-war council houses on the plain of
Stirling, leading the Scottish Tourist Board's consultants to
observe that 'it lacked the magic of the real'. The battlefield
consists of a flagstaff erected next to the Borestone in 1889, a
rotunda and memorial built in 1957, and the statue of Bruce
erected in 1964 the 650th anniversary of the battle. The
attempt is to create a spiritual heritage space, despite the fact
that the wider environment is not particularly conducive to it.
More generally, Bannockburn is one point in a key triangle of
a Scottish historical landscape with Stirling Castle and the
Wallace monument (erected in 1856) being the other nodes.

Bannockburn has also acquired political significance since
the 1950s when the nascent Scottish National Party began to
hold annual rallies at the site. As the Party's fortunes have
waxed, it appears to have become more ambivalent about the
annual pilgrimage and, in 1982, at the height of a period of
internal feuding between Right and Left, and fundamentalists
and gradualists, there was a proposal to discontinue the event.
In 1990 the party held its rally in Edinburgh, and in 1994
cancelled it to concentrate on the Monklands East by-election.
On the other hand, the more extreme group *Siol nan
Gaidheal* (seed of the Gael) which was expelled from the
Scottish National Party in 1982 has attempted to re-symbolise
the battlefield as an icon of Scottish nationhood. Given the
relatively small numbers visiting the heritage centre (it is on a
par with Walter Scott's Abbotsford House near Melrose, and
Camperdown Wildlife Centre in Dundee), and the ambivalence of the nationalist political party to make it a sacred site,

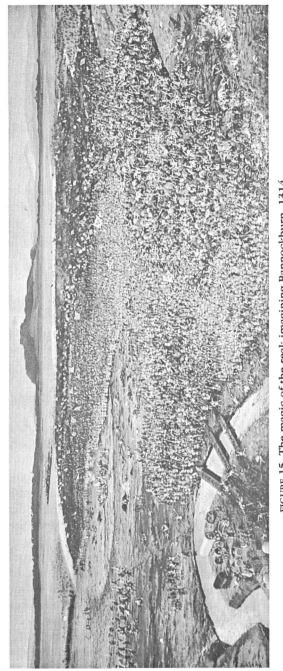

FIGURE 15 The magic of the real: imagining Bannockburn, 1314.

FIGURE 16 The real Bannockburn, 1983.

Bannockburn has not (yet) become a mass identity symbol for Scots.

In recent years there have been attempts to re-mythologise Bannockburn, most obviously by radical nationalists (like Siol nan Gaidheal), but also by militarist-religious groups like the Knights Templar who claim to have played a key role in Bruce's victory in 1314. This coupling with Scotland's militaristic past connects to a strong identification with myths about the fighting qualities of Scots, from Pictish resistance to the Romans, through to the celebration of Scottish regiments in the British army. Such is the power of this identification that even the Scottish National Party has lent its support to a campaign to save the Scottish regiments in the British army from amalgamation in the 1990s.

As we have seen, Bannockburn has traditionally been a shared icon across political parties in Scotland, from Nationalists to Unionists (like Ian Lang). This consensus was undermined from the Right after the Conservative Party won control of Stirling District Council in 1992. This council while under Labour control had adopted the logo of Bruce's statue with Stirling Castle in the background. The leader of the incoming Tory group instigated a change, with the comment: 'A knight on horseback does not give the impression of an open accessible council that cares about its customers' (*Stirling News*, 13 August 1992). In response, both the Scottish National Party and Labour pointed out the commercial absurdity of surrendering a unique weapon in the programme of economic regeneration (*The Scotsman*, 18 August 1992). This episode might well stand as an exemplar of the diminishing political strength of the Conservative Party in Scotland, namely, that despite Ian Lang's claim for the linearity of the Union of 1707 with Bannockburn of 1314, it has failed to associate with key aspects of Scottish iconography. Bannockburn as heritage is not a guarantee of political success in Scotland, but to deny its sacredness seems too much like political suicide.

CULLODEN

The third heritage monument which is central to Scottish identity is the battlefield at Culloden[3] – on Drumossie moor near Inverness. Like Bannockburn, it is 'in the care' of the National Trust for Scotland who describe it in their guidebook thus:

Scene of the last major battle fought on mainland Britain.
The final Jacobite uprising ended here on 16 April 1746,
when the army of Prince Charles Edward Stuart was
crushed by the Government forces led by the Duke of
Cumberland. The battlefield has been restored to its
original moorland state and the adjacent Old Leanach
Cottage, which survived the battle being fought around
it, is open to the public. Also in the Trust's care are the
graves of the Clans, the Well of the Dead, the Memorial
Cairn, the Cumberland Stone and the Field of the English.
The Visitor Centre has been enlarged and improved to
include a colourful historical display, auditorium with
multi-lingual audio-visual programme (English, French,
German, Italian and Japanese), study room, bookshop and
self-service restaurant with home baking. (*NTS Guide
1994*:26)

The heritage centre is visited by around 124,000 people a
year, not including the non-paying, and non-recorded, visitors
who visit the battlefield itself. Culloden is a site with considerable mythopoeic qualities. Historians have pointed out that
the struggle took the form more of a civil war within Scotland
than a national fight for independence between Scotland and
England, yet the prevailing myth is that it represented a military defeat for Scotland and its final incorporation into the
'English' state. As Colin McArthur points out in an analysis of
its abiding significance, it is an excellent example of a
powerful and historically deep-seated pre-existing narrative
which shapes the tone and substance of cultural work. Above
all, Culloden lets flow a 'deluge of tearful, breast-beating
elegaicism' (1994:1).

Despite the 'ancient' character of the site, McArthur shows
that it is of quite recent provenance. The existing commemorative cairn dates only from 1881, and it was not until 1944
that it passed from private hands to the care of the National
Trust for Scotland. Since then, the Trust has steadily acquired
more and more of the adjacent land – over 100 acres in 1981
from the Forestry Commission, and in 1989 the 'Field of the
English' (sic), the battle-stance of the government army. The
Trust has embarked on a programme of removing the trees
from the site to restore the battlefield to its 'original' state, and
with it 'the magic of the real'. This 'magic' is a recent creation.
McArthur shows that the elegaic quality dates from the second

FIGURE 17 Heritage reconstructed: David Morier's *An Incident in the Rebellion of 1745* was painted within a few years of the battle using captured Jacobite soldiers.

half of the nineteenth century. In the 1770s the Culloden defeat was deemed to be a victory for 'progress', and it was not until the 1830s that it took on the aura of a romantic defeat following the 'symbolic appropriation' of the Highlands by Victorians. For example, the newspaper, the *Inverness Courier*, carried only one reference to Culloden pre-1822, and a mere four between 1825 and 1841. The centenary of 1846, McArthur comments, was marked in a carnivalesque rather than an elegaic frame, and while the foundation stone of a commemorative cairn was laid in that year, it was not built until 1881.

The second half of the nineteenth century saw a major creation of 'heritage', and with it all the necessary institutional apparatus – the National Museum of Antiquities of Scotland in 1851, the Royal Scottish Museum in 1854, the National Gallery in 1859, and the Scottish National Portrait Gallery in 1889, and the Royal Commission on Ancient and Historical Monuments in 1908 (following the Ancient Monuments Protection Act of 1882). When this Royal Commission was created (a few months before its sister organisations in England and Wales), its remit ran as follows:

> to make an inventory of the ancient and historical monuments and constructions connected with or illustrative of the contemporary culture, civilisation and conditions of the life of the people of Scotland from the earliest times to the year 1707 such as:
>
> 1. sepulchral cairns and other burial places;
> 2. forts, camps, earthworks, brochs, crannogs, and other defensive works, either overground or underground;
> 3. stone circles and standing stones, and rock surfaces with incised or other sculptings;
> 4. architectural structures, ecclesiastical and secular, whether ruinous or in use, including sculptured or inscribed memorials;
>
> and to specify those which seem most worthy of preservation. (Dunbar, 1992:18)

This flourishing of national iconography drew on the 'discovery' of the Celtic/Saxon distinction (discussed extensively by Chapman, 1992), and the revival of sentimental Jacobitism to such an extent that writers like Pittock claim that it had and has major radical potential in Scottish culture (Pittock, 1991). McArthur comments that the choosing of a cairn as a form of commemoration avoided affiliation with other artistic forms with politico-religious overtones. (Anything in the Gothic style might have had overly Catholic or Episcopalian associations.)

In all three heritage sites we can see iconographic ambiguities. Culloden has taken on an elegaic quality, through both the defeat of the 'real' Scotland, and the place's association with Jacobitism which, as we have seen, is still a powerful myth north of the border. What was a military defeat has been turned into a moral victory, overcoming contrary historical evidence that whatever else it was about, it was not a Scottish-English battle. Now it has come to stand for Scotland, especially as it has acquired the patina of heritage. Its power as an icon derives from its contemporary cultural-political meaning rather than from its eighteenth-century significance.

It is interesting too that Culloden attracts twice as many paying visitors to its heritage centre as Bannockburn, which, although it too has acquired meanings which are modern rather than ancient, does not appear to have the same resonance in contemporary political-cultural life. It is of course less easy to reconstruct the site into a visualisation of its fourteenth-century image. Removing the apparatus of twentieth-century living – houses and motorways – is not as easy as clearing away trees. Nevertheless, Bannockburn too has taken on new meanings. It stands for Independence which was not lost in war but in peace. For nationalists it represents what was fought for and won, and has to be fought for again (this time peacefully). Its legacy of Independence was, it is argued, betrayed by a 'parcel of rogues in a nation' who have their contemporary exemplars in modern politicians. Bannockburn stands for the possibility of being 'a nation once again'. Scotland's historic nationhood as represented by this site can be 'imagined' (in Benedict Anderson's phrase (1983)) without too much difficulty.

Finally, the central Scottish icon – Edinburgh Castle – attracts almost eighteen times more paying visitors than Bannockburn, yet it too is a muted icon. Like all castles it is by definition a terrain of power, but this power is contested and unclear. As a tourist icon it 'belongs' to its visitors, but, as the controversy over its refurbishment in the 1980s makes plain, it is not the inalienable possession of tourists. Neither, however, does it belong unequivocally to the Scottish nation, as it is dominated by the military representatives of the British state. It is the Union flag not the saltire which flies on its ramparts. It is not clear who the army has the power over, what it is for, and what it is against. Despite its strong association with the British state, it is not (yet) contested by nationalists in Scotland as a symbol of alien power.

ETHNICITY, IDENTITY AND HERITAGE

'He's dreaming now,' said Tweedledee, 'and what do you think he's dreaming about? Why, about you! And if he left off dreaming about you, where do you suppose you'd be?'

'Where I am now, of course,' said Alice.

'Not you!' Tweedledum retorted contemptuously. 'You'd be nowhere. Why, you're only a sort of thing in his dream!'

'If that there king was to wake,' added Tweedledum, 'you'd go out – bang – just like a candle!'

'I shouldn't!' Alice exclaimed indignantly. 'Besides, if I'm only a sort of thing in his dream, what are you, I should like to know?'

(Lewis Carroll, *Through the Looking Glass*)

Heritage has uncommon power in Scotland because it is a stateless nation. We do not accept, as many writers do, that only formal political power, ultimately sovereignty, is the only guarantee of nationhood. The political slogan 'A nation once again' is inaccurate because since the Union of 1707 Scotland never ceased to be a nation. In large part its institutional autonomy as a distinctive civil society, with its holy trinity of law, education and religion, has helped to underwrite the continuing and strong sense of national identity north of the border (Paterson, 1994). While most Scots accept some form of dual identity – that it is possible to be both Scottish and British – it is clear that they are six times more likely to give Scottishness priority over Britishness. Even Conservative voters in Scotland are three times more likely to do so.

And yet, a persistent theme of the years since 1707 has been the fear, or rather the threat, of submersion into a much bigger British state in which Scots are demographically out-numbered by around 10:1. The fact that this state is in consti-tutional terms a unitary rather than a federal one adds to this sense of potential loss of identity. Like Alice's dream, what if Scotland went out like a candle? Is it only imagining Scotland that keeps it alive? Does it only exist in dreamtime? As we have tried to show in this book, Scotland is rich in dreams. There is no shortage of myth-making icons with which to imagine Scotland. The importance of tourism, and around it the heritage industry, gives commercial expression to nation-al identity.

We might consider Scotland's heritage in its iconographic form as 'inalienable wealth', a concept borrowed from the social anthropologist Marcel Mauss to describe cultural objects which still attach to their original owners even when they have become circulated among others. Annette Weiner's account of inalienable wealth has direct relevance to Scottish heritage:

> Inalienable possessions are imbued with affective quali-ties that are expressions of the value an object has when it is kept by its owners and inherited within the same family or descent group. Age adds value, as does the ability to keep the object against all the exigencies that might force a person or group to release it to others. The primary value of inalienability, however, is expressed through the power these objects have to define who one is in a historical sense. The object acts as a vehicle for bringing past times into the present, so that the histories of ancestors, titles, or mythological events become an intimate part of a person's present identity. To lose this claim to the past is to lose part of who one is in the present. (1985:210)

In Scotland the weight of identity has conventionally been placed since the Union on cultural rather than political mat-ters. We might reflect, for example, on Ian Lang's claim that Bannockburn is the key event in Scottish history at which he would most wish to have been present. It may seem somewhat strange to find the representative of a Unionist party claiming this sacred nationalist icon. The key to resolving the apparent contradiction lies in Lang's final comments:

> From then on [after Bannockburn] as a nation, we have never looked back. So much so that it was our king James IV (sic) who succeeded to the throne of England in 1603: and it was his great grand-daughter – another Scot – who oversaw the Union of the nations of Scotland and England in 1707. This is the real legacy of Bannockburn, and it is one of which I am very proud. That is why I would like to have been there in 1314. (*The Scotsman*, 27 November 1993)

This claim that Unionism and Nationalism are reconciled in this way may strike those of us of the late twentieth century as somewhat odd. We have grown accustomed to an antithesis between the two, at least as they are expressed in conventional political forms – that is to say the Conservative Party and the Scottish National Party. The dominant wisdom in contemporary Scotland is that Scottishness and Conservativism are strange bed-fellows. In a poll in August 1990, four out of every five Scots questioned agreed with the statement that 'The Conservative Party is mainly an English party with little relevance to Scotland'. Even a majority (56 per cent) of Conservatives questioned agreed with this statement. However, as we saw in Chapter 7, there is no inevitable contradiction between these views. The dominant view of our sample of life members of the National Trust for Scotland showed them to be, by definition, cultivators of Scottish heritage while at the same time being of Conservative political disposition.

Recent historical work, moreover, shows that 'unionist-nationalism' has a central pedigree in Scottish life. Graeme Morton (1993) has argued convincingly that in the mid-nineteenth century a view prevailed that it was only because Scotland won and retained her Independence in 1314 that she was able to enter the Union of 1707 as an equal partner, with England, in the British state. So, the National Association for the Vindication of Scottish Rights, founded in 1853, expressed, for example, a sense of patriotism which allowed it to proclaim admiration for its partner, England. Similarly, the erection of the monument in Edinburgh to Walter Scott which was begun in 1833 stresses the Scottish contribution to

English heritage. Perhaps more surprisingly (given Scott's political Toryism) those who raised funds for monuments to the two prime Scottish patriots, William Wallace and Robert the Bruce, did so by stressing a contribution to the Union. The Earl of Elgin who claimed descent from Bruce took the chair at the inauguration in 1856 of the movement to build the Wallace monument, spoke in the following terms:

> if the Scottish people have been able to form an intimate union and association with a people more wealthy and more numerous than themselves, without sacrificing one jot of their neutral independence and liberty – these great results are due to the glorious struggle which was commenced on the plain of Stirling and consummated on that of Bannockburn . . . And, gentlemen, if time permitted, I would even undertake to show that it is the successful struggle carried on under Bruce and Wallace that it is that the Union between Scotland and England has not only been honourable to the former but profitable to the latter . . . [With reference to the troubles in America and Ireland] I believe, therefore, that if the whole truth were to be told in this matter, we might show that England owes to Wallace and Bruce a debt of obligation only second to that which is due to them by Scotland. (Morton, 1993:215)

Such a discourse seems to contemporary Scottish ears anachronistic, because political developments in the twentieth century make the separation of 'nation' from 'state' less and less possible. We have grown used to the state encroaching on civil society, and civil society making increasing demands on the state. The cultural and political dimensions become increasingly fused. We have seen in our study that there is a considerable body of opinion which celebrates Scottish heritage while giving allegiance to Conservatism. We have seen too that heritage is not some distant cultural hobby, but has the power to define who one is in a historical sense. Heritage in Scotland has the power not only to mobilise politically but to define who people are to themselves and others. In this respect Scotland's past has a vibrant if indeterminate future.

The Iconography of Place

Heritage is a powerful commercial weapon, reinforced by the view of the Scottish Tourist Board that there is no business in Scotland which does not benefit financially from tourism (*The Scotsman*, 4 February 1992). There is little doubt that Scotland has marketing integrity. In 1994 the Scottish Tourist Board appointed a new chief executive who had learned his trade in food marketing. 'Scotland is a very rich country in the sense that it has many points of uniqueness; whisky, textiles, meat,' he said, 'They all have in common the environment' (*The Herald*, 29 March 1994).

When it comes to tourism, the Scottish tourist industry presents Scotland as a 'land out of time', as an 'enchanted fortress in a disenchanted world' (Rojek, 1993:181), and the 'real' Scotland is bracketed out. The images seem to overpower the reality of Scotland. If Scotland is presented as a 'land of dreamtime' then this is compounded by the dissociation of the cultural from the political realms. The marketing of dreams is, of course, a ploy common to all tourist bodies in all countries. What is the point of selling the same as back home?

Scotland has one major feature which embellishes its presentation, its assocation with the 'wilderness'. And wilderness is presented as the antithesis of culture, as the quintessential escape area in modern society. After all, the claim is that Scotland is the last great European wilderness. We also know, of course, that much of this wilderness is fabricated. The last great wilderness in Europe tag is achieved in spite (or perhaps because of) the exploitation of timber, minerals, livestock, wild life and water power. The key to the 'wilderness' tag is that it is a social construction. By the end of the eighteenth century the Highlands were discovered as a scenic game park replete with 'nature and its game – salmon, deer and grouse. Such has been the reconstruction of the Highlands in particular that we find it impossible to 'see' them in any other way. They have, in Womack's words, been 'colonised by an empire of signs' (1989:1). He points out that whereas 'botanically no doubt 'calluna vulgaris' [heather] is exactly as it was in the 1730s, semiotically it has been irrevocably hybridised' (ibid.:2), that is to say, it has been given a social meaning evoking Highland and, through it, Scottish culture. In other words, the Highlands were romanticised, they were the result of a process 'at an identifiable point in time, in response to specific ideological requirements and contradictions which are both exhibited and disguised by its eventual form' (ibid.:2).

From even a cursory reading of Scottish and Highland history it is clear that the cultural construction of the region was the result of political and commercial forces, often acting together. What undoubtedly had been a distinctive region in geographical, linguistic and economic terms before and after the Union of 1707 became invested with cultural qualities and meanings. These meanings were not generated randomly but were the result of double defeats for Highland Gaelic Scotland – first from a Lowland-dominated Scottish state, and after 1745 and the Culloden defeat, by a wider British political system. The distinction between the Lowlands and the Highlands has always been a shifting and contentious one in practice, given that the linguistic, economic and geographical boundaries do not coincide with each other. There is, however, little doubting the cultural divide in the sense that the Highlands were invested with the symbolism of being 'foreign' and exotic. The irony is that by the end of the eighteenth century Scotland as a whole was being colonised by this powerful sign.

The period between Culloden and the beginning of the nineteenth century saw the pacification of the Highlands under the aegis of 'Improvement' (Womack, 1989). Highland life was judged to have no ideological autonomy other than the one foisted on it by the wider state, and an 'associative web' was spun by the politically dominant Whigs to equate its opponents as Tories-Jacobites-Highlanders-Scots. Womack comments:

> That all Scots wear tartan, are devoted to bagpipe music, are moved by the spirit of clanship, and supported Bonnie Prince Charlie to a man – all these libels of 1762 live on as items in the Scottish tourist package of the twentieth century. (1989:20)

Some, like Murray Pittock, argue that there is little that is 'libelous' in this association insofar as the Stuart Jacobite myth has continued to carry much greater political potency than it is usually given credit for. Pittock argues that the loss of the Stuarts (his spelling) was closely bound up with the loss of

Scottish independence as a whole. Jacobitism provided a continuing relevant critique of Scotland in the Union, 'as well as
being a potent myth-creator and 'myth-kitty' for the Scottish
identity' (1991:151). In other words, having lost its political
independence, Scotland mobilised the Jacobite myth which
fed into both Right-wing and Left-wing causes. The myth,
Pittock argues, retains a powerful mythopoeic quality in the
Scottish imagination. Others, notably Christopher Smout, are
less convinced that Jacobitism was such a reservoir of social
and political dissent in Scotland, given the significant politico-
religious claims of the Protestant ascendancy north of the
border (Smout, 1994).

Be that as it may, it is clear that the Highlands in particular
and Scotland in general have come to be associated with alternative cultures. Womack comments:

> Processes which promoted capitalist accumulation in the
> lowlands through economic integration with England
> simultaneously exaggerated Highland difference . . . For
> the Scottish bourgeoisie, therefore, the Highlands had
> the aspect of a residual historical nation . . . so the
> Highlands acquired the role of representing Scotland 'for
> the English'. (1989:148)

As Scotland was becoming industrialised in the late eighteenth century, so the symbols and myths of Highland
Scotland were appropriated by Lowland Scots as evidence of a
distinctive culture. The irony was that the Highlands had been
reviled by Lowland Scots as barbaric, backward and savage.
Other writers, notably Chapman (1978 and 1992) as we
described in Chapter 3, showed how this cultural distinction
was given linguistic substance through the mobilising of racial
stereotyping of 'Celts' and 'Anglo-Saxons'. Scotland as a whole
settled for a Celtic or Gaelic definition in contradistinction to
England, and 'the face that Scotland turns to the rest of the
world is, in many respects, a Highland face' (1978:9).

By the end of the eighteenth century, then, the elements
were in place for the construction of modern tourist icons.
From then on, and especially in their literary exploitation by
Walter Scott in the early decades of the nineteenth century,
the Highlands in particular became the focus for 're-discovery'
of the wilderness. Mairi MacArthur observes that visitors in
1883 remarked that 'the farther we went the more we were

reminded that to travel in Scotland is to travel through the Waverley novels' (1993:23). Guidebooks and travel memoirs highlighted three themes: the wild grandeur of the landscape, remoteness and peace, with a dash of romantic (preferably tragic) history.

In some circumstances landscapes may have to be re-imagined, and even re-drawn. Donald Horne (1984) draws our attention to the exhibition mounted by the National Gallery of Scotland in 1978, entitled 'The Discovery of Scotland: the Appreciation of Scottish Scenery through Two Centuries of Painting'. The exhibition contained two landscape paintings by the eighteenth-century artist Paul Sandby. The first, painted in the mid-eighteenth century, was the kind of view demanded by the market at the time showing straightforward and realistic detail. The second is an engraving made thirty years later in which the same mountains are made higher and more rugged, with fir trees and a man in a kilt added for greater 'authenticity'. Before the transformation, mountains are shown as barren and desolate, while after, they come to symbolise the spirit of a tough and rugged people.

These, then, enter into the elements of the modern heritage industry in Scotland. It is clear that its iconography relates closely to historical, economic and political events in the last 300 years of Scottish and British history. It is not difficult to show that the 'emptiness' of the landscape is a fairly modern phenomenon, and that it results from a system of double oppression, first by lowland Scots and then by the British state after Culloden in 1746. In showing that the landscape and its iconography are not 'natural' it is not necessary to claim that it is simply an empty vessel into which post-modernity can pour any meanings it has to hand. The ones it has result from a complex of economic and political processes to which they can be related.

We are dealing here with what the geographer Denis Cosgrove has called 'terrains of power' (1994). He observes: 'Nature, landscape and environment are semiotic signifiers, deeply embedded in the cultural constitution of individual European nations and integral to the distinctive identities of Europe's peoples'. The point he is making is that these 'constitutions' relate to systems of power, not in any predetermined way, but as ideological constructs which reflect, often in attentuated ways, its operation. The 'imagined geography' of England focuses on 'woods of downland pastures of South-East England's 'home counties', 'Constable' country in Suffolk and Wiltshire water meadows, and the hawthorn-squared ploughlands of the Midland counties'. On the other hand, 'Welsh and Scottish nationalisms have constructed their own meaning from mountain landscapes, valleys and glens, drawing as heavily on the natural world as upon their separate language to construct differences from England'.

Here Cosgrove is making a crucial point. It is not simply that the iconography of the Highlands or of Scotland carries a unique message which speaks only to the powerful who might use it as a holiday playground. The iconography 'leaks' in such a way that it can be turned to radical uses, in respective nationalist and oppositional discourses. 'The wee bit hill and glen' of the anthem 'Flower of Scotland' may make weak poetry but strong politics. The ability of different political forces to 'read' into the landscape a suitable message is the key here. It is not that only one message can be read off the heritage signs, or that the viewer can read in what he or she wants. The signification is not 'depthless'. Rather, as Cosgrove comments the imaginative bonds between 'nature' and 'nation' are deep across Europe (1994).

The links between nature and nation, between landscape and lineage, have been made by a number of authors. Raymond Williams, for example, in his classic account, *The Country and the City* (1973), discussed the importance of place as ideological constructs. 'Country' and 'city' come to stand for powerful expressions of human experience:

> On the country has gathered the idea of the natural way of life: of peace, innocence, and simple virtue. On the city has gathered the idea of an achieved centre: of learning, communication and light. Powerful hostile associations have also developed: on the city as a place of noise, worldiness and ambition; on the country as a place of backwardness, ignorance, limitation. (1973:9)

Similarly, the historian Martin Wiener has argued that among the English élite, 'if England was an old country, it was also, at heart, country' (1985:46). In other words, despite being the world's foremost industrial power and one of the most urbanised societies in the world, the image of England was essentially a rural one, and it is interesting, as we have seen, that this was echoed by the current Prime Minister, John Major, in his evocation of 'Britain' as 'the country of long shadows on county grounds, warm beer, invincible green suburbs, dog lovers, and – as George Orwell said – old maids bicycling to holy communion through the mist' (address to the Conservative Group for Europe, 22 April 1993). In this regard, England has never become culturally an 'urban' society. We should not forget, however, that such imagery as John Major's is not the sole preserve of a particular class or power group, and that anti-urbanism has a deeper pedigree in these islands. Raymond Williams, for example, points out that in Ireland, Wales and Scotland, 'different versions of community [from England] have persisted longer, nourished by and nourishing specific national feelings' (1973:322). Radical as well as conservative messages can be read from the landscape in these 'Celtic' countries. The key is the important distinction between the nation and the state.

CONCLUSION

To be sure, Scotland did not create the heritage industry, but it can be taken as an excellent example of the genre. As George Rosie comments:

> Scotland now has museums dedicated to a quite astonishing range of subjects. There are museums about coal mining, highland clans, fisheries, the Scottish rugby team, railways, slate quarrying, bicycles, motor cars, wirelesses, gaol conditions, aeroplanes, shipping, fossils, gem rocks, textiles, the Roman occupation, the savings bank movement, and the Loch Ness monster. There is even a museum called The Cornice (in Peebles) which is all about the arts of decorative plasterwork. (1992:158–9)

The idea that Scotland is a land out of time chimes with its political status as a stateless nation. In Chapter 3, we outlined the powerful critique of Scottish culture which claims that it is deformed and deracinated precisely because it does not have proper political expression in a state of its own. The relationship between politics and culture in Scotland is one of the main themes in literature, and there is little doubt that the

conventional wisdom is that since the Treaty of Union in 1707
the two dimensions are ill-connected. Here, for example, is
Marinell Ash commenting on the nineteenth century:

> at the time that Scotland was ceasing to be distinctively
> and confidently herself was also the period when there
> grew an increasing emphasis on the emotional trappings
> of the Scottish past. This is the further paradox, and its
> symbols are bonnie Scotland of the bens and glens and
> misty shieling, the Jacobites, Mary Queen of Scots, tartan
> mania and the raising of historical statuary. (1980:10)

There is, then, considerable suspicion of cultural presentations
of Scotland, and still more of their commercial exploitation.

Why can't we take 'heritage' for granted and at face value?
Does it not simply refer to those items of value, commercial
and national, which need to be preserved? The problem with
this perspective is that it takes the interesting and important
questions for granted. Value is not intrinsic to the object, but
added. Objects are 'valued' because they are judged to be so,
and not for any necessary intrinsic merit. The historian
David Cannadine has pointed out that by conferring heritage
status on 'stately homes' aristocratic bric-a-brac comes to have
commercial and social value which is then compounded by
drawing a paying crowd on opening days (1990). Objects are
valued because people pay to see them. They pay to see them
because they are valued. There is also a process of reification
involved in heritage. Among the major beneficiaries of the
strategy of letting heritage define itself have been the owners
of stately homes, that curiously oxymoronic construction of
the grand and the domestic, the political and the personal. As
we saw in Chapter 5, their owners have latched on to this
'nationalisation' of heritage as a means of financial upkeep,
and more significantly, of cultural legitimation. By setting
themselves up as keepers of the 'national heritage', the lairds
have managed to fuse dynasty and nation in a hostile political
environment. Monuments become the expressions of heritage,
and are objectified. The meaning comes to be embedded in
the object, even although as we have seen in Chapter 7, people have a capacity to read behind the object to its meaning.
The appeal of heritage over history is that it evokes key social
and cultural processes which help to embed people in time.

The other reason why we cannot take 'heritage' for granted

is that its meanings are frequently contested. It has a capacity to evoke different and contradictory meanings for people. Further, the debate on heritage in the last decade has focused on its 'fabrication', the construction of significance rather than its taken-for-granted quality. We have seen just this in the making of 'new' heritage places and activities with only tenuous connections to their actual locations. A considerable literature has grown up to debunk heritage, to show that much of it is a modern fabrication with dubious commercial and political rationales. Being able to show that heritage is not 'authentic', that it is not 'real', however, is not the point. If we take the Scottish example of tartanry, the interesting issue is not why much of it is a 'forgery', but why it continues to have such cultural power. That is the point which critics like Hugh Trevor-Roper (1984) miss. As his fellow historians Raphael Samuel and Paul Thompson show, myths are no mere archaic relics but potent forces in everyday life. Myths are constantly reworked to make sense of memories and lives (Samuel and Thompson, 1990).

The remarkable growth of heritage coupled with the manifest 'fabrication' of much of it has encouraged writers to cast around for more general theories of cultural consumption, and none has been more potent than 'post-modernism'. In Chapter 2, we examined the arguments for heritage as a form of 'staged authenticity' in which image has replaced reality and simulacra masquerade as heritage as a form of history that never actually existed. Places become centres of spectacle and display, and the nostalgia associated with heritage is a powerful emotion. In this interpretation, heritage is set within the frame of tourism in the late twentieth century. Whereas leisure within 'modernism' was characterised by a quest for genuine authenticity and self-realisation, or so the argument goes, in 'post-modernism' the consumption of leisure is purely or largely for the signs over the content. Spectacle has replaced meaning, and sensation overpowers value. More generally, modern culture is characterised by depthlessness, fragmentation and reproduction. Meaning can in theory be bestowed on any form of activity, such is the almost complete dissociation of form from content in this frame of understanding. When it comes to consuming heritage, simply experiencing the monument is not it is argued, enough (or even the point). What we are looking for are the meanings which go with it. In itself the monument may not speak to us, but the images and interpretations do. So why not miss out the 'real thing' in favour of consuming the image? Given that the object cannot speak to us directly in the sense that we cannot read back in time to its original purpose, then why not take away its contemporary significance to us? This 'depthless' quality of monuments and objects is what interests those working within a post-modern paradigm. The object and its meaning have become so thoroughly attentuated that in this canon it means what we want it to mean.

What began as a process of deconstructing the meaning of objects – showing that it was not embedded in the objects themselves – has, within post-modernism, become a process for separating out the form and content of objects. We can, then, choose to read into them what we want, for they do not have historical legitimacy. We encounter here some deeper epistemological arguments. The argument that depthlessness is now a generalised quality of cultural relations is close to an idealist one that there is no such thing as a material world existing independently of our consciousness. Marshall Berman's observation that 'all that is solid melts into air' (Berman, 1982) seems to us to give up on the task of relating culture to material interests.

In this book we have taken a more orthodox sociological approach of *cui bono?* – who benefits from the cultural representations of Scotland in its heritage. That is why we have focused on the manufacturers of heritage, those agencies like the Scottish Tourist Board, Historic Scotland, and the National Trust for Scotland, as well the stately-homes industry North of the Border. We are not arguing for a straight one-to-one translation of material interests into cultural forms. Heritage does not carry within it a single, oppressive social message. For example, the appropriation of tartanry by the Victorian monarchy and its strong associations with the landed élite in Scotland, does not prevent its having possibilities for a radical interpretation of a more populist kind. Neither do we not want to substitute a realist approach, as if the meaning of heritage and its monuments is actually embedded in the object. It is, however, one thing to argue that the consumption of meaning does not come automatically with the package, but it is quite another to imply that any meaning can be poured into whatever receptacle we have to hand. There is, of course, much to criticise in an over-determined view of cultural consumption and of heritage. Such a perspective is plainly underpinning Hewison's analysis of the heritage industry, and to some extent Wright's. Both writers, as we have pointed out, appear to assume an uncritical, passive consumer on the receiving end of whatever meaning commerce or the state happens to have in store. Baudrillard may believe, on the other hand, that the real is no longer real, that linear history has disappeared, but our analysis of Scottish heritage and its consumption does not bear this out, nor does it bear out the view that the consumer is a passive receptacle.

Taken to extremes, the view that what matters is authenticity as performance can quickly be reduced to a kind of double reflexivity – tourists watch a 'native' performance which is put on for them by knowing actors, and what's more the tourists know that. In sum, what is on offer is 'playful' behaviour, and no harm seems to be done. However, as Bruner points out in his essay on Third World tourism, the conventional touristic discourse that the tourist self is transformed by the experience while the native African experience remains inert and frozen, is more likely to require inverting. His argument is that 'despite claims of the touristic discourse, the very opposite occurs in experience, that the tourist self is changed very little by the tour, while the consequences of tourism for the native self are profound' (Bruner, 1991:242).

What lessons does this carry for Scotland? Tourism is predicted to be the world's largest industry by the year 2000. Scotland's share of that market is at best static, and the Scottish Tourist Board has set out to win back a market share, to create in its own words 'Scotland the Brand'. There is no shortage of raw materials in the form of heritage, and Scotland has been in the forefront of the heritage business for at least two centuries. That looks to be an advantage. But Scotland is, currently at least, a stateless nation in which there is very little direct democratic control over the means of its own cultural reproduction. Its capacity to shape its representation is severely limited. Until such time as this is regained, then the charge that Scotland exists simply as 'land of dreamtime' will remain.

NOTES

1. We are indebted to Jennifer Trimarchi who carried out an analysis in the late 1980s under our direction of the cutural significance of Edinburgh Castle for her BA dissertation at Vassar College, USA. We have drawn on some of her work, while the interpretations are our own.
2. We are drawing here on the work of Tim Edensor who wrote his MA dissertation in 1992 on Bannockburn while at Lancaster University.
3. The forthcoming 150th anniversary in 1996 of the Battle of Culloden is likely to call forth a number of plangent and romantic assessments of the event. Colin MacArthur has begun important and critical work on its significance, as well as the reactions to it. We are drawing here on his important analysis which appeared in *Scottish Affairs*, 9, 1994.

Appendix

All studies are in large part the outcome of the methods used to collect the data. As sociologists we were interested in the production and consumption of heritage, and accordingly we set out to collect primary data in the form of interviews, and secondary data as documentary evidence during 1991 to 1993, the period in which our study was funded by the Leverhulme Trust.

Our first aim was to describe and analyse the key agents involved in the heritage 'industry', and our reading led us to identify the Scottish Tourist Board, Historic Scotland, and the National Trust for Scotland as the main entrepreneurs. Accordingly, we interviewed at some length the following: at the Scottish Tourist Board, the marketing director, the director of investment and planning, and the head of research; at Historic Scotland, its director, and marketing manager; and at the National Trust for Scotland, the director, and the past president. Along with the interview material, we collected key documents from these organisations, notably their annual reports, and newsletters for members. We also joined the National Trust for Scotland and Historic Scotland, and received over a two-year period the promotional material and literature which is sent to all members. Over this period we made visits to more than sixty heritage sites in Scotland and collected the appropriate brochures and guidebooks. We also carried out interviews with Scottish Civic Trust, the chief executive of Scottish Natural Heritage, the director and marketing manager of the Scottish Museums Council, Faulds Advertising (agents for Historic Scotland), and Jenni Calder, the author of a book on the National Trust for Scotland.

The second year of our study was taken up with the planning and completion of our interview programme with life members of the National Trust for Scotland. Our aim in so doing was to understand the meanings and motivations of a group of committed supporters of heritage in Scotland. We rejected a strategy of sampling from the list of ordinary (annual) members because it was likely to contain too many 'casual' members who had joined to take advantage of cheaper daily rates, and to whom 'heritage' was unlikely to be a central life-interest. We explored the possibility of sampling from lists of life members of Historic Scotland, as well as the National Trust for Scotland, but we could not obtain access to Historic Scotland lists. Nevertheless, as our aim was to explore the meanings and motivations of committed supporters of heritage, we were pleased and grateful to have access to life members of the National Trust for Scotland.

With the agreement of the membership secretary of the Trust, we used a procedure which maintained the security of the life members' list. The secretary and his staff selected from the alphabetical listing names and addresses to which they wrote explaining our project, expressing the hope that they would co-operate, and asking members to indicate any objections they may have had to being interviewed by us. Once a suitable period of time had elapsed to allow for refusals, the Trust passed on the names and addresses to us so that we could contact members. At no stage did we have access to the membership lists themselves, and we relied on the organisation's staff to use random selection from the alphabetically arranged lists under our guidance. We then wrote to members elaborating the purpose of our project, and followed this up with a phone-call to arrange an interview visit. This sampling procedure which was necessary to protect the confidentiality of the Trust's lists produced a response rate of 72 per cent – some ninety-seven individuals – of those initially contacted excluding those who were no longer at the given address.

The Questionnaire

I'd like to start with some membership details:

1. How long have you been a life member of the National Trust for Scotland?

2. Why did you become a life member?
   Were you originally an ordinary/annual member?
   When did you join? (year)
   Have you been a member continuously since that time?

3. Are you a member of any other heritage organisations (for example, Historic Scotland, English Heritage, Architectural Historical Society of Scotland, Scottish Civic Trust)? Which ones?
   How long have you been a member of each (year when joined will do, or roughly how long)?
   We are interested in the number and range of other associations and organisations which people belong to. Perhaps I could ask you about these, starting with the ones you are *currently a member of.*

4. Do you belong to any *locally based organisations* (e.g., the Womens' Rural, Rotary Club, Womens' Guild, Church groups, Young Farmers, etc.)?

5. Do you belong to any *recreational, sports or leisure clubs* (e.g., a football or rugby club, flower arranging society, recorder group etc.)?

6. Are you a member of any *local interest groups, councils, or committees* (e.g., Residents' Associations, Housing Associations, Community Councils, Stair Care groups)?

7. Do you regularly support a *particular charity* (e.g., Save the Children Fund, RSPCA, RSPB, RSPCC, World Wildlife Fund, Lifeboats, Marie Curie, Green Peace, etc.?). Which one(s)?
   What form does your support take (e.g. making a donation, contributing regularly, via tax covenant etc., collecting and participating in the association)?

8. Do you support any other *social or political cause* (e.g., a political party, Amnesty International, CND etc.)?

9. Are you a member of any *work-related association*, e.g. a professional body, trade union?

10. Thinking now of associations or organisations you *used to be a member* of, could you indicate which these are, and when, approximately, you joined, and when you left? (List association with starting and finishing dates if possible: if not, give rough approximates.)

Frequency of Visits and Favourite Properties

11. Turning now to your membership of the National Trust for Scotland, can you recall which Trust properties you visited in the last twelve months?

12. Was this a typical year? *yes/no*
    If not, in what ways did it differ from previous years (e.g. more/less/different pattern)?

13. Did you visit any National Trust properties in England, Wales or Northern Ireland?

14. Which other heritage sites, if any, did you visit in the last twelve months? [*Prompt if 'heritage sites' is unclear: e.g. What about those owned by Historic Scotland? Or by private owners, e.g. stately homes?*]

15. To what extent are such visits an important part of your leisure activities?

16. Can you tell me which three National Trust for Scotland properties you like best?

17. Why do you like these three best?

18. Are there other heritage sites not owned by the Trust which you like? What are they and why do you like them?

19. Have you ever visited the same heritage property more than once? *yes/no*
    If yes:
    Which ones?
    Why was that?

20. When you visit National Trust for Scotland properties, do you usually go on your own or with other people?

If 'with other people', are they mainly family, friends, visitors?

21. Have you ever taken an overseas visitor to visit a Trust property?
    If yes:
        Which property/properties did you take them to?
        What was their reaction to the visit(s)?

22. Have you ever taken an English visitor to visit a Trust property ?
    If yes:
        Which property/properties did you take them to?
        What was their reaction to the visit(s)?

23. I understand that members of the National Trust for Scotland can use their membership cards to visit National Trust properties in England. Have you ever taken advantage of this? [*try to get sites and dates/year.*]

Heritage and Holidays

24. Now I would like to ask about your holiday and leisure patterns. Did you have a holiday(s) in the last twelve months, and where did you spend it?

25. Was this a fairly typical holiday in terms of where you went and what you did?

26. When you are on holiday, do you organise it around visits to heritage sites?

27. Do you tend to take your holidays in Scotland? Why or why not?

28. Do you make a point of visiting Trust or other heritage properties while you are on holiday?

Value for Money

29. Being a life member of the National Trust for Scotland obviously costs money. Do you consider it to be good value for money? *yes/no*

30. Why do you say that?

31. Do you feel that value for money is not what being a life member is about?

The Meaning and Importance of Heritage

32. We hear quite a lot these days about 'heritage'. Can you tell me what you understand by the term?

33. Do you think that there is a distinction between 'heritage' and 'history'?
    What makes you say that?

34. As a life member of the National Trust for Scotland you obviously care about heritage. Can you tell me why you consider heritage to be important?

35. How would you describe Scotland's heritage in particular?

36. Are there any important differences between heritage in Scotland and in England?
    Why is this?

37. In Britain the impetus for looking after heritage comes mainly from voluntary organisations such as the National Trust for Scotland, the National Trust, the Architectural Historical Society of Scotland, the Scottish Civic Trust etc., and the role of the state is relatively small. Do you think that heritage in Britain should remain mainly in the hands of voluntary organisations or should the state take a more active role?

38. Should private owners of heritage properties play a greater/lesser role in promoting heritage?
    Why do you say that?

39. Should local government be more/less involved in promoting and protecting heritage?
    Why do you say that?

40. Are there any books about Scotland's heritage you would

recommend to someone who wanted to find out more
about it?

41. We are interested to know how people living in Scotland
    see themselves in terms of their nationality. Which of
    these statements on this card best describes how you
    regard yourself?
    [*hand respondent card*]
    Scottish, not British
    More Scottish than British
    Equally Scottish and British
    More British than Scottish
    British, not Scottish
    [*Note: If respondent sees him/herself as 'English',
    'Welsh', 'Irish' or whatever, ask the question in these
    terms, e.g. 'English, not British' etc.*]
    Why do you describe your nationality in this way?

    Social Description
42. To finish with, I'd like you to tell me a bit about yourself.
    For instance, where were you born?
    Your date of birth?
    Your marital status?

    Job History
43. Are you currently in paid employment?
    If yes, what is your current occupation?
    If no, are you retired/unemployed?

44. Could you give me details of the main jobs you have had
    since leaving school (starting with the first job)?

45. What does your spouse or partner currently work at (if
    appropriate)?

46. If currently retired, unemployed, housewife/househus-
    band, what was their last job?

47. What job was your father doing at the time you left
    school?

48. What did your spouse's father work at when he/she left school?

Education

49. What was the last secondary school you were at?

50. What type of school was it (local authority, fee-paying, private etc.)?

51. Did you stay on at school after reaching the school leaving age? *yes/no*

52. Have you had any further education of any kind since you left school?
    If yes:
       Institution
       Kind (correspondence, evening, day, full-time, etc.)
       Subjects
       Qualification
       Duration

Income

53. How people spend their leisure time frequently depends on how much money they have. I would like to ask you about your total gross family income from all sources in the last twelve months. Could you tell me which of the following income categories you are in? [*show card*]
       Below £10,000 p.a.
       £10,000–£20,000 p.a.
       £20,000–£30,000 p.a.
       £30,000–£40,000 p.a.
       Over £40,000 p.a.

Politics

54. As you no doubt know, political parties have begun to pay more attention to heritage in their programmes. [*Prompt if necessary: e.g. Scottish Natural Heritage, Minister for Heritage etc.*]
       If there were a general election tomorrow, can I ask you which political party would you vote for?

55. Have you always voted for that party ?

If yes, why have you done so?
If no, why would you vote for them now?

56. Could you tell me what you think the various political parties stand for?
    Conservative
    Labour
    Liberal-Democrat
    Scottish National Party

57. Which political party, in your opinion, is most concerned about heritage?

58. Why do you think this is the case?

Additional comments

59. I've asked you quite a few questions about heritage, and it has been very helpful. Is there anything else about heritage you would like to talk about?

Bibliography

PRIMARY SOURCES

Official Records

Association of Scottish Visitor Attractions, *Visitor Attractions
Survey 1992.*
Cultural Trends in Scotland (1992), London: Policy Studies
Institute.
Cultural Trends (1991), vol. 12, London: Policy Studies Institute.
– (1992), vol. 15, London: Policy Studies Institute.
– (1993), vol. 19, London: Policy Studies Institute.
Debrett's Peerage and Baronetage (1990), London: Debrett's
Peerage Ltd and Macmillan.
European Travel Commission/Europa Nostra (1974), *Tourism and
Conservation: Working Together. Recommendations to the
Governments and peoples of Europe.*
Henley Centre for Leisure Forecasting (1986) *Leisure Futures*,
London: Henley Centre.
Historic Scotland (1991), *Framework Document*, April.
– (1993), *Annual Report.*
– (1991–4), *Welcome.*
– *The Popular Choice*, n.d.
Myerscough, J. (1991), *Monitoring Glasgow 1990*, prepared for
Glasgow City Council, Strathclyde Regional Council and Scottish
Enterprise.
National Trust for Scotland (1991–4), *Heritage Scotland.*
Social Trends (1990), vol. 20, HMSO.
– (1994), vol. 24, HMSO.
The Department of National Heritage (1992), *Passenger Survey.*
The National Heritage Memorial Fund (1980–1), *Annual Report.*
The National Trust For Scotland (1993), *Annual Report.*
– (1994), *Annual Report.*
– (1993), *Heritage Scotland*, Summer.
The Scottish Tourist Board (1989), Arthur Young International:
Visitor Attractions Report.

– (1991), *Development, Objectives and Functions*.
– (n.d.), *Visitor Attractions: a Development Guide*.

Pamphlets and Guidebooks

Bowhill (1981), Derby: Pilgrim Press Ltd.
Drumlanrig Castle (1984), Selkirk: Buccleuch Recreational
   Enterprises Ltd.
Floors Castle (1984), Derby: Pilgrim Press Ltd.
TIMESPAN: *The Highland Experience* (1991), Highlands and Islands
   Development Board.

Secondary Sources

Ambrose, T. and Runyard, S. (eds) (1991), *Forward Planning: A
   Handbook of Business, Corporate and Development Planning
   for Museums and Galleries*, London: Henley Leisure Forecasts.
Anderson, B. (1983), *Imagined Communities: Reflections on the
   Origin and Spread of Nationalism*, London: Verso.
Anderson, E. (1979), 'The Kailyard revisited', in I. Campbell (ed.)
   (1979), *Nineteenth-Century Scottish Fiction*, Manchester:
   Carcanet Press.
Ascherson, N. (1986), 'The Lost Capital', *The Observer*, 20 July.
Ash, M. (1980), *The Strange Death of Scottish History*, Edinburgh:
   Ramsay Head Press.
– (1990), 'William Wallace and Robert the Bruce: The Life and
   Death of a National Myth', in R. Samuel and P. Thompson (eds),
   The Myths We Live By, London: Routledge.
Bain, R. (1968), *The Clans and Tartans of Scotland*, Glasgow:
   Collins.
Barnes, B. (1992), 'Status Groups and Collective Action', *Sociology*,
   vol. 26.
Baudrillard, J. (1983), *Simulations*, New York: Semiotext.
Bennett, Alan (1989), 'Back-to-Back to the Future', in *Weekend
   Guardian*, 16–17 December.
Bennett, T. (1988), 'Museums and "the People"', in R. Lumley (ed.),
   The Museum Time Machine, London: Routledge.
Berman, M. (1982), *All That Is Solid Melts Into Air*, London: Verso.
Beveridge, C. and Turnbull, R. (1989), *The Eclipse of Scottish
   Culture*, Edinburgh: Polygon.
Blair, K. (1989), 'Making Economic History', *Scottish Business
   Insider*, November.
Bourdieu, P. (1984), *Distinction: A Social Critique of the
   Judgement of Taste*, London: Routledge and Kegan Paul.
Boyne, R. and Rattansi, A. (1990), *Postmodernism and Society*,
   London: Macmillan.
Bruner, E. (1991), 'Transformation of Self in Tourism', *Annals of
   Tourism Research*, vol. 18, 2.

Calder, J. (1990), *Scotland In Trust: The National Trust for Scotland*, Glasgow: Richard Drew.

Callander, R. F. (1987), *A Pattern of Landownership in Scotland: With Particular Reference to Aberdeenshire*, Aberdeen: Haughend Publications.

Campbell, I. (1981), *Kailyard*, Edinburgh: Ramsay Head Press.

Campbell, R. H. (1985), *Scotland Since 1707: The Rise of an Industrial Society* (2nd ed.), Edinburgh: John Donald.

Cannadine, D. (1990), *The Decline and Fall of the British Aristocracy*, London: Yale University Press.

Carter, I. (1976), 'Kailyard: the literature of decline in nineteenth-century Scotland', in *Scottish Journal of Sociology*, vol.1, no.1.

– (1979), *Farm Life in North-East Scotland, 1840–1914*, Edinburgh: John Donald.

Caughie, J. (1983), 'Scottish Television: What would it look like?', in C. McArthur (ed.), *Scotch Reels: Scotland in Cinema and Television*, London: BFI Publishing.

Chapman, M. (1978), *The Gaelic Vision in Scottish Culture*, London: Croom Helm.

– (1992), *The Celts*, London: Macmillan.

Cheape, H. (1991), *Tartan: the Highland Habit*, Edinburgh: National Museums of Scotland.

Checkland, S. and Checkland, O. (1984), *Industry and Ethos: Scotland 1832–1914*, London: Edward Arnold.

Clarke, J. and Critcher, C. (1985), *The Devil Makes Work: Leisure in Capitalist Britain*, London: Macmillan.

Collins, R. (1986), *Weberian Sociological Theory*, Cambridge: Cambridge University Press.

Collins, B. and Robbins, K. (eds), (1990), *British Culture and Economic Decline*, London: Weidenfield and Nicolson.

Cormack, P. (1976), *Heritage in Danger,* London: New English Heritage.

Corner, J. and Harvey, S. (eds) (1991), *Enterprise and Heritage*, London: Routledge.

Cosgrove, D. (1984), *Social Formation and Symbolic Landscape*, London: Croom Helm.

– (1994), 'Terrains of Power', in *Times Higher Education Supplement*, 11 March.

– and Daniels, S. (eds) (1988), *The Iconography of Landscape*, Cambridge: Cambridge University Press.

Craig, C. (1982), 'Myths Against History: Tartanry and Kailyard in nineteenth-century Scottish Literature', in C. McArthur (ed.), *Scotch Reels: Scotland in Cinema and Television*, London: BFI Publishing.

Crawford, I. (1986), *Held in Trust: The National Trust for Scotland*, Edinburgh: Albany.

Dennis, N., Henriques, F. and Slaughter, C. (1969), *Coal is Our Life:*

an Analysis of a Yorkshire Mining Community, London: Tavistock.

Donaldson, W. (1986), *Popular Literature in Victorian Scotland*, Aberdeen: Aberdeen University Press.

Dunbar, J. G. (1992), 'The Royal Commission on the Ancient and Historical Monuments of Scotland: the First 80 Years', in *Transactions of the Ancient Monuments Society*, vol. 36.

Durie, A. (1992), 'Tourism in Victorian Scotland: the Case of Abbotsford', in *Scottish Economic and Social History*, vol. 12.

Eco, U. (1987), *Travels in Hyper-Reality: Essays,* London: Pan.

Edensor, T. (1992), 'Bannockburn Heritage Site: Tourist Practices and Modes of Transmission', MA dissertation, University of Leeds.

Fergusson, J. (1949), *Lowland Lairds*, London: Faber and Faber.

Featherstone, M. (1988), 'Leisure, Symbolic Power and the Life Course', in A. Tomlinson, J. Horne, and D. Jary (eds), *Sport and Social Relations*, London: Routledge and Kegan Paul.

Filor, S. (1990), 'Landscape, Heritage and National Identity', paper presented to the Conference of the Landscape Research Group, September (mimeo).

Fisher, M. and Owen, V. (eds) (1991), *Whose Cities?* Harmondsworth: Penguin.

Fowler, P. J. (1989), 'Heritage: A Post-Modern Perspective', in D. Uzzell (ed.), *Heritage Interpretation*, London: Belhaven Press.

– (1992), *The Past in Contemporary Society: Then, Now*, London: Routledge.

Fry, M. (1987), *Patronage and Principle: A Political History of Modern Scotland*, Aberdeen: Aberdeen University Press.

Giddens, A. (1990), *The Consequences of Modernity*, London: Polity Press.

– (1991), *Modernity and Self-Identity*, London: Polity Press.

Goffman, E. (1973), *The Presentation of Self in Everyday Life,* New York: Overlook Press.

Goldthorpe, J., Lockwood, D., Bechhofer, F. and Platt, J. (1969), *The Affluent Worker*, Cambridge: Cambridge University Press.

– (1987), *Social Mobility and Class Structure in Modern Britain*, Oxford: Oxford University Press (2nd ed.).

Hardy, F. (1990), *Scotland in Film*, Edinburgh: Edinburgh University Press.

Harvie, C. (1991), 'Modern Scotland: Remembering the People', in R. Mitchison (ed.), *Why Scottish History Matters*, Edinburgh: Saltire Society.

– (1992), 'Scottish Politics', in A. Dickson and J. H. Treble (eds) *People & Society in Scotland*, vol. 3, Edinburgh: John Donald.

Hewison, R. (1987), *The Heritage Industry: Britain in a Climate of Decline*, London: Methuen.

– (1989), 'Heritage: an Interpretation', in D. Uzzell (ed.), *Heritage Interpretation*, vol. 1, London: Bellhaven.

– (1991), 'Commerce and Culture', in J. Corner, and S. Harvey (eds), *Enterprise and Heritage*.

Hobsbawm, E. and Ranger, T. (eds) (1983), *The Invention of Tradition*, Cambridge: Cambridge University Press.

Horne, D. (1984), *The Great Museum: The Re-Presentation of History*, London: Pluto Press.

Howson, A. (1993), '*No Gods and Precious Few Women*', in *Scottish Affairs* No. 2, Winter.

Hoyau, P. (1988), 'Heritage and "the Conserver Society"": the French Case', in R. Lumley, (ed.), *The Museum Time Machine*.

Hutchinson, I. (1986), *A Political History of Scotland 1832–1924: Parties, Elections and Issues*, Edinburgh: John Donald.

Jarvie, G. (1991), *Highland Games: The Making of the Myth*, Edinburgh: Edinburgh University Press.

Johnston, T. (1911), *Our Scots Noble Families*, Glasgow: Forward.

Jameson, F. (1984), 'Postmodernism, or the Cultural Logic of Late Capitalism', in *New Left Review*, vol. 146.

Keat, R. and Abercrombie, N. (1991), *Enterprise Culture*, London: Routledge.

Kidd, C. (1993), *Subverting Scotland's Past: Scottish Whig Historians and the Creation of an Anglo–British Identity, 1689–c.1830*, Cambridge: Cambridge University Press.

Knowles, T. D. (1983), *Ideology, Art and Commerce: Aspects of Literary Sociology in the Late Victorian Scottish Kailyard*, Gothenborg: Acta Universitatis Gothoburgensis.

Lash, S. (1990), *Sociology of Post-Modernism*, London: Routledge.

Lee, M. J. (1993), *Consumer Culture Reborn: the Cultural Politics of Consumption*, London: Routledge.

Levitt, I. (1989), 'Welfare, Government and the Working Class: Scotland, 1845–1894', in D. McCrone, S. Kendrick and P. Straw (eds), *The Making of Scotland: Nation, Culture and Social Change*, Edinburgh: Edinburgh University Press.

Lowenthal, D. (1985), *The Past is a Foreign Country*, Cambridge:Cambridge University Press.

Lumley, R. (ed.) (1988), *The Museum Time Machine*, London: Routledge.

McArthur, C. (1983), 'Scotch reels and after', *Cencrastus*, 11.

– (1994), 'Culloden: a pre-emptive strike', in *Scottish Affairs*, vol. 9.

MacArthur, M. (1993), 'Blasted Heaths and Hills of Mist', in *Scottish Affairs*, vol. 3.

MacCannell, D. (1974), 'Staged Authenticity: arrangements of social space in tourist settings', *American Journal of Sociology*, vol. 79, 3.

– (1992), *Empty Meeting Grounds*, London: Routledge.

McCrone, D. (1992), *Understanding Scotland: the Sociology of a Stateless Nation*, London: Routledge.

MacDougall, H. A. (1982), *Racial Myth in English History: Trojans, Teutons and Anglo-Saxons*, Montreal: Harvest House.

MacEwen, J. (1977), *Who Owns Scotland? A Study in Land Ownership*, Edinburgh: Edinburgh University Students Publications Board.

MacLaren, A .A. (ed.) (1976), *Social Class in Scotland*, Edinburgh: John Donald.

Miller, D. (1987), *Material Culture and Mass Consumption*, Oxford: Blackwell.

Millman, R. (1971), *Maps of Scottish Estate Boundaries in 1970*, Edinburgh: Scottish Record Office.

Montagu of Beaulieu (1967), *The Gilt and the Gingerbread: or How to Live in a Stately Home and Make Money*, London: Michael Joseph.

Morton, G. (1993), *Unionist-Nationalism: The Historical Construction of Scottish National Identity, Edinburgh 1830–1860*, PhD Thesis: University of Edinburgh.

Nairn, T. (1975), 'Old Nationalism and New Nationalism', in G. Brown (ed.), *The Red Paper on Scotland*, Edinburgh: Edinburgh University Students Publications Board.

— (1977), *The Break-Up of Britain*, London: Verso.

— (1988 and 1994), *The Enchanted Glass: Britain and its Monarchy*, London: Radius.

Ousby, I. (1990), *The Englishman's England: Taste, Travel and the Rise of Tourism*, Cambridge: Cambridge University Press.

Parkin, F. (1979), *Marxism and Class Theory: a Bourgeois Critique*, London: Tavistock Publications.

Overton, J. (1988), 'The Taste of Newfoundland: Tourism, Commodity Aesthetics and The Imagined Community', conference paper at the Seventh Atlantic Canada Studies Conference (mimeo).

Paterson, L. (1994), *The Autonomy of Modern Scotland*, Edinburgh: Edinburgh University Press.

Pittock, M. (1991), *The Invention of Scotland: the Stuart Myth and the Scottish Identity, 1638 to the Present*, London: Routledge.

Prebble, J. (1988), *The King's Jaunt: George IV in Scotland, 1822*, London: Collins.

Prentice, R. J. (1971), *Conserve and Provide: A Brief History of the National Trust For Scotland*, Edinburgh: G. Waterson & Sons Ltd.

Pringle, T. (1988), 'The Privation of History: Landseer, Victoria and the Highland Myth', in D. Cosgrove and S. Daniels (eds), *The Iconography of Landscape*, Cambridge: Cambridge University Press.

Rojek, C. (1993), *Ways of Escape*, London: Macmillan.

Rosie, G. (1992), 'Museumry and the Heritage Industry', in I. Donnachie and C.Whatley (eds), *The Manufacture of Scottish History*, Edinburgh: Polygon.

Samuel, R. and Thompson, P. (eds) (1990), *The Myths We Live By*, London: Routledge.

Scott, J. (1991), *Who Rules Britain?*, Cambridge: Cambridge University Press.

Scott, J. and Hughes, M. (1980), *The Anatomy of Scottish Capital*, London: Croom Helm.

Shepherd, G. (1988), 'The Kailyard', in D. Gifford (ed.), *The History of Scottish Literature, volume 3, The Nineteenth Century*, Aberdeen: Aberdeen University Press.

Smout, T. C. (1986), *A Century of the Scottish People, 1830–1950*, Glasgow: Collins.

– (1994), 'Perspectives on the Scottish Identity', in *Scottish Affairs*, vol. 6.

Sorensen, C. (1988), 'Theme Parks and Time Machines', in P. Vergo (ed.), *The New Museology*, London: Reaktion.

Taylor, P. (1993), 'The Meaning of the North: England's "foreign country" within?', *Political Geography*, vol. 12, 2.

Thrift, N. (1989), 'Images of Social Change', in Hamnett et al. (eds), *The Changing Social Structure*, London: Sage.

Timperley, L. (1980), 'The Pattern of Landholding in Eighteenth-Century Scotland', in M. L. Parry, and T. R. Slater (eds), *The Making of the Scottish Countryside*, London: Croom Helm.

Trevor-Roper, H. (1984), 'Invention of Tradition: the Highland Tradition of Scotland', in E. Hobsbawm and T. Ranger (eds), *The Invention of Tradition*, Cambridge: Cambridge University Press.

Trimarchi, J. (1987), 'Scots on the Rocks: Tourism and Cultural identity at Edinburgh Castle', BA dissertation, Vassar College, USA.

Urry, J. (1990), *The Tourist Gaze: Leisure and Travel in Contemporary Societies*, London: Sage.

Vergo, P. (ed.) (1989), *The New Museology*, London: Reaktion.

Walsh, K. (1992), *The Representation of the Past: Museums and Heritage in the Post-modern World*, London: Routledge.

Weber, M. (1978 ed.), *Economy and Society*, London: University of California Press.

Wiener, A. (1985), 'Inalienable Wealth', in *American Ethnologist*, vol. 12.

Wiener, M. (1985), *English Culture and the Decline of the Industrial Spirit*, Harmondsworth: Penguin.

Williams, R. (1973), *The Country and the City*, London: Chatto and Windus.

– (1977), *Marxism and Literature*, Oxford: Oxford University Press.

Wills, D. (1984), 'New Images of Scotland: New Questions', *Cencrastus*, 15.

Winchester, S. (1982), *Their Noble Lordships: Class and Power in Modern Britain*, New York: Random House.

Womack, P. (1989), *Improvement and Romance: Constructing the Myth of the Highlands*, London: Macmillan.

Wright, P. (1985), *On Living in an Old Country: The National Past in Contemporary Britain*, London: Verso.

— (1986), 'Misguided Tours', in *New Socialist*, vol. 40.

Index

National Trust, 3, 23, 29, 45, 98–100
National Trust for Scotland, 3, 16,
    26, 41, 45, 73, 78, 86, 98–109,
    110, 122, 138, 140–1, 143,
    156–7, 192, 208, 211, 212
    image of Scotland, 106–9
    life members of, 143–55, 163–7

Ousby, Ian, 24
Overton, James, 46

Parkin, Frank, 125
Paterson, Lindsay, 6, 70, 196
patrimoine, 13, 26, 74, 141, 158
Pittock, Murray, 195, 201
post-modernism, 11–12, 42–8,
    207–8

Quebec, 6

reality, virtual, 10–11
regiments, Scottish, 5, 52, 186, 191
Rojek, Chris, 45–6
Rosie, George, 205
Royal Commission on the Ancient
    and Historical Monuments of
    Scotland, 194
Roxburghe, Duke of, 110–11,
    113–14, 116, 118, 120, 122,
    127, 130–1

Samuel, Raphael, 23, 32–3, 207
Scotland
    compared with England, 167–71,
        181
    as 'stateless nation', 6, 209
Scott, John, 128
Scott, Walter, 4, 7, 51, 60–1, 111,
    127, 133, 188, 198, 202
Scottish Museums Council, 73, 76–7,
    137
Scottish National Party, 5, 87,
    156–7, 175–7, 181, 188
Scottish Natural Heritage, 72, 76

Scottish Tourist Board, 5, 16, 26, 72,
    76–88, 140, 200, 208, 209, 211
    image of Scotland, 81–2, 89
Smout, T. C., 60, 202
Sobieski Stuarts, 51
Sorensen, C., 11
'stately homes', 27, 31, 110–34, 206,
    208
status group, 122–6

tartanry, 5, 7, 50–6, 69, 182, 207,
    208
Taylor, Peter, 24
Thatcherism, 15, 29–33, 89, 156
Thrift, Nigel, 23
Timespan Ltd, 10
Timperley, Lorraine, 117
tourism, 2, 9–10, 35, 43, 78–9, 182,
    207
    'post-tourism', 35
    tourist gaze, 35, 44, 209
tradition, invention of, 9, 60
Trevor-Roper, Hugh, 5, 60, 207
Trimarchi, Jennifer, 210n.
Turnbull, Ronald, *see* Beveridge,
    Craig

Union, Treaty of (1707), 70, 129,
    196, 201, 206
Unionist-Nationalism, 197–9
Unna, Percy (Unna Rules), 109
Urry, John, 12, 21, 34–6, 39–43, 48

Vergo, P., 2
voluntarism, 152–4

Wallace, William, 129, 199
Walsh, K., 2
Weber, Max, 122–5, 139
Wiener, Annette, 8
Wiener, Martin, 111, 126, 204–5
Williams, Raymond, 6, 20, 50, 204–5
Womack, Peter, 56, 200
Wright, Patrick, 14, 15, 21–3,
    28–33, 100–1, 131, 209